The Concept of Self

African American Life Series

A complete listing of the books in this series can be found at the back of this volume.

Series Editors

Melba Joyce Boyd
Department of Africana Studies, Wayne State University

Ron Brown
Department of Political Science, Wayne State University

The Concept of Self

A Study of Black Identity and Self-Esteem

RICHARD L. ALLEN

Wayne State University Press

Detroit

Manufactured in the United States of America.
05 04 03 02 01   5 4 3 2 1

Library of Congress Cataloging-in-Publication Data
Allen, Richard L., 1946–
The concept of self : a study of Black
identity and self-esteem / Richard L. Allen.
p. cm. — (African American life series)
ISBN 0–8143-2898–9 (alk. paper)
1. Afro-Americans—Race identity. 2. Afro-Americans—Psychology. 3.
Afro-Americans—Social conditions. 4. Self-perception. 5. Group
identity. 6. African diaspora. I. Title. II. Series.
E185.625 .A46 2001
305.896'073—dc21
00–009539

CONTENTS

**PART 1: THE BLACK SELF: TRENDS,
INFLUENCES, AND EFFECTS**

**PART 2: THEORETICAL AND EMPIRICAL
EXAMINATIONS OF THE BLACK SELF**

PART 3: THEORY CONSTRUCTION

FIGURES

TABLES

ACKNOWLEDGMENTS

My enduring thanks go to my best known ancestors, Mack and Jane Allen, my parents, two humans that I love so deeply and miss so thoroughly. They remain with my thoughts, actions, and aspirations. They will be with me as long as the river flows and the sun rises. They are very much alive with me, and I hope that they have a certain fulfillment in the knowledge that I carry them with me wherever I go. Also, I am pleased to voice my appreciation of my brothers and sisters, Mack, John, Gloria, and Irene, beautiful branches from sturdy roots.

The successful consummation of my writing was most directly influenced by a Faculty Career Development Grant from the University of Michigan. Dr. Lester Monts was instrumental in making this happen. *Asante sana*, brother. The data for a substantial portion of the empirical analysis were provided by Dr. James S. Jackson. I am indebted to him. He has been quite generous. Also, I cannot forget my friend and a good human being who assisted me on my various research projects, Richard Bagozzi, a real jazz man. Finally, my friends, Keith Reeves, Barbara Cressman, and Lourdes Ortega Perez, have been helpful and insightful critics, and my soulmates, Iris Ferrer Labanino, Salome Gebre-Egziabher, and Saba Kidane have been my inspiration and the embodiment of Maat.

A hearty *yebo* is extended to my former colleagues at the University of Texas at Austin and to my many friends in Austin. They have been very supportive of all my academic endeavors. Special thanks go out to John S. Butler, Horace Newcomb, Thomas Schatz, Paula Poindexter, Terry, Ali, Prince Aligbe, and Herman Gray.

INTRODUCTION

T*he Concept of Self: A Study of Black Identity and Self-Esteem* explores
the many and varied issues leading to and manifesting themselves in the
African American's dynamic sense of self. The book examines critical issues
influencing the black self-concept through an analysis of two important and
relevant data sets. It examines the historical basis for the widely misconceived
ideas on how Africans think of themselves individually, and how they relate
to being part of a group that has been subjected to challenges to their very
humanity. Also, as an evolving work in progress, it systematically investigates
the past research on the self-esteem and black identity of African Americans.
Much of this research has been useful and has served as the foundation for a
more detailed theory-driven and empirically based inquiry. In my pursuit, I
attempted to separate the wheat from the chaff, hoping that I kept only the
wheat. But I am not one to make that determination.

Part One lays out the historical arguments for the importance of studying
the self-concept of the African, including its past conceptions. I trace the
significance of the many forces that have impinged on the lives of African
Americans and point to the uniqueness of their position. In Chapter 1,
with its emphasis on the impact of the vestiges of enslavement, I attempt
to show how the kinds of relationships developed during that period are
reproduced even today. Further, I reveal how many institutions in the United
States formed and perpetuated certain images of Africans, past and future.
Communication and mass media are especially identified as the culprits in
conveying and purveying pejorative and dehumanizing images of Africans. I
provide a wide range of examples of this practice both then and now. Relatedly, I present the acts of contestation—the many and continuous instances
of resistance that Africans have carried out throughout all of their contacts
with their oppressors. The latter part of this chapter invokes DuBois's
concept of double consciousness, which is further developed throughout
the book. The chapter ends with a compilation of my research questions.
Chapter 2 develops the many issues and questions explored in the research
literature on self-esteem and black identity. I define a host of terms and try
to provide conceptual clarity to much of the work in this area. I also point to
a number of theoretical and empirical flaws that hamper this line of inquiry
and critique the presumed existence of a black self-hatred, making the case
that research does not confirm the widespread existence of this phenomenon.

Part Two focuses on the empirical tests of my initial formulation of the self-concept of African Americans. The major source of data is the National Survey of Black Americans, a national survey of African Americans on a wide range of political, social, and psychological issues. I used both the cross-sectional and longitudinal data provided by that study. Chapter 3 looks entirely at the concept of self-esteem. It begins with a navigation into the diverse theoretical frameworks that have been employed to predict and explain the black self-concept, then moves to an empirical assessment of various theories or theoretical frameworks. Here, social structural variables (class and various demographic variables) are introduced into the analysis to examine the extent to which they are important to the black self. Chapter 4 takes a similar approach, but addresses many different black or group identity measures. Based on my previous research investigations of the African American belief system, it offers an assessment of the utility of previous theories. From the many measures of black identity, I selected two popular ones: closeness to the masses and closeness to the elites. I then attempted to find out which of the many theories available best fit the data. Chapter 5 combines the analysis of the self-esteem and black identity constructs. I wanted to test several of the formulations that have been developed to explain the relationship of self-esteem to black identity. Borrowing from some of the empirical literature and paying careful attention to the assumptions about the relationships suggested by scholar-activists, I examine the stability, the correlation, and the causality associated with the two sets of self-constructs (self-esteem and closeness to the masses and the elites).

Part Three turns to theory construction. Using the ideas put forth by DuBois, and tapping into some of the African-centered theorizing about the black self, I provide a set of interrelated hypotheses. Chapter 6 synthesizes the results from all the previous studies and presents a litany of assumptions based on alternative conceptions of the black self. The newly constructed theory incorporates select antecedents, with the additional inclusion of both majority media and black media processes that most influence the black self—closeness to the elites and the masses and self-esteem. Also, I incorporate a construct called African self-consciousness and the ethnic identity. Drawing upon recent work, I conceive of the African self-consciousness construct as embracing the ideas introduced by a number of African-centered scholars concerning the black self-construct. In brief outline form, I suggest some of the methodological considerations when exploring the proposed theory. Finally, I subject my theorizing to empirical tests with a new set of data. Chapter 7 includes a compilation of the findings, speculations, and, perhaps most important, ideas about how Africans might create and use the African worldview for the upliftment of the *we*, in the service of the group and, ultimately, in the service of all humankind.

PART I

THE BLACK SELF: TRENDS, INFLUENCES, AND EFFECTS

CHAPTER 1

The Context of the Issues: Historical Events and Considerations

History is best qualified to reward our research.
—Malcolm X

To know the present we must look into the past and to know the future we must look into the past and the present.
—Walter Rodney

This chapter provides the groundwork for the examination of a number of issues and problems concerning the self-concept of Africans, with an emphasis on those born in the United States. It presents a historical context for the proffered research questions. Specifically, it highlights how African people have been presented subsequent to their enslavement and outlines the purported impact of such an event on their self-concept. The following major topics are examined: the denigrating portrayals of and ideas about African people over time in various political, academic, and lay circles, and how they are conveyed by the mass media and non-mass media; the nature of the Africans' resistance to attacks on their humanity, and how they actively created alternative images through alternative means (e.g., black media). The concept of "double consciousness" is introduced here, and pursued throughout the study, to pinpoint the dynamic and ongoing struggle that Africans engage in to maintain a sense of their humanity.

This study embraces the contention that people of African descent in the United States can be understood fully only when both the African cultural and Western hemispheric political realities are taken into account. "For nearly four hundred years, the slave trade, colonization, segregation, and racism—highly sophisticated systematic strategies of oppression—have been the massive political and economic forces operating on African people.

These forces have influenced the culture, the socialization processes, and the very consciousness of African people" (Hilliard, 1995, p. 7).

Focusing broadly on the slave trade, this chapter argues that the enslavement of Africans had major repercussions that are manifest even today (Hartman, 1997) and that it is impossible to understand the social, political, and cultural history of Africans in the United States without understanding what happened before and after the holocaust of slavery. Over time, there has been a striking absence of political will in this nation to address the legacy of slavery until events have forced it to do so.

The slave system was both psychological and physical. "The slaves were taught discipline, were impressed again and again with the idea of their own inferiority to 'know their place,' to see blackness as a sign of subordination, to be awed by the power of the master, to merge their interest with the master's, destroying their own needs. To accomplish this there was the discipline of hard labor, the breakup of the slave family, the lulling effects of religion (which sometimes led to 'great mischief,' as one slaveholder reported), the creation of disunity among slaves by separating them into field slaves and more privileged house slaves, and finally the power of law and the immediate power of the overseer to invoke whipping, burning, mutilation, and death" (Zinn, 1995, p. 35).

In the past as well as in the present, major challenges to the racial status quo by the most dispossessed segments of the African American community have forced a response from the dominating group. It is with this understanding that Frederick Douglass (1857) offered his insightful observation many years ago:

> Power concedes nothing without a demand. It never did and it never will. Find out just what any people will quietly submit to and you have found out the exact measure of injustice and wrong that will be imposed upon them, and these will continue till they are resisted with words or blows or with both. The limits of tyrants are prescribed by the endurance of those whom they oppress.

It is not widely known and is rarely acknowledged that for most of their history Africans were major contributors to and shapers of world culture (Clarke, 1991; Drake, 1990). The accomplishments of Africans have been monumental. All too often, scholars restrict their writing and research to Africans on the periphery of civilization, presenting them as stunned survivors from the trauma of colonization and slavery. These survivors have been thought to be unable to deal with the conundrums of high cultures or civilizations. DuBois (1915, p. 707) noted:

> Always Africa is giving us something new or some metempsychosis of a world-old thing. On its black bosom arose one of the earliest if not the

earliest, of self-protecting civilizations, and grew so mightily that it still furnishes superlatives to thinking and speaking men. Out of its darker and more remote forest vastness came, if I may credit many recent scientists, the first welding of iron, and I know that agriculture and trade flourished there when Europe was a wilderness. . . . Nearly every human empire that has risen in the world, material and spiritual, has found some of its greatest crises on this continent of Africa, from Greece to Great Britain.

Many people find it exceedingly difficult to see Africans as controllers of their own fate and builders of enduring civilizations (Amin, 1989). World histories and histories of civilizations, so popular in current academic circles, are based primarily on what is known as European civilization. This species of parochialism provides a false picture of human history. Few students learn that European civilization, historically speaking, is a product of the recent past, and that European culture was not indigenous but was derived from the older civilizations of Africa and Asia (Jackson, 1970, p. 302). The notion often put forth—that Africans waited in darkness for Europeans to bring light—is misguided because for most of human history the Europeans themselves were in darkness (Clarke, 1970).

Clarke (1970, p. 6) reported a speech by Richard Moore, a renowned Caribbean scholar, that captured the essence of African history and its significance:

> The significance of African history is shown, though not overtly, in the very effort to deny anything worthy of the name of history to Africa and the African peoples. This widespread and well nigh successful endeavor, maintained through some five centuries, to erase African history from the general record is a fact which of itself should be quite conclusive to thinking and open minds. For it is logical and apparent that no such undertaking would ever have been carried on, and at such length, in order to obscure and to bury what is actually of little or no significance.
>
> The significance of African history becomes still more manifest when it is realized that this deliberate denial of African history arose out of the European expansion and invasion of Africa which began in the middle of the fifteenth century with domination, enslavement and plunder. Hence, this brash denial of history and culture to Africa, and, indeed, even of human qualities and capacity for civilization to the indigenous peoples of Africa (pp. 6–7).

The history of Africa has considerable significance in the history of black people worldwide for two basic reasons: first, because people of African ancestry are dispersed worldwide, and second, because of the general derogatory image of Africans and black people everywhere that has been inherited from Western history. Malcolm X on several occasions talked about how the understanding of the historical achievement of African people was a required weapon in the struggle for liberation. He emphasized that an attachment to Africa was crucial. In a speech on the African and self-hate, Malcolm X (1990, p. 85) stated:

> You show me one of those people over here who has been thoroughly brainwashed and has a negative attitude toward Africa, and I'll show you one who has a negative attitude toward himself. You can't have a positive attitude toward yourself and a negative attitude toward Africa at the same time. To the same degree that your understanding of and attitude toward Africa become positive, you'll find that your understanding of and your attitude toward yourself will also become positive.

This perspective captures well the tension that has marked the presence of Africans in the United States and the origin of this tension in the general history of the race. Many scholars have emphasized that how Africans view their history determines how they act. They conclude that Africans in the United States must understand their history, starting on the continent, as well as the myriad ways in which current problems are informed by it.

It is customary for Africans to be viewed as objects of historical action rather than as historical actors. What is overlooked or downplayed, for example, is that the history of Africans is the history of *Homo sapiens sapiens* (Ben-Jochannan, 1988; Diop, 1974; Van Sertima, 1989). Not only did humans originate on the African continent, but the modern rendition also came from Africa (Diop, 1974; Krings et al., 1997; Tishkoff et al., 1996).

By treating Africans as either a problem or of little consequence, historians contribute to the "miseducation" of the population (Woodson, 1933). On questions concerning race, much historical writing has systematically camouflaged the shameful past of the United States (DuBois, 1935; Fredrickson, 1981). Litwak, at an annual conference of historians, exposed the distortions perpetuated by his colleagues and urged them to rectify this situation. He stated: "No group of scholars did more to shape the thinking of generations of Americans about race and Blacks than historians. . . . Whether by neglect or distortion, the scholarly monographs and texts they authored perpetuated racial stereotypes and myths" (Black Issues in Higher Education, 1987, p. 2).

Samples of This Thinking

Although historians have contributed substantially to these misconceptions, half-truths, and oftentimes unmitigated lies, they are accompanied by a cast of characters who were well known in the arts and sciences; in fact, several held positions of authority. Harris (1987), Gould (1981), Hilliard (1995), and others have provided us with a myriad of their expressions. To give only an adumbrated sketch:

The geographer Hallett (1761) stated:

> It is true that the centre of the continent is filled with burning sands,
> savage beasts and almost uninhabited deserts. The scarcity of water forces
> the different animals to come together to the same place to drink. It
> happens that finding themselves together at a time when they are in heat,
> they have intercourse one with the another, without paying regard to the
> difference between species. Thus, are produced those monsters which are
> to be found there in greater numbers than in any other part of the world
> (cited in Harris, 1987, p. 19).

The famous philosopher Hume (1768) asserted:

> I am apt to suspect the negroes . . . to be naturally inferior to the whites.
> There never was a civilized nation of any other complexion than white, nor
> even any individual eminent either in action or speculation. No ingenious
> manufacturers among them, no arts, no sciences.

Hegel (1901, cited in Harris, 1987, pp. 19–20) noted:

> It is manifest that want of self-control distinguishes the character of the
> Negroes. This condition is capable of no development or culture, and
> as I have seen them at this day, such have they always been . . . it is no
> historical part of the world; it has no movement or development to exhibit.

The renowned naturalist Agassiz (1850, p. 144) maintained that

> This compact continent of Africa exhibits a population which has been
> in example of the Egyptian civilization, of the Phoenician civilization,
> of the Roman civilization, of the Arab civilization . . . and nevertheless
> there has never been a regulated society of black men developed on the
> continent.

The historian Toynbee (1934, cited in Newby, 1969, p. 217) claimed:

> When we classify mankind by color, the only one of the primary races,
> given by this classification, which has not made a creative contribution to
> nay of our twenty-civilizations is the Black race.

Abraham Lincoln said:

> There is a physical difference between the white and black races which I
> believe will forever forbid the two races living together on terms of social
> and political equality, and inasmuch as they cannot so live, while they do
> remain together there must be the position of superior and inferior, and
> I as much as any other man am in favor of having the superior position
> assigned to the White race. . . .

> Negro equality, Fudge! How long, in the government of a God great enough to make and rule the universe shall there continue knaves to vend and fools to quip, so low a piece of demogogism as this (cited in Sinkler, 1972, p. 47).

Thomas Jefferson speculated:

> I advance it, therefore, as a suspicion only, that the Blacks, whether originally a distinct race or made distinct by time and circumstance, are inferior to the Whites in the endowment of both body and mind (cited in Gossett, 1965, p. 44).

It is worth noting that the hostilities toward the African did not escape even some white progressives. Fabian socialists, including George Bernard Shaw, were social imperialists who believed in white superiority and the manifest destiny of the British "race" (Lewontin, Rose, & Kamin, 1984). Drake (1987, p. 30) points out that even abolitionists had stilted views of the African. He asserted that one of the ironies of the eighteenth and nineteenth centuries is that a large proportion of non-Africans who fought to "abolish both slavery and the slave trade believed in the intellectual inferiority and esthetic repulsiveness of the people whose cause they espoused."

This racist legacy has placed a profound burden on historians seeking to truthfully and honestly reconstruct the history of the African. This history must rest on a solid historical base, engaging and demolishing the myriad myths fashioned by past Europeans and transmitted to the current scene (Harris, 1987). Gould notes that throughout the "egalitarian tradition of the European Enlightenment and the American revolution, I cannot identify any popular position remotely like the 'cultural relativism' that prevails (at least by lip-service) in liberal circles today, the nearest approach is a common argument that black inferiority is purely cultural and that it can be completely eradicated by education to a Caucasian standard" (Gould, 1993, p. 85).

Bernal (1991), in *Black Athena*, a book he found difficult to get published, is one of the recent scholars who has illustrated the nature of historical distortion concerning Egypt (Kemet). He noted that there existed an ancient model of the influence of Kemet upon early Greek civilization. This model held sway for many centuries, but was eventually overthrown without providing any new information. While Kemet was once believed to be the fount of European civilization, the modern model replaced Kemet, the pinnacle of Nile Valley civilization, with other, non-African sources of European civilization. Bernal contends that there were a number of forces that culminated in the primacy of the modern model, not the least of which was racism or white supremacy.

Davidson (1991), alluding to historical distortions and the way that Kemet, as part of Africa, was eliminated from world history, poses the question: "But isn't Egypt, other issues apart, quite simply a part of Africa? That, it seems, is a merely geographical irrelevance. The civilization of Pharonic Egypt, arising sometime around 3500 B.C. and continuing at least until the Roman dispositions, has been explained to us as evolving either in more or less total isolation from Africa, or as a product of West Asian stimulus. On this deeply held view, the land of ancient Egypt appears to have detached itself from the delta of the Nile, some five and a half thousand years ago, and sailed off into the Mediterranean on a course veering broadly towards the coasts of Syria. And there it apparently remained, floating somewhere in the seas of Levant, until Arab conquerors hauled it back to where it had once belonged" (p. 40) In this regard, Karenga (1993) observed that Egypt (Kemet) is the only country that has to justify its geographic location. That is, it has to answer the question of why it is in Africa, since anything of worth is assumed to have a European origin.

If the Eurocentrist cannot claim Egypt for Europe, he or she claims it for some strange wandering Asiatic people from Europe (Clarke, 1991). Why would any people build such an enduring high culture for another people and then vanish? Or build such a high culture away from home before they built a house with a window at home? (Clarke, 1994).

While the secular ideas concerning the African were devastating, various religious interpretations were at least as destructive. Metaphysical forces and religious doctrine were intertwined. The Creator God was used to underwrite and endorse white supremacist notions. Overlooking the major presence of blacks/Africans in the Bible, between the fourth century and the seventeenth and eighteenth centuries (Enlightenment), Europe recast the entire Bible into a saga of European people. The Western world basically accepted this interpretation as fact. While the Bible did not apply any racial labels, the idea of race subsequently became associated with the descendants of Ham as presented in the biblical interpretation of Noah's curse of Ham. The "curse of Ham" has since been identified as a postbiblical myth (African Heritage Study Bible, 1993).

The role of the African in the development and continuation of major "Western religions" (Islam, Christianity, and Judaism) has often been ignored and in many instances denied. Not only have Africans been major proselytizers of the development of major "Western" religions, many of the major philosophical concepts and ethical codes originated from earlier African religions or spiritual systems (Ben-Jochannan, 1991). As a consequence of the barrage of misinformation, it is a generally held view that almost all biblical characters are Caucasian or European when in fact Africa was the stage on which most of the biblical stories were acted out by actors who were black (African Heritage Study Bible, 1993; Ben-Jochannan, 1991).

Religions of exclusively traditional African origin have often been given such pejorative titles as "Paganism, Voodooism, Witchcraft, Fetishism, and

Black Magic," and considered to be of lesser status and significance than the religions thought to originate outside Africa (Ben-Jochannan, 1991). Jackson (1972, 1985) noted that "Western religions" have distorted the understanding of the origins of the Christ myth and its allegorical truth as it pertains to the African continent.

Clarke (1995) maintains that one of the most unfortunate consequences of the human degradation process that Africans have undergone is the replacement of their conception of the deity with that of their oppressor. More often than not their Lord and Savior has very little physical resemblance to them, an uncommon occurrence in human history (Jackson, 1970).

The Scientific Community

Although the impact of social and political views is profound in the analyses of the African, scientific views have taken on more significance than other forms of knowledge. Often science is viewed as the final word, the ultimate legitimator, in contemporary Western society. Science is accorded the authority that once went to the church. After all, scientists are ordinary human beings, unconsciously reflecting in their theories the social and political constraints of their times (Gould, 1977, 1995). Lewontin et al. (1992, p. 3) argue that

> science, like other productive activities, like the state, the family, sport, is a social institution completely integrated into and influenced by the structure of all our other social institutions. The problems that science deals with, the ideas that it uses in investigating those problems, even the so-called scientific results that come out of scientific investigation are all deeply influenced by predispositions that derive from the society in which we live. Scientists do not begin life as scientists, after all, but as social beings immersed in a family, a state, a productive structure, and they view nature through a lens that has been molded by their social experience.

With respect to Western scholarship, it has a long and torturous history of criminalizing the victim with a stamp of biological inferiority, in short, using biology as an accomplice to scientific racism (Franklin, 1991; Gould, 1977, 1995; Harding, 1993). Further, the history of this racism is characterized by the relatively few challenges it has received, particularly from mainstream science. Investigators have produced "scientific evidence" for blatantly racist views; this evidence has subsequently been found to be erroneous, but it has nonetheless been widely accepted and has contributed to repressive social policies (National Academy of Sciences, 1993). For example, despite obvious flaws and inconsistency in the data of Cyril Burt, who made a spirited attempt to show the heritability of IQ, a large segment of the academic community embraced his work and praised his name. Even after Burt was found to be engaged in wholesale fudging and distortion of his data, there were those who came to his defense (Lewontin, Rose, & Kamin, 1993). Although poorly armed, they attempted to defend their esteemed colleague. It is as if many members of the scientific community have a trained incapacity to see things differently (Kaplan, 1964). Biological determinist theory, despite its claims of being new scientifically, has a long history in Western societies. Determinists justify inequality as natural, fair, or both. Indeed, their theories provided the framework for addressing demands for equal economic reward and social status. Thus, the perspective that presents Africans as being intellectually deficient has important social purposes (Amin, 1989; Lewontin, Rose, & Kamin, 1984; Lewontin, 1992). One rendition of this thinking has come in the form of a book entitled *The Bell Curve*. It suffers from many of the same flaws in reasoning, analysis, and ideological commitment as exhibited by its predecessors (Fischer et al., 1996).

Unity of Africans and Africans in the Diaspora

The demand for cheap labor, the visibility of blacks, and European attitudes about Africans strengthened the institution of slavery by deeply embedding in Euro-American society conceptions that were used to justify slavery and black inferiority. The racial conditions in the Americas, particularly in the United States, followed from earlier attitudes about Africans, such as the myths that Africans had no history and no written language. While Africans, like other groups, have experienced the ebb and flow of fortune—the pinnacle and the nadir—the past five hundred years have been particularly dismal for African people taken in the aggregate. It led one scholar to speak of a five-hundred-year room of history in which African people experienced slavery, colonialism, anticolonialism, the African independence explosion, and the rise and decline of the human rights movement in the United States. As Robinson (1983, p. 95) explains, the development of economic structures and political institutions among Europeans over the past five hundred years has had a profound impact on the destinies of Africans. Europe's intrusion into African history during this period intensified the racism inherent in Western civilization and its self-destructive mechanisms, such as the use of totalitarian force. This period, which has been called the "Christopher Columbus era" even though it began before Columbus was born, has greatly benefited the Europeans, as it resulted in the "renewal of European nationalism, the expulsion of Moors, Arabs, and Jews from Spain in 1492, and the beginning of the holocaust of slavery that stimulated the economic life of Europe" (Robinson, 1983, p. 95). This led to the institution of genocidal processes, a resurgence of prejudice, notions of Western white supremacy, and ultimately to the entrenchment of the idea of black inferiority (Robinson, 1983).

Enslavement of the African in the New World

The enslavement of one group or another has a long history and no group has escaped the grasp of this institution at some point in its history. However, the concept of slavery is so profoundly associated with Africans, that unless otherwise modified, the term when used in this book refers to the experiences of the African.

The form of slavery introduced by the Europeans in the fifteenth and sixteenth centuries has no rivals in barbarity. In ancient societies, the enslaved were held for a limited time, for specific reasons. Often captured in local wars, the enslaved had some rights that enslavers had to respect. Further, skin color did not determine whether or not an individual was enslaved. One of the most striking contributions of the Europeans to the New World was the elaboration, perpetuation, and extension of the concept of black inferiority (Harris, 1987) and, in the context of the United States, the associated concept of white supremacy. Indeed, the social relations between Africans and Europeans were informed by the ideology of white supremacy or this "conscious and deliberate process of degrading Africans for economic and political ends" (Drake, 1990, p. xix).

Given the enormous impact of slavery on Africans in the New World, it is crucial to understand its operations so as to recognize its contemporary traces, especially its impact on the psychology of Africans. Although slavery formally ended more than a hundred years ago, its legacies remain. When one explores the nature of this peculiar institution, it comes as no surprise.

Forcing individuals to submit to the bondage of slavery required extraordinary techniques and procedures, all intended to change an independent, self-supporting individual into a totally dependent person. The desired outcome was the subjugation of the mental processes or, more generally, cultural genocide. Of paramount importance to slavers was destroying the identity of the enslaved. "Slaves were torn from their motherland; separated from their kin; denied and forbidden their names, customs and religion; and stringently prohibited from securing formal education or marriage. To the extent that it was possible, they were forced to face enslavement in a new land singly, one by one, alone and without even the understanding and promise which their families had infused into their highly personal names" (Hodge-Edelin, 1990, p. 37).

Oppressed Africans had to contend with attempts to alienate them from the possibility of a functionally realistic perception of reality, knowledge of self, self-esteem, and fellow Africans (Wilson, 1990). There were attempts to preclude any identification with positive, undistorted images of Africans and African culture. Attributing the source of the problem to the broad category of education, Woodson (1933) states that this was the ultimate device for control and that it has continued with certain institutional social practices.

With an eye toward providing context, Drake (1987) urges us to keep in mind the fact that racist thinking has been bestowed upon various European and Asiatic groups and that white racism has operated in the oppression of Asians as well as Africans. He notes, however, that since the "sixteenth century black people everywhere have been subjected to the most sustained and severe racist assaults upon their bodies and psyches. The reasons for the extreme animus against 'blackness' require an explanation separate from that which accounts for White racism in general." Optimistically, he claims that the "epoch of constant, relentless derogation of Africans and peoples of African descent is drawing to a close because of forces convergent since World War II. But in attacking the color prejudice that remains as a legacy of slavery and colonial imperialism, consideration must be given to the way in which Blacks became the central target of White Racism. The crucial factor, of course, was the traffic in black bodies which flourished from the sixteenth century through part of the nineteenth century, and the enslavement of black people throughout the Americas. With the end of slavery, colonial imperialism on the continent of Africa shifted the scene of exploitation of African laborers to their home soil and reinforced antiblack ideologies that had emerged during the slavery period" (pp. 23–24).

In a similar vein, Karenga (1993) provided a penetrating rendition of the impact of slavery on Africans, both in the diaspora and on the continent. He said the enslavement through mass murder, physical destruction, and dislocation resulted in depopulation of the continent, with estimates running as high as 100 million; resulted in the loss of young people and skilled personnel, which adversely affected the scientific and cultural development of Africa; perpetuated patterns of life and material achievement which led to uncertainty and insecurity; and influenced economic activity by distorting and in some cases abolishing market industries. Significantly, it subordinated and grafted economies onto the commerce of the enslavement industry, and led directly to the underdevelopment of Africa and the overdevelopment of Europe. While chattel slavery was devastating, it was overshadowed by a worse form of slavery; namely, one which "capture[d] the mind and imprison[ed] the motivation, perception, aspiration and identity in a web of anti-self images, generating a personal and collective self-destruction" (Akbar, 1996, p. v).

On the individual level, Nkrumah (1964, p. 5) referred to the situation in which the colonized African students, whose roots were in their own society, "[were] systematically starved of sustenance, introduced to Greek and Roman history, the cradle history of modern Europe, and then encouraged to treat this portion of the story of man, together with the subsequent history of Europe, as the only worthwhile portion. This history [was] anointed with a universalistic flavouring that titillate[d] the palate of certain African intellectuals so agreeably that they [became] alienated from their own immediate society."

Extending the above idea, Rodney (1972, p. 255) stated that the "formal school system and the informal value system of colonialism destroyed social solidarity and promoted the worst form of alienated individualism without social responsibility." Chinweizu (1987, p. 9) maintained that the African mind must be decolonized by overturning the authority that alien traditions exercise over the African. "The decolonisation of the African mind must therefore be seen as a collective enterprise, as a communal exorcism through an intellectual bath in which we need one another's help to scrub those nooks of our minds which we cannot scour by ourselves."

The Nature of the Resistance

Even under slavery, colonization, segregation, and apartheid, African peoples have resisted in many different ways at many different times. While it is important to delineate the forces that have impacted on the position in which Africans now find themselves, it is equally important to specify their response to this unparalleled oppression. This has been an ongoing, perpetual struggle that has varied in intensity, depending on the level and intensity of the onslaught. Or, as Ture and Hamilton (1992, p. 194) observed, Africans have demonstrated the law of human nature: where there exists oppression, there exists resistance; and where oppression increases, resistance increases.

Africans worldwide have had to contend, to varying degrees, with the following strategies of subordination: elimination of all personal identities; the separation of language groups and the forced acquisition of a foreign language; inculcation of fear, primarily through violence; dissemination of the family unit; sexual abuse of African women; creation of the color caste system; forced religious conversion to the Europeanized version of Christianity; and continuous propagation of the myth of African as a savage. Used with excruciating constancy, these were forces that the enslaved African had to overcome (Latif & Latif, 1994).

Several instances of resistance have been noted (e.g., Bennett, 1962; Blassingame, 1972; Harris, 1987; Paris, 1995). Bennett (1962) noted that many revolts took place before the slave ship departed. The slave ship rebellions were so common that a new type of insurance was introduced— "insurrection insurance." Moreover, there are many examples of physical resistance to enslavement on the African continent. In the Caribbean and in the United States revolts and conspiracies were plentiful, which ultimately led to the abolition of slavery in those areas (Aptheker, 1944; Bennett, 1962; Jackson, 1970).

Double Consciousness

After emancipation, Africans not only fought against other forms of physical imposition (e.g., sharecropping and later the "Black Codes"), but also against all attempts to control their perception of the world and their self-image. DuBois (1964, pp. 16–17) characterized this tension-filled "double consciousness" as

> this sense of always looking at one's self through the eyes of others, of measuring one's soul by the tape of a world that looks on in amused contempt and pity. One ever feels his two-ness—an American, a Negro—two souls, two thoughts, two unreconciled strivings, two warring ideals in one dark body, whose dogged strength alone keeps it from being torn asunder. The history of the American Negro is the history of this strife—this longing to attain self-conscious manhood, to merge his double self into a better and truer self.

This construct of double consciousness has had a profound influence on scholars operating within the African-centered paradigm (Gaines & Reed, 1994), but it is by no means confined to it. The aforementioned statement has been identified as one of the most popular and often cited among DuBois's many insightful statements and comments proffered during his long and illustrious career (Reed, 1998). The construct has been used in a wide range of disciplines and among a diverse group of scholars operating from markedly different ideological perspectives. This has led one scholar to argue that "sundry intellectuals misread DuBois ahistorically and instead project their own thinking onto him" (Reed, 1998, p. 92). While in some instances this may be true, the value of the construct remains. Moreover, there is no a priori reason for not extending, expanding, or otherwise refashioning the construct to fit within one's own research or activist endeavor as long as its sources are duly noted. The major value of the construct seems to reside in its richness as a source for the generation of compatible conceptions.

One of the important elements of the double consciousness construct and how it was developed by DuBois is that it encapsulates the psychological and sociohistorial realities of oppression and points to the strength of the African American culture. This is particularly noteworthy as African culture had been defined as lacking or deficient or, in some instances, nonexistent. Further, DuBois's conceptualization suggests that although the culture and the people are under constant attack, the culture provides the people the wherewithal to develop a positive sense of self or the means to "resolve the tension between pride and shame in self" (Gaines & Reed, 1994, p. 12).

In this study, the underlying theme is double consciousness. Along with Gaines and Reed (1994, 1995) and several other scholars, I maintain that double consciousness is a predictable consequence of being a member of a group that has been exploited, dominated, and otherwise oppressed for a long time in recent history. It supplies the framework for the research problem and serves as the basis for several hypotheses concerning the African American's self-concept, especially black identity and self-esteem. Specifically, I acknowledge the sundry negative forces impinging on the African American's attempts to build a positive self, broadly defined, and I embrace the notion that this leads to an internal struggle to fashion a functional self. I view double consciousness as a phenomenon and a dynamic process that changes in direction and strength based on the response to ever-changing external factors and to the present state of the culture. The thrust of this research is to test, with appropriate data, some of the major implications of double consciousness and its expansion in the context of the study of the self-concept of African Americans.

While DuBois's explication of double consciousness has great value as originally conceptualized, it needs to be clarified. In agreement with several other scholars—Holt, (1995), Lewis (1993), and Sundquist (1993)—I argue that DuBois's conceptualization and discussion of double consciousness leads to neither assimilation nor separation but to a permanent tension, a certain hyphenated identity. I thus present a theoretical perspective that argues for a resolution of the double consciousness. It suggests that the individual synthesizes the many positive forces that impinge on his or her sense of self, and directs them to the development of a person deeply engaged in the essence of African culture. Thus, the struggle identified by DuBois is fashioned into a self-defining thrust toward the fostering of a new and optimal self in step with the interest of the group.

Conceiving cultural identity in broad terms and manifested along three different dimensions—linguistic, psychological, and historical—Diop (1991) asserts that Africans in the diaspora, while having the linguistic bond severed, have tenaciously held on to the historical and psychological bonds to Africa. Extending this idea, Kambon (1992) contends that the personality of the African American is molded and defined by the African worldview, where consciousness is wholistic and relational, and where the person obtains his or her significance only within the framework of the community. For the most part, this worldview is decidedly unconscious and firmly anchored, yet frequently disguised and distorted.

Resistance to the Pejorative Images

The major trend in the portrayal of Africans has been created and nurtured by several generations of white image makers. Nonetheless, its obverse has been created and sustained by African image makers, who have exposed the omissions and distortions in the imagery fostered by whites. Referring to this "war of images," Dates and Barlow (1993) assert that the definition and control of images of African people in the mass media have been contested from the outset along racial lines. Attempts at white cultural domination have been met with African cultural resistance. Gray (1995) fashioned the issue as an ongoing struggle between the claims made by various dominant commercial institutions of image making and representation, defining and framing "blackness" in the imagination of the majority, and claims originating from the subjects themselves. Indeed, many scholars have pointed to the need for African people to define themselves, to reclaim their history and their identity from "cultural terrorism, from the depredation of self-justifying white guilt" (Ture & Hamilton, 1992, pp. 34–35). An interesting development has taken place recently. Beginning in the 1980s, African American youth, building on their skepticism and oftentimes cynicism toward the majority media, garnered powerful and pervasive alternatives in various areas of popular culture. Similarly, and not necessarily independently of the aforementioned youth, African American cultural purveyors—writers, filmmakers, hiphop and rap artists, musicians and painters—introduced many powerful conceptions of the world and African Americans' place in it (Gray, 1995).

Black writers cognizant of the images and stereotypes presented of Africans have striven to submit alternative views. These alternatives have taken several forms, reflecting various phases of the ongoing struggle for free expression and survival in the context of the prevailing white order. While historically trying to resolve their own inner tensions, black writers have tried to provide a content that derives from a double vision arising from oral and literary conventions of both African and European symbol systems (Bell, 1987; Wa Thiong'o, 1986).

Neal (1968) contends that all African American writers have had to deal with this aforementioned double consciousness, either to make peace with it or to make war against it. Further, he says, double consciousness cannot be ignored, and every African American writer has taken a stance toward it, whether he or she admits it or not.

One may, however, distinguish which stance toward double consciousness was more dominant at any given time among these African American writers. Of relevance to this discussion is the period starting from the 1800s, which Karenga (1993, pp. 416–429) referred to as the period of "protest" literature during which African American writers voiced disapproval against the established order, enslavement, exploitation, oppression, and white supremacy. Almost all writers who published during this time wrote in the protest mode. Some of the foremost names in this period were George Moses Horton (*Hope of Liberty*), Frances Harper (*Poems on Miscellaneous Subjects*), Anna Cooper (*A Voice from the South*), and Martin Delaney (*Blake*). Several powerful and penetrating political autobiographies were written during this period, including those of Frederick Douglass (*Life and Times*) and William Wells Brown (*Narrative of William Wells Brown*).

The next era, called the "Pre-Harlem Renaissance Period," saw the rise of a number of powerful scholar-activists such as James Weldon Johnson and his brother John, Ida B. Wells, Paul Laurence Dunbar, and W. E. B. DuBois. This period led into the "Harlem Renaissance," one of the most fruitful periods for African American writers, when African Americans explored their African roots for rejuvenation and intellectual sustenance, and emphasized black culture and black pride. It was a period when Marcus Garvey issued a call for black self-reliance. Alain Locke spoke of a "New Negro." Claude McKay urged Africans to fight their oppressors rather than "die like dogs." Cruse (1984, pp. 11–12) contends that in the twentieth century Harlem became the most strategically important community of black America. Harlem, he says, is still the major location of the black world's search for identity and salvation. Black America will follow the lead of Harlem. More generally, he states that in terms of political, economic, cultural, and ethnic reasons, Harlem is the key community for the entire black world.

While this Renaissance period was eclipsed by the Great Depression, its momentum continued into the 1950s with the work of writers like James Baldwin and Gwendolyn Brooks. Often called the "Second Black Renaissance," the 1950s and 1960s manifested tremendous literary and political diversity. This decade was preeminent in self-conscious goals and achievements. The human rights movement was both a result and a consequence of heightened black identity and self-worth. Aside from destroying structural obstacles to black progress, the movement also emphasized the elimination of psychological barriers (Morris, 1992). And these barriers were most effectively dealt with by the advocates of Black Power during the latter part of the 1960s and the early 1970s (Smith, 1995).

Karenga refers to the 1960s as a very important period in the evolution of African people and culture—a time in which there was a building of economic institutions, alternative educational institutions, and the black student movement; the construction of black studies programs; the linking of African people on the continent and those in the diaspora; the examination of the idea of armed struggle and self-defense as a right and obligation; the casting of the world in black images and interests; and the securing of the groundwork for benefits experienced in the 1970s. As a lasting legacy, the 1960s taught African people that any liberation struggles depends primarily on the struggle on the people themselves, no matter the sincerity and support of allies. As a period, Karenga (1993) submits that it was the most important decade in African history and that its achievements were substantial and enduring.

Although the writing from the next period, the 1970s, did not have the intensity of the Second Renaissance, it did speak to African peoples' life chances, aspirations, and struggles. The greatest gains during this period were the victories in electoral politics, but also of significance is the beginning of a very candid and open discussion among black men and women concerning their relationship. Such discussions were standard fare in many old and newly created black journals and other publications. Finally and relatedly, the 1980s and 1990s (a period of major challenges to African people) gave rise to a plethora of works by and about black women. There was also a continuing expansion of African American criticism as well as specific womanist criticism. A very insightful historical overview of some of this work is provided by Watkins (1997). A third aspect of this era was the tendency for authors to "distance themselves from the long literary tradition of social engagement as members of the African American community." Politically speaking the 1990s witnessed the Los Angeles Rebellion, a manifestation of injustices heaped upon African people and other oppressed groups. Court is still in session on the outcome of the 1990s, but it is clear it was a decisive decade with conflicts and challenges that have shaped and will shape the future of this country (Karenga, 1993; Oliver & Shapiro, 1998; Smith, 1995).

Communication and Media Contribution:
The Continuation of a Struggle

Communication and the media have often been used to justify the power of whites over blacks, Europeans over Africans. In fact, white literature and the mass media have participated in fostering the notion of black inferiority. Further, these images are not harmless products of an idealized popular culture. They are typically socially constructed images that are selective, limited, superficial, and distorted in their portrayal of African people (Dates & Barlow, 1993; Riggs, 1988, 1991a,b). A typical theme running through these historical characterizations is the connection between Africans on the continent and Africans in the diaspora. The explicit link made was that it is from the root (Africa) that the presumed problems in the branches (Africans in the United States and the Americas in general) have arisen. Images from television, newspapers, radio, and other media have rarely presented Africans in heroic roles. Most of the time they are not portrayed seriously at all. The media may be viewed as a form of invented reality that colonizes information about the world just as nations colonize people (Clarke, 1991).

Semmes (1992) argues that over time the media images of African Americans have been informed by a normative orientation of white supremacy, manifested in the limited images and roles given to them and the establishment of a subordinate role to whites. Beginning in the antebellum period, these images persisted as technological changes ushered in motion pictures, radio, and television. He further states that the changes witnessed came about only after protracted struggle. He points to the human rights and black consciousness movements as instruments in modifying the grotesque stereotypes and expanding the range of roles that African Americans could play. He maintains that the independent African American media was largely responsible for presenting alternatives to their characterization. More will be said about this later.

Examples reflecting the distorted media coverage of African Americans abound. One such glaring instance was the media treatment of the Charles Stuart case in Boston, where an upper-class white claimed that he had been shot and his wife and unborn child had been murdered by a lone African American male. The shameless coverage by the white media of the presumed murder is a classic in racism and media bias. Not only was the alleged assailant indicted by most of the media but so was the entire African American community. Despite the fact that the accusations were bogus, the major media refused to admit that they had done "much of anything wrong" (Gomes & Williams, 1990). The case raised the unsettling question of why Stuart's folly or lie could have been so readily and pervasively accepted, if race and crime, especially African Americans and crime, were not so ingrained in the American psyche. This phenomenon has been documented by several scholars (e.g., Entman, 1992; Jamieson, 1990; Oliver, 1994).

Putting the problem in a larger context, Gomes and Williams (1990) observed that although the exploitation of African Americans and divisions among America's working strata are enabled by various cultural institutions, such as the government and schools, the mass media are key in affecting attitudes about race relations and the presumed symbiosis between race and crime.

Following the White House perception of race, certain majority media have provided more coverage of "reverse discrimination" as contrasted with such issues clearly more important to African Americans: eliminating poverty, broadening educational opportunities, and furthering previous human rights advancements. This may be meaningfully interpreted as an example of the media's proclivity to present government priorities camouflaged as objectivity (De Uriarte, 1994; Herman & Chomsky, 1989).

A number of scholars have observed certain patterns or themes running throughout literature that have characterized the African. Brown (1968) referred to seven overlapping stereotypes or enduring values that mark white authors' writings about Africans: the contented slave, the wretched freedman, the comic darky, the black brute, the tragic mulatto, the local-color clown, and the exotic primitive. Brown asserted that all of these stereotypes are exemplified by either exaggeration or omission; they all agree in stressing the African's divergence from an Anglo-Saxon norm to the flattery of the latter.

Many scholars have used classification schemes or some modification thereof to analyze the treatment of Africans in the media, especially print.

For example, these seven categories identified by Brown have been collapsed into three categories by Finkenstaedt (1994). The brute and the exotic primitive were combined into one category (retaining the label "brute"). The second category combined the contented slave, the comic darky, and the local-color black (retaining the label "contented slave"). The wretched freedman and the tragic mulatto represented the third category (retaining the label of "mulatto"). The first category captures the predominant theme in the white literature, depicting the black as the symbol of subversion of white civilization, that is, the symbol of the "unregenerate, non-Christian, non-European man" (Finkenstaedt, 1994). This stereotype does not accord the black even human status but associates him with animal nature. The African is presented as an unintelligent and vicious denizen of the savage jungle. In contrast, the contented slave, while also presented as an inferior to whites, is characterized as amicable, almost always sexless, with undying love for whites and shouldering their problems as his problems. Finally, the third category, the mulatto, is similar to the brute but is depicted as a tragic entity, malicious and destructive, with the emotions of a black but the cleverness of a white.

The Press

Africans have long been suspicious of the white press, accusing it of shunning issues that Africans consider important. Unless their views echoed those of the dominant white culture, Africans rarely had an opportunity to be heard. The white press was not trusted to tell the truth about Africans and their experiences. Moreover, many Africans have charged this press with directing an inordinate amount of attention to racial conflict, crime, and negative news about Africans, while avoiding favorable news (Kerner Commission, 1968). The majority press is still inclined to present African Americans as lazy, heavy drug users, and major welfare recipients and to condemn black crime without consideration of one of its main causes—white supremacy (Lusane, 1991). When journalism discovered "crack" in the latter part of 1985, it signified the start of rapacious coverage in which the race and class connection was redefined. No longer a glamour drug associated with white impropriety, it "became increasingly associated with pathology and poor people of color isolated in America's inner cities—the so-called urban underclass" (Reeves & Campbell, 1994, p. 74).

European Americans have dominated the general press, or publications directed at the general population. Historically, blacks had no voice in this press. It is possible to identify the treatment of African Americans and other groups of color in developmental stages. For example, Wilson and Gutierrez (1995) maintained that there were five interrelated phases that may historically be identified as (1) exclusionary, (2) threatening issue (blacks, for example, being considered a threat to the social order), (3) confrontation, (4) stereotypical selection, and (5) multiracial coverage. The first four phases, they say, were so common and regularly practiced by the news media that they essentially acted as latent policy. On the other hand, the fifth phase, which represents the present era, has yet to be achieved but is the desired goal.

As in the other media, African Americans responded to these different phases by creating their own activist, involved, and committed press. This press was dauntless in pressing images to mold self-esteem and opinion, and in setting the public agenda of African Americans (Dates, 1990a). Presently, it is the black press which is intimately involved in the definition of what constitutes multiracial coverage.

Initially, in the early 1800s, the black press consisted essentially of newspapers. A little more than a century later, however, other types of print media gained popularity. Partly because of the self-imposed limitations of these newspapers, magazines merged and took over the organizational journals' role previously assumed by newspapers. Today, the black press has furthered its tradition of struggle and advocacy. For example, it has been in the forefront in support of affirmative action and in the challenge of the ever-present academic and institutional assault on black intellectual abilities and capabilities.

Presently, on numerous major issues, especially those pertaining to African Americans, one can see the substantial differences in interpretation by the black press and the white or majority press. Of great importance for many African Americans, the black press provides alternative perspectives, thus clarifying their fit within society and the position or agenda that might or should be endorsed on given issues (Dates & Barlow, 1993; Wilson & Gutierrez, 1995).

Film

With the advent of film came a renewal and magnification of the stereotypes of Africans that were first made an integral part of common culture in earlier pulp fiction, magazines, and newspapers (Cripps, 1993). Further, the various images, although false, for many whites were reality, as a greater number of whites learned about Africans primarily through newspapers, books, films, and other mass media.

Winston (1982) states that Africans have been presented in the cinema as one gigantic illusion. He maintains that Africans have been subordinated, marginalized, positioned, and devalued in every possible manner to glorify and relentlessly hold in place the white-dominated symbolic and racial hierarchy of the United States. Taking the extended view, the image of the African in commercial film has been constantly shifting, with a constant barrage of insults. It has had fleeting illuminations and revelations, and even brief instances of a true range of black existence.

Bogle (1994) has provided a historical timeline of the various representations of Africans from film's earliest days to the present. He sees various decades as being characterized by distinctive images of Africans, all of which persist in some form to this day. According to Bogle, five basic types of Africans—toms, coons, mulattos, mammies, and bucks—dominated film imagery in the early years of the twentieth century. During the 1920s, the image of the jester developed, followed by the images of African Americans as domestics during the 1930s and as entertainers, singers, and dancers clad in zoot suits and sequined gowns during the 1940s.

By the end of the 1950s—perhaps the most prodigious decade for blacks in film—Africans were being viewed as a peculiar set of people. This trend continued into the 1960s, as cinema reflected the turmoil of an era of stupendous change and the synthesis of old and new. Many of the films during this decade explored provocative topics and controversial subject matter—poverty, exploitation, interracial cohabitation—and the activist African took center stage.

In contrast to and yet as an extension of the 1960s, the 1970s were characterized as "Bucks and a Black Movie Boom." In this contradictory era, the movies were markedly different from those of previous decades, yet old images frequently reemerged with slight variations. Unparalleled in movie history in its energy and importance, this era opened with films making political commentary and ended with movies that were notably more escapist.

The decade of the 1980s was the Era of Tan. It was a period during which films would strive to obliterate the blackness of a black star. Frequently, a black star appeared in a general release movie, but he or she had not a semblance of cultural identity; it was smoothed out of the star's essence and submerged within a white cultural framework. In other words, characters were not white and were not black, they were more like a tan blend.

The present era introduced new stars, new filmmakers, and a new African American cinema. In the early 1990s, new black artists received leading roles, others had important supporting roles, and some received considerable notoriety. Another aspect of the era was the rise of African American filmmakers who created a new kind of cinema, often inventively using symbols and icons from the African American community. Within the domain of Hollywood films' treatment of black life, even for critically acclaimed films, there still remains to a large degree an emphasis on the agency of whites. More concretely, Gray (1995, p. 156) observed that "Black agency and subjectivities are framed and made possible at the behest of sympathetic whites such as the contentious but benign Miss Daisy in *Driving Miss Daisy*, the ambitious but dutiful young white officer in *Glory*, and the transgressive but loyal Idgie in *Fried Green Tomatoes*."

Black Cinema

African Americans responded to the barrage of insulting portrayals of black characters in the film industry by creating an alternative black film movement, which emerged in the late 1920s and grew into the 1930s. Filmmakers took charge of presenting a more accurate picture of the African. Although filmmakers were constrained by meager funds as well as technical and distribution problems, many films they produced during this period were outstanding (Bogle, 1994). While the black film fizzled in the 1940s, the demand for an alternative to the Hollywood images resulted in a new set of black filmmakers in the 1980s and 1990s. Their films typically reflected contemporary social problems. Given the tradition from which they sprang and the reasons for their existence, it is likely that these films will continue to contest various images of Africans in the motion picture industry. In order to sustain themselves and continue to grow, black filmmakers will undoubtedly have to express the culture, consciousness, and commitments of the African American community while maintaining box office profitability.

Television

When Africans have found themselves in opposition to viewpoints or images presented in print media, radio, or film, they have created an alternative channel; however, the rise of the television industry presented a unique set of challenges. Besides the prohibitive cost of obtaining a television station, there are a host of other impediments. Thus, the attempts to change black images or suggest materials for inclusion on television required African Americans to put public pressure on television networks and stations. As a consequence of organized resistance to certain images and shows presented on television, the industry has made noticeable changes. Public television, which was developed as an alternative outlet to cater to the needs and interests not accommodated by the commercial industry, has a better report card when it comes to serving blacks. It, too, had to respond to pressures from black and other progressive sources. By the late 1980s, the Public Broadcasting System began to include several positive images and to portray a broader range of relevant issues to diverse groups, including Africans (Dates, 1990c; Frederickson, 1971). It has moved closer to its mandate, but it remains "thin and superficial" (Unger & Gergen, 1991).

Television, which incorporates the technical attributes of sound and visual and the artistic attributes of theater and literature, however, may be the ultimate medium. Clearly, it is the most popular. Initially touted as the great democratizer, it was hailed as a tool in the resolution of age-old social problems. Given its "commercial imperatives, formal character, texts, organizational and industrial structure, technical apparatus, and relationship to everyday life," television fosters contradictory manifestations (Gray, 1995, p. 9). To succeed in fulfilling its task of making meaning and providing entertainment, television operates on basic assumptions about the shared experiences and awareness of its viewers. Gray (1995, p. 10) further states that "black representations in commercial network television are situated within the existing material and institutional hierarchies of privilege and power based on class (middle class), race (whiteness), gender (patriarchal), and sexual (heterosexual) differences." This situation is even more pronounced concerning race or ethnicity, where the "very presence of African Americans in television discourse appeals to this normative 'common sense,' this working knowledge of the history, codes, struggles, and memories of race relations in the United States."

Although the older electronic media had presented Africans in less than flattering roles or with a limited range of human possibilities, the new electronic medium was supposed to be different. Some maintained that Africans would be provided an equal chance to participate in the medium. Whereas other media—literature, film, and newspapers—were purveyors of stereotypical images and generally enshrined the notion of black inferiority, television was to be a harbinger of change.

In analyzing the relationship that television has had with African Americans, MacDonald (1992) has identified three eras. The formative first decade (1948–57) was the "Promise Denied" or, perhaps, the "Dream Deferred." While making an initial pass at authenticity and accurate and broad representations of Africans, the stage ended with the well-worn stereotypes. The presentations turned out to be little more than an extension of the same story lines and themes of submissiveness and black inferiority reflected in the earlier electronic media, film and radio. The second era was the "Age of the Civil Rights Movement" (1957–70). During this period, television portrayals moved toward a more equitable position for Africans, yet still contained major shortcomings. By the end of this period, television was shying away from many of the pressing social issues that it had briefly entertained at the beginning of this era. Lastly, the 1970s to the present has been described as the "Age of the New Minstrelsy," in which African Americans are more visible in programming, yet still susceptible to racial ridicule. Historically, there has not been a period in which so many African Americans have been presented on television with such stereotypical images (MacDonald, 1992).

Winston (1982) stated that television develops a "set of symbols used not only to convey racial messages, but also to define racial reality in terms that accord with the cultural, social, and political fact of white supremacy." Similarly, a number of scholars have argued that the media, and television news in particular, are responsible for fostering modern racism or a slightly veiled "anti-black affect," expressed in antagonism, resentment, and anger toward blacks' wishes, and a lack of sympathy with claims on resources traditionally reserved for whites. For example, the media, and especially television, covers issues concerning drug use and race as if young African Americans are the major users and suppliers (Hutchinson, 1994). Contrary to the mass media depiction of a young African American spread-eagled on the ground or as the target of a highly visible drug raid, whites dominate the drug trafficking industry and are its major users.

While the above characterization is clearly evident, it is important to recognize other representations that have managed to survive. That is, there were, although less frequent, and there still are oppositional representations on commercial television. Such programs as *The Cosby Show, Frank's Place, A Different World*, and *In Living Color* have been identified as meaningful if not exemplary alternatives (Gray, 1995). For example, *The Cosby Show*, the focus of extensive debate about its meaning (Dyson, 1989; Jhally & Lewis, 1992), was highly significant for its often overlooked expression of African American diversity and its articulation and exhibition of black possibility. Indeed, it may be seen as an important base for the development of crucial expansion of African American representation on television.

While the above comments have focused primarily on entertainment television, that is, that which explicitly attempts to entertain, what is also worthy of greater consideration is television news, that is, that which explicitly attempts to inform. Recognizing that television news is generally considered the main source of information on political issues, it is worth examining its content offerings. In doing so, we find that the same pattern is evident. Television news often reflects racial stereotypes that have engendered white hostility and fear of African Americans. This portrayal suggest that African Americans are violent and a threat to whites, with a proclivity for demanding from the political system more than they deserve. In short, as a group they are presented as a problem (Entman, 1994; Gandy, 1994; Herman, 1997). The most devastating aspect of this portrayal is most clearly seen in the news about crime and violence, politics and poverty (Entman, 1994, Herman, 1997).

Music

Black music is perhaps the richest and most vibrant domain of African American culture, where the representation, revelation, celebration, and debate of African American culture and experiences have taken place (Baraka, 1991; Gray, 1995). Black music, including gospels, spirituals, blues, jazz, and rhythm and blues, represents an identifiable legacy or tradition. At the same time, it has social, political, and artistic content, which represents a reaction to middle-class industrial values.

There have been many different and related conceptions of black music. Cone (1991), for example, defines black music in five fundamental ways.

First, as unity music, integrating the hope and despair of African Americans and directing them to total liberation. Second, as functional music, with its objectives being connected to the consciousness of the African American community. Third, as social and political music—a "rebellion against humiliating deadness of western culture," and a "rejection of white culture values" and affirming a political alternative for African Americans. Fourth, as theological music, relating the spiritual force that drives African Americans to self-reliance. Fifth, as a vibrant living entity, engulfed in the paradox if not contradiction of black existence.

In its most advanced forms black music is completely antithetical to middle-class values and standards (Baraka, 1967). Historically, black music reflects the pain, the hurt, and the sadness of an oppressed and uprooted people, while simultaneously expressing feelings of release, oftentimes ecstasy. It is at the same time expressions of grief and joy, love and stultification, hate and forbearance (Finkenstaedt, 1994).

During the Harlem Renaissance, when writers and painters submitted their creative edge to "the paternalism and indifference of their white sponsors," it was black music which remained steadfast in maintaining its fundamental character (Finkenstaedt, 1994). Cruse (1970), surveying the artistic landscape from 1920 to 1960, noted that it was only jazz that did not retrogress in the face of external pressures. However, even in the case of jazz, one may easily observe the intrusion by commercial interests that have often recolored its creative landscape. Existing within the confines of a consumer society with consumer ethics, Baraka and Baraka (1987) observed that jazz also had to vigorously fight to maintain its space. When a new jazz form attains a certain developmental stage, it is "duplicated by corporations, diluted commercially bowdlerized, for the sake of mass profit" (p. 264), which is a variation on an exploitation theme entitled "black roots white fruits" (Chapple & Garofola, 1993).

Barlow (1993) saw the growth of the commercial record industry in the United States as having a profound and paradoxical influence on black music, both encouraging and impeding its development as a black working class art form. On the one hand, with the swift reproduction of millions of spirituals, jazz, blues, and rhythm and blues discs the music was made more accessible to the general public and specifically to African American people. Moreover, the creation of the African American race record industry permitted blues, jazz, and other types of black music to emerge as a national entity by the 1920s.

On the other side of the positive, Barlow says, was the transformation of music traditions into "commodities to be sold in the commercial marketplace." It turned out that the profits garnered from the sale of race records went to white businessmen who owned or managed the record companies, with the producers of the cultural output receiving a very small percentage of profits from their labor. Second, and more substantively, the record companies "went to great lengths to get African American music to conform to their cliched, formula-prone, Tin-Pan Alley standards, and they often expected black recording artists to conform to racist stereotypes inherited from blackface minstrelsy" (p. 26). Finally, another record industry practice that had adverse effects on the development of black music, according to Barlow, was the popular practice of presenting white artists to perform "cover" versions of popular blues and jazz tunes (Garofalo, 1993). In doing so the record industry was attempting to get the white audience to buy the record, and it was contended, to upgrade or commercialize the music— bringing it more in tune with European American musical traditions while adding to it the appearance of white American respectability.

Clearly, black music has been affected by economic and political forces, but it has maintained its creative impetus against enormous odds (Garofalo, 1993). Black music has retained its tradition, but has renewed and extended itself. As in the past, black music has brought African American scholars and activists into intimate connection with their aesthetic heritage.

While the other black music forms have reconfigured themselves, a new black music form, commonly called rap or hiphop, has recently developed that speaks to the black masses. It has had a significant influence on the African American community and a noticeable impact on other communities, both here and abroad. It has been credited with rebuilding a disintegrating sense of community among the young and has related to them in a special way, with its most developed form adding to political consciousness raising (Karenga, 1993). Moreover, despite some of its crude forms and representations, this music has been influential in grappling with the issue of self-definition in the African American community and in combating the many forces of inferiorization.

Sambo Across Media

A recurring comic image that is not specific to any medium or channel but cuts across all of them is the popular cultural image of the Sambo. This image has taken a number of forms spanning many decades and is highly resistant to change in its essence. The origin of Sambo has been traced back to the seventeenth-century American colonist. It is likely, however, that Sambo was conceived in Europe and came to life during the slavery period. Boskin (1986) provided five metamorphoses of the portrait of the comic Sambo in the United States. In the 1850s, the portrait is what he called the plantation darkie. A decade later it was the minstrel man, an image that lasted for slightly over thirty years. This portrait was eclipsed by African jokes, which began in the 1890s and lasted into the 1900s. The 1920s brought in the "Postcard Buffoon." The 1930s witnessed the arrival of the portrait called the "Movie Chauffeur." Boskin noted that these images have suffered a devastating blow from pressures by Africans, but that subtle occurrences still exist.

A number of images that are not medium-specific are presented in advertising. Many past portrayals are startling in their viciousness, and some of these stereotypical and denigrating images persist to this day, albeit somewhat updated. Old-time figures such as Aunt Jemima, Rastus, and Uncle Ben migrated from the plantation kitchen into the modern American mind-set (Kern-Foxworth, 1994).

The Essence of the Problem

Given the physical and social constraints placed on Africans, along with the sustained attacks on their humanity and on the group to which they belong, several fundamental issues emerge: What effect do these forces of inferiorization currently have on Africans in the United States? How has the often cited phenomenon of "double consciousness'" manifested itself? Undoubtedly, some Africans have accepted, at least partially, the perspectives developed by Europeans. Others, however, have been able to ward off the major brunt of these forces. Hodge-Edelin (1990) observed that, although not monolithic or devoid of tension, an African American identity can be detected in the behaviors and preferences of the majority of Africans. People of Africa have gone through a cultural and psychological crisis and have basically accepted the European version of things (Rodney, 1972). But what has this acceptance, either full or partial, entailed? Have these forces intruded on the individual's concept of self? Or have they been confined only to perspectives the individual has concerning the group rather than the self? What are the antecedents that molded the African's conception of self and the group? Have these different individual or group conceptions changed substantially over time? Do they operate the same across different elements or groupings within the African American community?

The complexity and timeliness of these issues have resulted in an abundance of conceptualizations, theories, and theorizing by many scholars. The next chapter explores these questions. I focus essentially on the writings that address the self-concept of African Americans. The overriding theme of this inquiry will be the ongoing struggle of Africans to fashion an identity under the pressure of a double consciousness.

CHAPTER 2

Conceptualization and Presentation of the Self-Concept

When I discover who I am, I'll be free .
—Ralph Ellison

The previous chapter framed the issues in terms of conflicting forces warring for dominance. On the one hand, there are the powerful and enduring forces that have systematically worked to place African Americans in inferior positions and to present them as inferior beings, most often responsible for their own degradation. On the other hand, African Americans have developed strong, tenacious, and ever-vigilant forces not only to resist the onslaught, but also to fashion an alternative healthy being or, as Fanon (1964) stated, to put a new human afoot. These system-level forces, according to the scenario I outlined, have a major impact on the self-concept, whether that concept applies to the individual or to the group to which he or she belongs. While many terms have been used to characterize this situation, I have explicitly referred to this phenomenon as DuBois's (1964) double consciousness. I suggested a conceptual framework for understanding some of the forces that have contributed to the shaping of the self-concept of Africans, especially African Americans. I noted that the onslaught on the African self has a long and tortuous history, with various strategies employed to subjugate the African, some institutionalized, others personalized, some individual, and some societal. Originating from many different sources (e.g., governmental and nongovernmental, religious and secular, academic and lay), the major thrust has been toward what has been called inferiorization (Karenga, 1982, 1993), dehumanization (Kovel, 1970), and control of the self-image (Akbar, 1984).

The essence of the ensuing struggle is embodied in this question: Who has the authority to define the African? The outcome of this struggle is crucial for the individual's and collective's sense of identity. Ture and Hamilton (1992) expressed the importance of Africans' being able to define themselves and to reclaim their history and their identity. Africans, they said, have to struggle for the "right to create [their] own terms through which to define [themselves] and [their] relationship to the society, and to have these terms recognized." Clarke (1991) insisted that what African Americans do for themselves is contingent on what they know about themselves and that when other people control what African Americans think about themselves, they will also control what Africans do for themselves. It is this control of information and its interpretation that has been the basis for an ongoing historical struggle. In the previous chapter, I outlined a perpetual struggle between powerful contradictory external forces and described the ways in which the African has, through a wide array of alternative strategies, tenaciously engaged these forces. This situation has fascinated and inspired several social observers to predict, explain, and, in a number of instances, change the nature of the contestation. This is best exemplified in the study of the self-concept.

Approaches to the Self-Concept

Under the rubric of self, observers have examined how the individual has developed a sense of himself or herself and a sense of the group to which he or she belongs. The concept of self has commanded the attention of scholars in many different fields and disciplines and has generated an extensive research literature (Akbar, 1995; Kitayama, Markus, & Matsumoto, 1997; Nobles, 1973; Markus & Kitayama, 1991, 1994; Rosenberg, 1986, 1989). Although suspect early in the development of the social sciences (Rosenberg et al., 1995), it has undergone a rebirth lately (Gecas, 1982; Phinney, 1990; Rosenberg et al., 1995; Mruk, 1995). Although a considerable overlap exists among the different disciplinary foci on the concept of self, there are several marked distinctions among them as well. Further, many of these conceptual and empirical laborers do not seem to be familiar with the literature of other disciplines (Oyserman & Markus, 1993; Phinney, 1990; Rosenberg, 1989).

Just as there has been substantial cross-disciplinary concern with the concept of self, there have been many metatheoretical orientations, as Wilson (1983) uses the term; many ideological positions, as Chomsky (1989) uses the term; and the self has been studied at various levels of theory and units of analysis. This diversity of approaches or observations can be readily seen when one explores the work done on the self-concept of the African American, the major focus of this inquiry. Underlying questions that have informed many of these studies are: How do oppressed groups deal with the reality fostered by dominating groups? To what degree do elements within the culture of oppressed groups buttress the aforementioned reality or provide an alternative reality? Given the recent history of the encompassing oppression of the African, these questions have taken on much more meaning. Psychoanalytic theory and techniques have been employed, behavioristic approaches have been implemented, and a number of strategies for change have been considered in an attempt to understand and, in some cases, alter the self-concept of the African American. The diversity and intensity of interest in the self-concept of the African American have not abated, but rather have increased as the launching of new journals and alternative perspectives attest. Recent research has exploded long-held notions about the African American self-concept.

Considerable agreement has accrued concerning the following idea: awareness of self—what constitutes humanness, the "shoulds" of how one feels, acts, and finds happiness and success, what constitutes failure, and what is valuable or what is not—is intimately related to the particular cultural, historical, and institutional contexts within which we live. Oyserman and Markus (1993) have pointed out that although individuals all tend to have a sense of self, the "content, processes, and structures of that sense are bound to sociocultural context and thus are likely to be different." They go on to say that there are myriad questions to be examined concerning the interdependence between the elements of sociocultural content and the operation of the self-system. Stating an interest in the content, structure, and function of the entire self-concept, they contend that little is understood about how numerous conceptions of self are synthesized in a way that allows an individual to attain a oneness or continuity. The available insights, they suggest, which lead to such phenomena as identity and self-esteem should be viewed as "plural and diverse even within the individual." They contend that it is no longer meaningful to speaking of *THE* self-concept, but rather the working self-concept. That is, the self-concept is always in the process of being formed; it is a dynamic entity. This position, they say, does not deny that any healthy individual always has a habitual and accessible self-concept, but it does suggest that the self-concept is usefully viewed as a continually active, changing, and dynamic body of self-knowledge. The term *self-schemas* has been used to refer to interpretive structures that assist the individual in making sense of his or her past life experiences, of generalizations about present actions, and of likely future outcomes (Markus, 1977).

Concept names for the various notions of the self-concept abound, but there have also been demonstrably different and innovative conceptualizations of the self-concept. Kitayama and Markus (1993) conducted an insightful inquiry, and based on many sets of studies they conducted in various Asian countries, they asserted that the "European-American view of the self and its relation to the collective is only *one* view. There are other, equally powerful but strikingly different, collective notions about the self and its relation to the collective." This idea is expressed in Zulu as *umuntu umuntu ngabantu,* which translated into English means "a person is a person through other people."

Many theories and theoretical orientations have been advanced to examine the self-concept, broadly defined. Nobles (1973) outlined four primary theoretical approaches to the concept of self: phenomenological, behavioral, existential, and symbolic interactional. The phenomenological approaches, he says, argue that the manner in which an individual perceives stimuli is a major influence on an individual's behavior, and "the study of self in the phenomenal senses refers to the continuum of clarity in the phenomenal or conscious field." Typically explored through introspection, the self-concept was thought to be a preestablished entity. A more empirical treatment has shared in the investigation in this area, challenging whether the preestablished self-concept can be derived only by introspection. The empirical work in this area, he noted, reflects different variations of self-awareness, for example, self-characteristic, self-esteem, and self-regard.

The behavioral approaches, he states, conceive behavior as either a product or antecedent of the self-concept, the value of this approach being thought to reside in its usefulness in predicting and explaining the self-concept. Focus has been placed on how behavior explains self-esteem and how self-esteem explains behavior.

The third, or existential approaches, are critical of some of the assumptions embodied in the social scientific method. Nobles describes this approach as a rejection of the attempt to reduce the whole to its parts. Those operating from this perspective are critical of methods or techniques that ostensibly can yield abstract laws; they maintain that that gap between the law and the dynamic, changing individual is generally large. Within this approach the self is a perceiver of others, the self is perceived by others, and the self is interacting with others. Further, the self is viewed as a reference for the awareness of self called "I."

Finally, the symbolic interaction approach, originally conceived by Cooley (1902) and said by Gecas (1982) to still function as the major influence on the concept of self, operates from the assumption that one's concept of self is an ongoing product of social interaction with other people. Under this thesis, what an individual incorporates as his or her own is based on information about oneself received from others, that is, the "looking glass self." According to Nobles, this approach was also embraced by Mead (1934), who extended it by suggesting that the self was a basic internal process with two analytically discernible phases. Nobles (1973) contends that

Mead's "I" was the perception of oneself as reflected by the shared meanings and values of "others." He suggested that the incorporated attitudes

ʒs and values) of others constituted the organized "me"; that the
ɔerceived the "me" constituted the "I"; and that both combined
ᵈ the nature of "self."

It is the "I," "me," and "we" as an expansion of Mead's phases, Nobles maintains, that is important in arriving at a clearer understanding of black self-concepts. Both Cooley and Mead contend that social interaction is the basis upon which an individual builds his or her self-concept. More will be said about the relevance of this conceptualization for studies of the African community.

Self-Esteem

Rosenberg, Schooler, and Schoenbach (1989) acknowledge many other theories that do not address the broad concept of self but rather one of its important components: self-esteem. They focused on two—self-esteem theory and self-consistency theory. In self-esteem theory, it is proposed that self-esteem is a fundamental human motive. Although given many different labels (e.g., self-maintenance motive [Tesser & Campbell, 1983], self-enhancement motive), the essence of these theories is that humans possess an insatiable desire to protect and refine their feeling of self-worth. Within this self-esteem theory, Rosenberg (1986) pinpointed three principles: reflective appraisal, social comparison, and self-attribution. The former was implicit in the work of Cooley and Mead, that is, the notion that people's feelings about themselves are informed by their judgments of what others think of them. Social interaction is thus viewed as the driving force of self-esteem. Additionally, the principle of social comparison contends that given no objective information about self, the person judges himself or herself based on comparisons with relevant others. Finally, self-attribution holds that naive observers credit motives, causes, intentions, and disposition to themselves based on their observation of their own actions.

Crocker and Major (1989) present an exciting and thought-provoking literature review of the social psychology literature on the self-esteem. They focus on the definition of self-esteem in terms of generalized feelings of self-worth or self-acceptance (i.e., the definition proffered by Rosenberg, 1981, 1989), and include within the category of "stigmatized" or "oppressed" groups such diverse groups as Africans in the United States, the mentally challenged, homosexuals, the insane, and the physically unattractive. Within this conceptual scope, they reviewed three perspectives—reflected appraisals, self-fulfilling prophecies, and, efficacy-based self-esteem—and identified several others—equity theory, social exchange theory, social comparison theory, and social identity theory—that were said to be in concert with the prediction that stigmatization has a negative effect on self-esteem. As

Africans are the most stigmatized group in the United States, it may be reasonably assumed that their self-esteem, defined as self-worth, would be particularly diminished. A finding to the contrary is often considered counterintuitive, and a stimulating debate has ensued concerning the proper interpretation of some of the recent evidence on race and self-esteem (Taylor & Walsh, 1979; Baldwin, Brown, & Hopkins, 1991).

From a slightly different perspective, Mruk (1995) describes several major perspectives, representing each using a major theory, which have been used to explain self-esteem: psychodynamic, sociocultural, learning theory, humanistic, and cognitive. First, he argues that each of these perspectives can in some way lead to a sound general theory of self-esteem. In this regard, he says, they all have the potential to provide a theoretical understanding of self-esteem. These perspectives have the capability of uncovering different dimensions of self-esteem. Second, despite the unique aspects of each perspective, he notes, each has aspects that may serve as the foundation for a more descriptive and expansive theory. Conversely, while each of the theories, growing out of the perspectives, reveal important dimensions of self-esteem, there is sparse communication among them.

Identity

Focusing on identity, or more specifically ethnic identity, Phinney (1990) identified three broad, often overlapping theoretical frameworks for studying ethnic identity. (This framework is expanded in Chapter 4.) The first, and clearly the most frequently employed, is social identity theory, formulated by Kurt Lewin (1948) and elaborated by Tajfel and Turner (1979) and Tajfel (1986). The scope of this theory is quite broad in comparison with other social psychological theories of intergroup behavior. It attempts to deal with the full range of responses that dispossessed or stigmatized group members might invoke in attempting to ameliorate their individual and group positions (Taylor & Moghaddam, 1994). Social identity theory is consistent with several other theoretical frameworks (see Crocker & Luhtanen, 1990; Taylor & Mogadam, 1994). It assumes that people tend to maintain or improve their self-esteem and to strive for a positive self-concept (Tajfel & Turner, 1979), and that membership in a group instills in the individual a sense of belonging that leads to a positive self-concept. Social identity frames two different aspects of the self: personal identity and group identity. According to Crocker and Luhtanen (1990), personal identity points to one's individual characteristics, whereas group identity refers to the characteristics of one's group, which do not necessarily characterize oneself as an individual. Moreover, social identity theory was said to shed light on the issue of participation in two cultures.

A second framework of identity is acculturation. Sometimes mistakenly equated with ethnic identity, the acculturation framework explores the changes in attitudes, values, and behaviors that make subjective culture a consequence of contact between two distinct cultures.

Finally, the ethnic identity formation framework encompasses the study of how identity forms over time and the decisions made by individuals concerning the meaning their ethnicity has for them.

Since each group's sense of identity is particular to that group because of historical circumstances and setting, care has to be taken in extrapolating from one group to another. The relationship of group identity to self-esteem is therefore based on varying approaches to both self-esteem and group identity. Attempts to generalize are constrained by diverse theoretical orientations, the diversity of measures employed and corresponding measurement problems, and the lack of consensus about the fundamental components of each of these constructs (Crocker & Major, 1989; Crocker & Blanton, 1999; Cross, 1991; Gordon, 1977; Jenkins, 1982; Markus & Kitayama, 1994; Phinney, 1990).

The study of oppressed or stigmatized groups other than Africans may prove to be useful (Adams, 1978; Winant, 1998) in that it would provide a broader theoretical context for the relationship of minority status and self-development (Porter & Washington, 1993; Phinney, 1990). In fact, many such theoretical journeys have been planned. Such studies may illuminate the thinking on the effects of prejudice and discrimination on victimized groups.

No matter which disciplinary focus is used, it turns out that the self-concept—and the two components I am most interested in here, self-esteem and group identity—have myriad definitions and are conceptualized in incompatible ways (Banaji & Prentice, 1994; Crocker & Major, 1989; Cross, 1991; Gordon, 1977; Rosenberg et al., 1995; Wylie, 1977). For example, terms such as self-image, self-impression, ego identity, self-esteem, identity, self-formation, self-satisfaction, and self-enhancement have been used to convey the more general construct of the self. In many instances the definitions of the self-concept must be inferred from the methodology (Gecas, 1982; Gecas & Schwalbe, 1983; Gordon, 1977; Rosenberg & Simmons, 1971). Further, imprecision, inattention to definitional boundaries, and interchangeability of terms have characterized this use. It is not uncommon for several different concept names to be used to express the one notion of self or of the self-concept.

Careful explication of the self-concept is rare. As a consequence, confusion abounds and people tend to have major communication problems (e.g., the debate between Adams, 1978 and Pettigrew, 1978) and to overlook key elements of past research. It is also striking to observe how, for example, scholars have equivocated on the use of one important indicator of the self-concept, namely, self-esteem. In the many debates surrounding the results of self-esteem studies, a scholar will at one point think of self-esteem as incorporating elements of self-worth or the extent to which an individual considers himself or herself adequate, but at another point talk about self-esteem as representing feelings of arrogance, superiority, or overconfidence.

Depending on what outcome the person is in favor of, the inferences drawn will reflect that preference. Since theoretical definitions, which provide meaning to the concept, are usually not explicit, many scholars who produce work on the self-concept and those who interpret such work can easily vary in their usage. When theoretical definitions are not provided and when the operational definitions are indirect, this problem is exacerbated. Even when both theoretical and operational definitions are supplied, thus adding meaning and measurement, there may be a poor linkage between the two. In reference to the concept of identity, Phinney (1990) noted that while there is no generally agreed-upon definition of identity, a large majority of the work provides no explicit definition of the construct. For example, ethnic identity is often defined as the ethnic component of social identity (Phinney & Chivira, 1992).

The Self: Self-Esteem and Group Identity

Apart from this more elaborate, innovative conception of the self, many theorists are beginning to question several other fundamental issues concerning the theory and research practice in examining the concept of self. For example, with respect to European Americans, Martin, Krizek, Nakayama, and Bradford (1999, p. 28) asserted that this group has a privileged status in society and conceive of their identity as the "norm and the standard by which other groups are measured, and this identity is therefore invisible, even to the extent that many whites do not consciously think about the profound effect being white has on their everyday lives." Similarly, white identity, more recently referred to simply as "whiteness" (Ignatiev & Garvey, 1996), has been characterized as an "unmarked category against which difference is constructed; whiteness never has to speak its name, never has to acknowledge its role as an organizing principle in social and cultural relations" (Lipsitz, 1998, p. 1).

In a classic piece on black identity, or what was called race consciousness, Pitts (1974, p. 667) contends that black consciousness behavior is very evident in African American behavior and can take on different forms in different historical periods, as well as in different regional and international settings. Its significance, he argues, has become more pronounced since the Second World War and as a normative behavior it "develops in a society where racial stratification is present." Citing Brown (1931), he reports that it is through race consciousness that members of a race become a historical group, aware of a past present, and future; it is a social entity struggling for status in society and as such race consciousness is a result of conflict, which increases the sense of solidarity. While Pitts refers to race consciousness with respect to African Americans, Brown (1931) views the construct in more general terms as applying to all groups in a racially divided society.

Using the term *self-esteem* rather than *self-concept*, Porter and Washington (1979) separate it into two components: the racial and the personal. Others working from a social identity perspective view self-concept as having two components: personal identity and social identity. Crocker and Luhtanen (1990) retained the component of personal identity but replaced social identity with the concept name *collective identity*. A useful distinction for my purposes pertains to the content of self-conceptions (e.g., identities) versus that of self-evaluation (e.g., self-esteem). With respect to ethnic identity, researchers typically have attended to the individual's sense of belonging to the group, attitudes about group membership, and the involvement in the group's social, political, and cultural practices (Phinney, 1990). Several researchers have asserted that personal self-esteem and group identification are associated in profound and unobvious ways (Broman, Neighbors, & Jackson, 1988). Evidence has been accumulating which suggests, empirically, that personal identity and group identification may be separated (e.g., Jackson et al., 1981), and that black group identification is multidimensional (Allen, Dawson, & Brown, 1989).

Cross (1985, 1991) maintains that many of the disparate findings concerning the self-concept could be illuminated by dividing the self-concept into "personal identity" and "reference group orientation." Under the broader heading of reference group orientation, he includes the concept of group identity as well as racial identity, race awareness, racial ideology, race evaluation, race esteem, race image, and racial self-identification. Further, he conceptualizes and categorizes the self-concept in general terms as personal identity. Subsumed under this heading are the concepts of self-esteem, self-worth, self-confidence, self-evaluation, interpersonal competence, ego-ideal, personality traits, introversion-extroversion, and level of anxiety. By making these distinctions he has more usefully organized the empirical work, conceptualized diverse areas of research concern, and suggested many provocative hypotheses.

Cross observes that although a positive linear relationship was predicted for self-esteem and group identity (based on social identity theory), rarely if at all has it been empirically tested, and thus it has never been confirmed. He notes that between the years 1939 and 1960, researchers who employed group identity measures deemed it unnecessary to also employ self-esteem measures, as such information was assumed to be redundant. The consequence, he maintains, is that for most of the history of the study of black identity there are single-variable studies of either personal identity (PI) or reference group orientation (RGO); however, the interest is often in exploring the relationship between PI and RGO.

By the early 1970s, Cross (1991) states that the situation had changed and the studies had moved from univariate to correlational studies, although the magnitude of the shift had been exaggerated. When the shortcomings of several studies and omnibus literature reviews are considered, Cross (1991) states that there is not much support for a positive trend between self-esteem and group identity for African Americans. The next chapter explores these ideas in more detail.

The Black Self-Concept

Given the aforementioned experiences of African Americans at the hands of the dominating culture, the issues that have captured the concern of social commentators and scholars pertain to how this experience has been internalized. That is, what are some of the effects of the historical and contemporary experience on the dominated African Americans? Underscoring this point, Nobles (1992) states that one cannot talk about the self-concept of Africans without talking about how this self-concept has been influenced by the Africans' domination by European peoples. He goes on to say that it is imperative that one gain a full understanding of the Africans' concept of self before sound research can be done pertaining to Africans.

Nobles (1973) stated that Mead's (1934) conception could be relevant to the study of the African self. As mentioned earlier, Nobles conceived the self as being constituted by shared meaning and values with others. This was the organized "me," and the manner perceived to "me" constituted the "I," and together this "I" and "me" culminated in the nature of self. Nobles argued that Mead "omitted the reference for oneself as being a member or part of the group (society), or what is descriptively discussed as the feeling of 'we-ness.'" His analytical expansion of Mead's phrase presents the notion of self as a social process within the individual which reflects the awareness of three referents for self: the "I"—the self as perceiver of oneself in relation to others' attitudes and feelings toward you; the "me"—the self as the internalized or incorporated perceptions of others; and the "I"—the self as the feelings or perceptions one has toward the group and being (or interacting with) the group. Further, he states that peoples of African descent, based on an "African perspective," are more inclined to adhere to the self as reflecting the principle of "I am because We are, and because We are, therefore, I am" (Nobles, 1991a, p. 300). One who holds this view would find it extremely important to maintain a strong, positive unit relation among his or her "I," "me," and "we" self-referents. With this expansion, Nobles posits that group membership is a germane referent for self, which he conceived as the "I." In doing so, Nobles introduces the variable of race into an analysis of the self-concept. He thus suggests that group identity is positively correlated with personal self-esteem.

Nobles (1991a,b) also argues that the black self-concept should be grounded in African assumptions and embody African-based analyses and theoretical frameworks. Or, as others have argued elsewhere, there is a distinction between African and European cosmologies (Akbar, 1991a; Azibo, 1989; Baldwin, 1981; Dixon, 1977).

Semmes (1992, pp. 93–94) introduced the concept of legitimacy, which "involves gaining recognition and respect for one's perspectives, beliefs, and actions" and noted that it is a fundamental component of all behavioral systems. African Americans, he says, are plagued by the feeling of nonrecognition and nonrespect as a consequence of white supremacy and other forms of oppression. The self-concept of African Americans is linked primarily to the black reference groups, but at some point in their life experiences they must "accommodate white secondary reference groups which have inordinate power and control to decide what should be recognized and what should be respected in society." As a consequence, the self-concept of African Americans may be informed by the peace they make with the reward system provided by the larger, dominant society and its needs. That is, they may respond in many different ways to the claims and challenges of the larger society, but it is not possible to ignore its existence. In short, Semmes maintains that the control of legitimacy influences the psychic harmony of African Americans, but identifies this quest for control as an ongoing battle.

The importance of taking into account the history, present societal position, and cultural experience of African Americans in any analysis of their sociopsychological orientation is a view entertained by many prominent African scholars (e.g., W. E. B. DuBois, E. Franklin Frazier, Harold Cruse).

Although this view has some detractors and several variations in interpretation, Nobles (1989, p. 254) captures the crucial element in this position:

> The fundamental and only substantive justification for the special treatment of African-Americans as a racial or ethnic group is that African people are culturally, philosophically, biologically, and spiritually distinct from other geo-political-socio-cultural groups. Consequently, the "meaning and definition" of the African psyche and African psychological attributes, qualities, and functioning would have to be conceptually grounded in the philosophical and cultural reality of African people.

Scholars have tended to view African Americans as a deviate from the European American norm. When the circumstances of their lives, their cultural background, and their experiences are understood, then their personality development is just as "rational" as the development of European Americans' personality, which includes their self-concept (Gaines & Reed, 1994, 1995). While Nobles and others acknowledge the damage of enslavement and the systematic attempts to denigrate Africa and everything African, and to fashion Africans into a colorful rendition of their oppressors, they maintain that the African's sense of self is not simply a response to European Americans or a consequence of oppression and exploitation.

Pointing out the importance of the thinking of DuBois, Gaines and Reed (1994) outlined the richness of the African heritage in the culture of Africans in the United States and the resilience of this culture despite the many and varied attacks upon it. Many scholars have overlooked the contributions of African culture. That is, the difference between African American culture and European culture and the retention of many aspects of African culture by African Americans have enabled African American culture to remain intact. Despite the relatively extended contact between Africans and Europeans in the United States, some contend that each group has different cultural systems and that the systems of consciousness, "self-knowledge," are distinct (Nobles, 1991a). This struggle to retain, restore, and reassert African culture continues over time with varying levels of success, which underscores the importance of the dynamic nature of the African self-concept.

Several other scholars have emphasized that the culture of the African population is very important and may be a crucial element in examining the self-concept. Increasingly, evidence across many disciplines and fields indicates that people from different cultures hold diverse conceptions about the self (Akbar, 1991b; Markus & Kitayama, 1994; Nobles, 1991b; Triandis,1994; Triandis, McCusker, & Hui, 1990). While entertaining the idea that there may be universal aspects of the self, Markus and Kitayama (1991) maintained that a number of other aspects of the self may be specific to particular cultures and that the content and structure of the self may differ markedly by culture. Taking caution to point out that culture is a vague construct, Triandis, Bontempo, Villareal, Asai, and Lucca (1988) and Triandis (1989, 1994) point out the importance of determining the dimensions of cultural variability. Citing Mead, Triandis et al. (1988) emphasize that cultures differ to the degree to which they emphasize competition, cooperation, or individualism. A promising area of research, they contend, is the individualism/collectivism dimension or the evaluation of self by a generalized other, and evaluation of self by a specific reference group.

Markus and Kitayama (1994) relied on the distinction between the degree of separation as distinct from the degree of connection with others. The self is viewed as a separate and autonomous entity, guided by internal orientations (called self-construals) and the self that is connected with others and informed at least partially by perceptions of others' orientations (called interdependent construals). They have hypothesized that the two different self-construals (independent and interdependent) are among the most general schemata of the individual's self-system, and are credited with organizing the more specific self-regulatory schemata. Further, Markus and

Kitayama (1991) argue that these cultural self-schema cannot be used to indicate a given person's articulated view of self. The self-concept, they say, issues from both the cultural self-schema and from the entire configuration of self-schemata and embodies the contents of race and one's particular social and development history. The majority of the research in this tradition has been directed at mapping out group differences in the self as a function of geographic location.

The selves and theories of selves have been constructed within a European-American cultural tradition or what is sometimes called the Western view of the individual (Akbar, 1985; Kambon, 1992; Gaines & Reed, 1994, 1995; Triandis, 1989, 1994). In this view (Markus & Kitayama, 1991, p. 224), the individual is seen as an independent, self-contained, monadic entity who (a) comprises a unique configuration of internal attributes (e.g., traits, abilities, motives, and values) and (b) behaves mainly as a result of these attributes. Thus, as a consequence, the understanding of these phenomena that are tied to the self in some way by scholars who subscribe to that view may be inappropriately limited. Nobles (1991a, pp. 298–299) provides a graphic rendition of the problem:

> if one examines the African world-view and compares it with the view of the European, one can readily note the differences and their implications for understanding black self-conception. Rather than survival of the fittest and control over nature, the African world-view is tempered with the general guiding principle of (1) survival of the tribe and (2) one with nature. In contrast with the European world-view, the values and customs consistent with the African world-view are characteristically reflective of the sense of "cooperation," "interdependence," and "collective responsibility." Similarly, the emphasis in African psycho-behavioral modalities is not on individuality and difference. The modalities consistent with the African world-view, I note, emphasize "commonality," "groupness," and "similarity. . . .
>
> The effects of these two different world views on the understanding of black self-concept concept is critical. The nature of the "processing" of data regarding black people and our self-conceptions was, in fact, filtered through the European world-view and to the extent that black people are African people, the "process" has significantly distorted the validity of black self-conception.

The Black Self-Concept and Self-Hatred

The history of literature on black self-hatred is extensive. In essence, it reflects the inability of many scholars operating from a dominant paradigm to conceive of Africans as not suffering from self-hatred. It was also difficult for many scholars to conceive of deflecting or resistive forces within the African community in the United States.

The theoretical formulations of Cooley (1902) and Mead (1934) have served as the source for this thinking. They both argue that social interaction is the basis upon which an individual formulates his or her self-concept (Gordon, 1977; Crocker & Major, 1989). Or stated differently, the Cooley and Mead models indicate that the individual's conception arises through interaction with other members of the society that constitute his or her significant social circle. Specifically, the social looking glass theory posits that one's self-conception is determined to a large extent by the way in which it is reflected or mirrored through the eyes of significant others. Thus, "European-American racism and racist practices are construed to represent the African American community's social looking glass (i.e., their generalized significant others) reflecting derogatory images of blacks. Through African American's *internalization* of and/or identification with the (generalized) European American racist attitude toward blacks, or through so-called objective comparison (housing, employment, income, etc.), blacks come to view themselves (cognitively and affectively) as whites view them. This black self-hatred may also take the disguised form of a defensive/displaced outward aggression" (Baldwin, Brown, & Hopkins, 1992, pp. 147–48). A few examples will prove instructive.

Allport (1954) emphasized the destructive effects of the above forces on African Americans when he stated that "since no one can be indifferent to the abuse and expectations of others I must anticipate that ego defensiveness will frequently be found among members of groups that are set off for ridicule, disparagement, and discrimination. It could not be otherwise."

Making the assumption that there is a relationship between black identity and self-esteem, Proshansky and Newton (1968) stated that Africans in the United States who feel hatred toward their own racial group are to some degree expressing hatred for themselves as individuals.

Albeit more focused, this view was echoed by Rainwater (1966), who stated that "to those living in the heart of a ghetto, black comes to mean not just 'stay back,' but also membership in a community of persons who think poorly of each other, who attack and manipulate each other, and who give each other small comfort in a desperate world. Black comes to stand for a sense of identity as no better than these distributive others. The individual feels that he must embrace an unattractive self in order to function at all." Similarly, Kardiner and Ovesey (1951, p. 297) remarked that African Americans had "no possible basis for a healthy self-esteem and every incentive for self-hatred."

In a critique of an article by Adams (1978), Pettigrew (1978) argued that coping with the oppression thesis, which assumes "that black responses shaped by racial oppression had negative consequences for black personality," is sound. Moreover, to assume otherwise would be to "deny a fundamental insight of social psychology" (p. 58).

Grier and Cobbs (1968) further underscored this theme of self-hatred by formulating a model of black psychological health they termed a "Black Norm" that all Africans in the United States were believed to share. As a reaction to racism, this "norm" was said to be manifested in cultural paranoia, cultural depression, and masochism (Ramseur, 1991).

Perhaps the most influential of the individuals who have provided research on the topic of African American self-hatred is Clark (1965), who asserted that the dominant culture plants in the dominated culture the seeds of a harmful hatred of self and of the group to which an individual belongs.

I could include an almost endless number of examples of the above explicit assumptions. Suffice it to say that this assumption has informed, and to some degree still informs, the hypotheses that were tested and the frameworks used in the interpretation of most research on African Americans. With self-esteem in mind and acknowledging the predictions derived from the Cooley and Mead models, Rosenberg and Simmons (1971) suggest that there is a firm basis for expecting that the low social status of Africans on important social structural dimensions (e.g., occupation, performance on standardized tests, and income) would bring into question their ability to "perceive themselves as worthy persons." Crocker and Major (1989), using the same self-esteem concept, noted that two other perspectives, namely, the self-fulfilling prophecy and efficacy-based self-esteem, predict the same relationship.

Although the theoretical literature overwhelmingly suggests that Africans would have low self-esteem (i.e., low self-worth or, more emphatically, self-hatred), the empirical literature does not support that hypothesis (Cross, 1991; Gordon, 1977; Porter & Washington, 1979, 1993; Rosenberg, Schooler, & Schoenbach, 1989), and indeed the test of any theory is its correspondence to the available evidence or data. Succinctly stated, there is a glaring gap between the theory and theorizing, the research and the findings. This gap often arouses uneasiness, astonishment, incredulity, and surprise among many scholars. The lack of agreement between theory and findings has led to a wide range of explanatory interpretations. The most pernicious "explanation" is that life experience and culture must have deleterious effects on the black psyche, and that if any researcher finds otherwise, this is undoubtedly the result of a faulty research strategy.

Assuming that all stigmatized groups are similar, Crocker and Major (1989) attempt to explain these ostensibly puzzling findings. They put forth three possibilities, or what they call mechanisms, that buffer the self-esteem of members of oppressed groups and those hostile toward them. The first mechanism involves giving negative feedback to prejudiced attitudes toward their group. A second buffer mechanism that oppressed groups may use is to make in-group comparisons in which some members would fare relatively better in comparison with other oppressed group members than with most members of the oppressing group. A third buffer mechanism is to put less value on some performance dimension that suggests that the individual or the group to which he or she belongs does poorly or not as well as other groups.

While not arguing whether such mechanisms should be used or might have negative consequences, Crocker and Major maintain that the defensive mechanisms are not necessarily mutually exclusive. Each may be employed simultaneously. They emphasize that oppressed groups are not passive receptors of damaging information, but may engage in active contestation or resistance—a point that is in accord with the arguments presented by a number of scholars concerning the black self-concept. Further, they describe the form and the intensity of that contestation by identifying moderating factors, one of which is the culture of the particular group under consideration. But that is just one attempt to explain why Africans in the United States are a stigmatized group, yet do not suffer from low self-esteem. There are those who have operated from a different paradigm who would not have predicted that African Americans would have low self-esteem in an absolute sense or lower self-esteem in a comparative sense (see Kambon, 1992; Nobles, 1992).

The black self-hate literature highlights several important issues that only recently have been entertained. First, after the early 1960s, even though most of the empirical literature converged on the finding that African Americans had a positive self-concept, hardly anyone scrutinized the models upon which the negative assumptions had been based. For example, most of these models assumed that Africans receive their sense of self from the European American community rather than the African American community. They failed to include the possibility that the African American community could have been a source of strength and nourishment more powerful than the very real external discrimination and disparagement, a point that was continually made by a pioneer scholar in the study of African peoples, W. E. B. DuBois (1903, 1964). And moving beyond the question of the models, even a cursory analysis of the research strategies and findings would have generated strong skepticism about the studies showing self-hate.

Cross (1991) separated his analysis into two major periods of activity concerning the African self-concept: 1939–60, which he called the Negro self-hatred period, when the self-hatred thesis was predominant; and 1968–80, which he called black identity transformation, or "nigrescence." During the 1939–60 period, Cross argues, black self-hatred gained a consensus in the press. He contends that during this period most of the scholars focused on either personal identity or black identity but not both. In this first period, findings based on studies of black identity showed black children demonstrating substantial attraction to "symbols representative of the white perspective." But what is seldom mentioned, he says, is that as black children got older they tended to have a black preference. The research results suggest that blacks have preference for whites. And since few significant studies of personal identity were conducted between 1939 and 1960, no meaningful conclusion can be drawn about black self-hatred in that era. On the other hand, during the 1968–80 period, according to Cross, black identity as group identity changed, becoming more positive, yet personal identity among blacks did not change substantially.

Exploring the studies that used measures of both personal identity and of black identity from 1939 to 1987, and examining Lewin's hypothesis of a positive linear relationship between personal identity and group identity, Cross reported that there was little evidence supporting the conclusion that African Americans had a negative self-conception. Few studies suggest that there was no correlation between the two measures of the self-concept.

Wright (1985) observed that there has been a noticeable shift to a more positive self-image for African Americans. Similarly, a literature review by Porter and Washington (1989) shows that personal self-esteem among African Americans tends to be fairly high, at least as high as it is for European Americans.

Nonetheless, prior to the 1960s, and in reference to children, the majority of research findings painted a picture of what had come to be called black self-hatred, although careful reassessment of the data casts serious doubts on the original conclusion (Baldwin, 1979; Baldwin, Brown, & Hopkins, 1991; Cross, 1985, 1991; Nobles, 1973, 1991a, b). The literature of the time said that African children were more likely than white children to reject their own race. More recent work concluded that African American loyalties have shifted (Baldwin, Brown, & Hopkins, 1991; Rosenberg, Schooler, & Schoenbach, 1989).

Given the major flaws and prominent omissions in the self-hatred literature, and the neglected areas in the study of the black self-concept, there is a great deal of theoretical and empirical work which remains undone. It is important to highlight the enormous gains in the area of theory and research. Not only have old myths been exploded, but many alternative conceptualizations and perspectives have been proffered with a variety of research questions to be investigated. A useful foundation has been built, and it awaits embellishment. Clearly, there is doubt about the veracity of the findings that black self-hatred was prevalent. But it is nevertheless important to define the black self-concept and to discover the dynamics of the relationship between personal identity and group identity. To these inquiries, other research questions might be pursued, including those suggested below.

Theoretical Orientation and Research Questions

A wide range of theories and theoretical orientations have been formulated to predict and explain the self-concept of African Americans. Usually different theories are employed for different aspects of the self. For example, there are theories that have been formulated for addressing self-esteem, and others for addressing group identity.

Based on recent empirical findings, making some allowances for the quality of the studies and borrowing from Cross (1991) and others (e.g., Baldwin, Brown, & Hopkins, 1991), I can summarize the major tendencies as follows.

(1) Going against most of the theoretical literature, Africans Americans tend *not* to have low self-esteem. In comparison with European Americans, African Americans tend to have the same or, in some instances, higher self-esteem than European Americans. The majority of the studies were conducted with children or adolescents as respondents and across a number of different paradigms.

(2) Operating from a number of different theoretical paradigms again, the empirical research indicates that African Americans have high group identification and that this identification increases over time. Some literature suggests that the results are less certain when very young children are examined or when different income groups are considered.

(3) There is some support for a positive relationship between black identity and self-esteem, but there are several studies that have found nonrelationships. Despite the popularity of this hypothesis (sometimes called the Lewinian hypothesis), there are few genuine tests of it.

Navigating in the empirical literature, it is important to be mindful of certain shortcomings that militate against having substantial confidence in the picture they portray. First, many of the measures of self-esteem and group identity did not have generally acceptable reliability, when they were reported at all. This was particularly the case for earlier studies (pre-1970s). Relatedly, many of the measures were nonvalidated (this was especially true for what Cross calls the "reference group measures").

Second, there are a wide variety of measures of self-esteem, with substantial different theoretical and operational definitions. Indeed, Rosenberg et al. (1995) showed that different operationalizations, related to different conceptualizations of self-esteem, can lead to demonstrably different outcomes. In reference to the study of African Americans, it is worth exploring the self-concept as it is defined and operationalized appropriately for the underlying culture—its experiences or social reality or culturally mandated task.

Third, most of the studies were conducted with children or in some instances adolescents. Few studies have investigated African American adults.

Fourth, since most of the studies were done with small samples, usually in experimental settings, the generalizability of the findings is unknown. Also, only a paucity of research has investigated the relationship of the self-concept within different categories of the African American population.

Finally, it is the rare study indeed that has empirically examined the influence of the mass media (majority and/or black-oriented) on the self-concept of Africans. There has been, however, an inundation of speculation about either the negative effect, overall, or the positive effect with respect to specific kinds of content.

This inquiry involves the following questions:

What is the relationship of several of the alternative conceptions of self?

Does the conception of the black self, which assumes the inappropriateness of separating self-esteem and black group consciousness, have different antecedents than those found for the more traditional conception of the black self?

What is the level of self-esteem and the level of black identity among black adults over time? Are they reliable? Are they stable?

What is the relationship between self-esteem and black identity? Are the two self-concepts correlated? Are they correlated over time?

Does having a greater black identity result in a stronger self-esteem? Or, does having a greater self-esteem result in a greater black identity? Is there a reciprocal relationship?

Do the media, as often speculated, influence self-esteem or black identity? Do the majority media, as compared to black media, influence these self-concepts differently?

Do the above relationships hold for different subgroups (e.g., age)?

How does class influence the self-concept? Is the "new black middle class," with its newfound privileges and status, less susceptible to the societal onslaught on sense of self?

In the chapters that follow, I attempt to replicate and substantially extend the several findings that appear to be on shaky evidentiary ground, using a large, more representative data set, with data collected at several points in time over an extended period. Also, and more important, I formulate a number of hypotheses derived from an alternative conceptualization of the black self-concept with alternative measures. My inquiry will be informed by an attempt to correct the errors identified in past theory and research and to extend the theory development and research questions examined. Further, as part of this extension, I examine in some detail the influence of the mass media on African Americans. Given that African Americans tend to have a comparatively large appetite for media fare, this brings into question its influence, especially in light of a burgeoning black media that, for the most part, presents more positive and diverse images of African people and their culture. Moreover, in the next four empirically based chapters that follow, I perform most of the analysis using structural equation modeling, sometimes referred to as analysis of covariance structures, LISREL models, or analysis of moment structures. In general terms, structural equation modeling (SEM) is a comprehensive statistical approach to testing hypotheses about relationships among observed and unobserved or latent variables. Although caution has often been voiced (e.g., Bollen, 1989), the development of these generalized techniques for testing hypotheses was considered to be one of the most important and influential statistical revolutions in the social sciences (Cliff, 1980). It is an extremely "flexible approach to research design and data analysis than any other single statistic model in standard use by social and behavioral scientist. Although there are research hypotheses that can be efficiently and completely tested by standard methods, the SEM approach provides a means of testing more complex and specific hypotheses than can be tested by those methods" (Hoyle, 1995, p. 15).[1]

PART II

THEORETICAL AND EMPIRICAL EXAMINATIONS OF THE BLACK SELF

CHAPTER 3

Some Issues, Questions, and Problems Surrounding the Black Self-Concept: Self-Esteem

If you have no confidence in self you are twice defeated in the race of life. With confidence you have won even before you have started.
—Marcus Moziah Garvey

This chapter builds on the two previous ones by using the insights obtained to explore the various conceptual and methodological issues pertaining to the frequently explored concept of self-esteem. Here, I provide an overview of some of the major conceptions presented by several disciplines. As part of the conceptualization, I place considerable attention on revealing the many and diverse theoretical and operational definitions of self-esteem, and on analyzing the voluminous past empirical research. Taking into account conclusions gathered from this literature and using cross-sectional data, I report a secondary analysis. Hypotheses derived from this aforementioned theorizing are tested. I include an examination of issues associated with the reliability and validity of the measures and more general measurement concerns.

Operating from a wide range of theories, disciplines, and ideologies over a very long time span, it has been argued that people have an abiding need for a strong sense of self (Allport, 1937, 1954; DuBois, 1903; Marcus & Kitayama, 1994; Nobles, 1973). According to Crocker and Luhtanen (1990), a number of theoretical perspectives posit that individuals strive to keep a high level of personal self-esteem and to also keep a high positive group identity. Whereas many variations of the concept of self have been proffered (e.g., Baldwin, 1979; Banaji & Prentice, 1994; Kambon, 1992; Nobles, 1991a), self-esteem in its many manifestations, variously conceived, has commandeered much of the research and theoretical attention, especially with respect to African Americans. Many disciplines and fields have studied the self, and they have brought with them their own respective paradigms, modes of inquiry, methodologies and theories, or fragments thereof. While this has enriched discourse in many ways and has provided insights not otherwise attainable from an interdisciplinary approach, many of these scholars are not familiar with the work in the other areas. Thus, it is not uncommon for people in different fields to use different concept names to talk about the same phenomenon or to use the same concept name but to define or operationalize it differently. It is imperative to set definitional boundaries and strive to be precise and explicit, with an eye toward eliminating possible confusion and vagueness.

While there are a number of different aspects of the self, I focus on only one of these in this chapter, namely, self-esteem. One prominent theorist in this area maintains that the self may be divided into the phenomena of self-esteem and identity (e.g., Tajfel, 1982; Tajfel & Turner, 1986), and this distinction has often been made in the literature. Several others have viewed the self as composed of personal identity and group identity or reference group identity (e.g., Cross, 1985, 1991). Further, the term *esteem* has been maintained, but the distinction has been made between personal esteem and racial esteem (e.g., Porter & Washington, 1979, 1993; Rosenberg, 1985a). This form of self-esteem may be more reflective of personal well-being than of group activity (Cross, 1985). Beyond the concept names employed, the designations pertain to phenomena that relate to the individual's self-evaluation and, conversely, that which pertains to the conception or evaluation of the collective (e.g., African Americans). More important, Cross (1991) makes the point that discussion of the black self-concept has assumed a relationship between group identity and self-esteem. Because of this, rarely have researchers bothered to collect independent assessments of each concept. The relationship was taken for granted so that if you collected data for either variable, you would have a reflection of the other. This practice persisted with few exceptions until the 1970s.

Within these two variously defined broad classifications—group identity and self-esteem—several different subcategories have been identified by various scholars. Noting that these two categories are related in complex ways, it has been argued by many that such distinctions are useful (Broman, Neighbors, & Jackson, 1988; Cross, 1985; Rosenberg, 1985). In one of the most comprehensive studies on the identity of Africans in the United States, Cross (1991) included the following concepts under the broad designation of personal identity: self-esteem, self-worth, self-confidence, self-evaluation, interpersonal competence, ego-ideal, personality traits, introversion-extroversion, and level of anxiety. Under the heading of reference group orientation, he included racial identity, group identity, race awareness, racial ideology, race evaluation, race esteem, race image, and racial self-identification. Personal identity, and its subcategories, was conceived as having universal significance, relating to traits or dynamics that exist in all humans. On the other hand, Cross maintains that the reference group orientation focuses on those elements of self that are culture-, class-, and gender-specific. Consistent with that position, Crocker and Luhtanen (1990) assert that personal identity concerns an individual's characteristics, whereas group identity or "collective identity" concerns the characteristics of one's group, which need not simultaneously characterize oneself.

Personal Identity as Self-Esteem

Although this chapter focuses on one aspect of personal self-esteem, this category has many different subcategories carrying different names or meanings. Much recent evidence suggests that self-esteem as self-worth or self-pride and group identity may be meaningfully separated. In fact, a considerable amount of the confusion in this area may be attributed to not making a distinction between self-esteem and group identity. Hence, results that pertain to blacks and group identity are often assumed to apply to the relationship of blacks and self-worth. It is assumed that to make a statement about your personal identity is also to make a statement about your group identity. This notion is exemplified in the oft-cited statement by Proshansky and Newton (1968) that Africans in the United States who have disdain or antipathy for their own group are expressing, at some level of awareness, disdain or antipathy for themselves. Acknowledging the variants within the mainstream view of black personality and identity, the basic model claims that in a white supremacist society—where African Americans are seen and responded to as inferiors, and where African Americans are poor in a poor community—they are inclined to internalize, early in life, negative beliefs about themselves and other African Americans. Interestingly, in one of the few studies that examined the empirical literature on the presumed relationship between self-esteem and group identity, no such relationship was found, but the number of these studies was small (Cross, 1985, 1991). I explore this relationship in greater detail in a later chapter.

Self-esteem has often been viewed as multifaceted, and people have been thought to develop different aspects of self in many different ways. For example, this development could be based on personal history or limitations placed on personal achievement or goal attainment (Clark & Clark, 1947; Jenkins, 1982). Self-esteem as a concept has most often been defined or interpreted in terms of self-worth. A further distinction made is self-esteem *qua* self-worth and whether it is global or specific. Measures of self-worth based on global assessment may predict quite different outcomes as compared to measures of specific elements of self-esteem (Rosenberg et al., 1995).

Theoretical Conceptions and
Orientations Toward Self-Esteem

From many different disciplines, several theories, hypotheses, and what some have called principles have been employed to explain the self-esteem of African Americans. At some points, there is conceptual overlap, and, in some instances, scholars from one discipline will use the theories formulated in another discipline. Further, many of the extant theories focus primarily on those processes that influence self-esteem; others attempt to explain how self-esteem influences other aspects of the individual's existence (Gecas, 1982). More recently, there has developed a body of literature that attempts in some way to incorporate these concerns (Banaji & Prentice, 1994). I present only a few of the major conceptualizations, as there tends to be substantial overlap in explanations employed to investigate the self-esteem (defined apart from racial esteem or any group-specific sense of worth) among African Americans.

Social Evaluation Theory

According to Porter and Washington (1979), people learn about themselves by making selective comparisons to relevant others. This process, it is said, results in positive, neutral, or negative self-evaluations as compared to the standard employed for comparison. Porter and Washington (1979) stated that African Americans tend to use whites as a referent group with regard to economic and social status issues, but for personal matters other African Americans are used as the referent. For most African Americans, it is the African American community that provides them with a frame of reference, and thus their sense of self-esteem or worth. As a further aspect of this theoretical orientation, it assumes that Africans who are in a comforting, nurturing environment (examples given were those in lower status positions and those in segregated settings) should demonstrate especially high self-esteem. Although some support has been found, Porter and Washington contend that the situation is unclear. They maintain that positive self-reports of the individual existing in a nurturing environment may not be accurate, but may in some cases reflect defensive reactions.

Locus of Control

The central theme of this theoretical orientation is that the individual has a perception that reward is based on individual behavior (internal control). Conversely, the individual's perception that rewards are controlled by external forces is an example of external control. Gurin and Epps (1975) maintain that the locus of control consists of three aspects: control ideology, sense of personal control, and the extent to which the individual blames himself or herself or the system. It is the latter aspect that is considered to be relevant to the prediction of black self-esteem. Since historical and current barriers are used to keep Africans in subordinate positions, any sense and awareness of external control may represent an awareness of real-world situations rather than submissiveness or some form of fatalism. Gurin and Epps (1975) suggest that it may reflect a healthy adjustment. System-blame is also more prevalent among the young; hence, it should tend to more strongly influence self-esteem in this age group.

The Tangle of Pathology

Porter and Washington (1979) state that the tangle-of-pathology approach has most often been used to analyze the self-esteem of the black lower class. They describe this framework by stating that "the lower-income subculture, which develops as an adaptation to economic and family problems and low self-esteem, cannot successfully bolster the self-image of lower-income blacks; they are aware of their failure by mainstream standards" (p. 55). They attribute this position to Clark (1965).

An elaboration of the approach, Porter and Washington (1993) state, substitutes a model of cultural determinism for economic determinism and places the onus of failure and low self-image not on the system, but on the individual's involvement in a subcultural tradition that emphasizes personal disorganization and fatalism. Identified as the "blaming the victim" approach, the major examples are embodied in what they call the "cultural-deprivation" and "culture-of-poverty" theses.

The support for this approach has been provided by the existence of higher personal self-esteem among middle-class African Americans when compared to poor African Americans. Porter and Washington note, however, that social evaluation theorists find that self-esteem among poor African Americans is higher in comparison to African Americans of higher status. This discrepancy, Porter and Washington suggest, may be due in part to methodological discrepancies. The social evaluation approach relies on objective self-reporting of personal esteem, in contrast to the tangle-of-pathology approach, which relies on participant observation or projective techniques, using small samples. Second, the tangle-of-pathology approach relies on what they call the "very bottom of the socioeconomic spectrum," and not on a combination of working and lower-class samples. Third, the support from the evaluation theory comes, to a large degree, from nonadult samples. The tangle-of-pathology evidence is based on adults who have already met economic disaster. Porter and Washington (1993) summarize the tangle-of-pathology approach by contending that it assumes that the lower-class African American environment is characterized by disorganized, unsupportive institutions and culture.

The Supportive African American Community

As an explicit recognition of the nature of the African American community and as a challenge to the tangle-of-pathology approach, the supportive African American community approach contends that the African American community is an organized, ongoing entity different from the European American culture but not deficient or pathological. It also claims that the African American community should not be interpreted relative to some presumably, healthy, European American community. To the contrary, given the historical experiences in this country and the cultural continuity retained from Africa (Holloway, 1990), Africans are exposed to an alternative culture that is strong, vibrant, and supportive. The socialization practices are such that they provide individuals ways to not only survive but also to flourish in a hostile, dominating society.

One of the major proponents of a distinctive African culture, Nobles (1991a) puts forth the argument that while the African American community is under attack and makes adjustments based on these onslaughts, it retains its essentially African base, which makes it different from the mainstream in fundamental ways. Nobles (1991a) states "one cannot, however, talk about the African self-concept without talking about the effect of African peoples being dominated, oppressed, and subjugated by European peoples. In noting that the juxtapositioning of Africans and Europeans affected the traditions of both the European and the African, I do not believe that the negative contact with Europeans resulted in the total destruction of things African. I do believe, however, that each system was different and that even now, after a relatively long period of contact, the systems of consciousness (i.e., self-knowledge) are still different" (p. 302). According to him, one important aspect of this enduring African culture is the strong concern for the collective, which allows it to withstand many horrendous experiences. He likens his position to the aforementioned comments by DuBois on double consciousness.

The essence of the above position was captured by Ramseur (1991, p. 365) when he pointed out that, based on recent research, (1) Africans often use other Africans as the referent for comparison; (2) a variety of means may be employed to foster black self-esteem; (3) a system-blame explanation of negative events uses African cultural as distinct from European cultural standards of evaluation; and (4) as distinct from Europeans, African Americans may not have equivalent assessments of different aspects of the self.

Self-Esteem Theory

A fundamental tenet of this theory is that self-esteem is a basic human motive. Given its many different names—for example, self-maintenance motive, the motive for self-worth, the self-reflected appraisals enhancement motive—it embraces the notion that people "protect and enhance their feeling of self-regard" (Rosenberg, Schooler, & Schoenbach, 1989). A number of different principles are associated with this theory: reflected appraisals, social comparison, and self-attribution (Hughes & Demo, 1989; Rosenberg, Schooler, & Schoenbach, 1989). Crocker and Major (1989) identified three perspectives that have a bearing on the question of social stigmatized groups and their sense of self-esteem. With one of the perspectives overlapping with a previously mentioned perspective (namely, reflective appraisal), they identified two additional perspectives: self-fulfilling prophecies and efficacy-based self-esteem.

Taking these perspectives in turn reflected appraisal argues that people's feelings about themselves are strongly influenced by the views others have of them. As such, the principle emphasizes the extent to which we are social beings, highly dependent upon others for our view of self. Relatedly, the social comparison theory contends that since we rarely have objective information about ourselves, therefore, we must judge our attitudes, abilities, and sometimes perceptions based on comparisons with others (Festinger, 1954). Self-attribution is the notion that people attribute certain causes and motives to themselves based on the success or failure of their actions (Rosenberg, 1989; Rosenberg, Schooler, & Schoenbach, 1989). Further, Africans in the United States are aware of past and continuing racist attitudes and practices that curtail, to a considerable degree, their life chances. It is thought that this notion, also examined under the heading of locus of control, allows African Americans to attribute a portion of the blame to shortcomings in the social system instead of entirely to themselves as individuals (Hughes & Demo, 1989).

The self-fulfilling prophecy, associated with Merton (1948), holds that when a perceived behavior is based on false beliefs about a target person, such that those beliefs come to be confirmed by the behavior of that target person, people tend to act in a manner that is compatible with the expectation of others and may change their self-concept as a consequence of their behavior (Crocker & Major, 1989; Major, Sciacchitano, & Crocker, 1993).

The efficacy-based self-esteem perspective assumes that members of a dominated group or a stigmatized group (e.g., Africans in the United States) should have lower self-esteem as they interact with the environment, an environment that puts limitations on their socioeconomic development. This in turn is thought to militate against high self-esteem. This idea of self-esteem, therefore, is very different from the self-worth notion that is more commonly used, yet it still predicts that African Americans will have low self-esteem.

Self-Hatred Revisited

With the exception of the strong African American community perspective and the one aspect of the locus of control perspective, the theories, approaches, and principles that I have identified (and they are clearly the most popular ones) hypothesize that African Americans will have a lower sense of self, or a lower self-worth, as compared to nonstigmatized or nondominated groups. But several other theories or orientations that have not been presented also make this prediction. For example, social identity theory, social exchange theory, and the social equity hypothesis all make this same prediction (Crocker & Major, 1989). Although most theories suggest that African Americans will have lower self-esteem as compared to members of nonstigmatized groups, in many of the writings it is also either stated explicitly or assumed that Africans will have low self-esteem in a noncomparative sense.

Rosenberg (1985b) provided two major reasons why, on the surface, one would think African Americans would exhibit self-hatred: (1) prejudice against Africans in the United States, which takes the form of denigrating stereotypes and claims of inferiority, has been pervasive and enduring and thus makes it difficult to see how people cannot *not* be adversely affected; (2) objective material conditions such as higher rates of unemployment, lower educational attainment, and other associated sociostructural elements would negate positive self-esteem. So pervasive is the notion that Africans will have a negative sense of self that it is accepted as a given, as Crocker and Major (1989) contend. They report Cartwright (1950) as saying that self-hatred and feelings of worthlessness tend to arise from membership in underprivileged or outcast groups of which Africans are thought to have membership Crocker and Major (1989, p. 611). They report Allport (1954) as saying that "group oppression may destroy the integrity of the ego entirely, and reverse its normal pride, and create a groveling self-image."

The Empirical Literature

The overwhelming body of empirical literature suggests that African Americans do not suffer from lack of self-esteem or self-worth (Cross, 1985, 1991; Crocker & Major, 1989; Rosenberg, 1979, 1985a,b). According to this research, African Americans are seen to have a healthy sense of self. Baldwin, Brown, and Hopkins (1991) stated that the proponents of the theoretical orientations that suggest Africans will suffer from self-hatred usually attribute this to the level of racial oppression to which they are exposed. Similarly, Taylor and Walsh (1979) stated that until the latter part of the 1960s, it was generally assumed that discrimination and segregation distorted African Americans' sense of self. However, contemporary research—almost in unison—shouts not so. In fact, the majority of the empirical studies fail to demonstrate that blacks have lower self-esteem, and some studies suggest that their view of self is higher than that of whites. As a consequence of this outcome, several alternative perspectives and theoretical orientations have been proposed. For example, Crocker and Major (1989) discussed three explanations that have been given; they considered each to be unconvincing. First, self-esteem is created early in life and, once established, does not fluctuate much. Second, those who exhibit racist behaviors toward African Americans do not constitute an important referent group for the victimized; thus, they do not have a negating effect on the individual's sense of self. Finally, since the victimizers' attitudes and behaviors toward Africans are often subtle, ambivalent, or not uniformly negative, they may not be communicated to the victimized. Consequently, self-esteem cannot be adversely affected.

As a critique of the theoretical literature which proposes that blacks are consumed by self-hatred, Baldwin, Brown, and Hopkins (1991) asserted that this thinking is based on the flawed conception that African people obtain their self-conception from the European American community rather than from the African American community. Several others have put forth the possibility that the conceptualization of black self-hatred may be more appropriate when talking about group identity than about negative orientation (Broman, Neighbors, & Jackson, 1988).

White and Parham (1990) rejected the idea that African Americans have a consuming self-hatred; however, they credit theorists in this domain of discourse with a certain perspicacity in pointing out that white America provides few positive images of the African and African American cultures. This denies African Americans the opportunity to see themselves as individuals or as a group from the perspective of those who look upon them with shameful disregard and disrespect. The essence of the problem with this idea, according to White and Parham, is that it is assumed that Africans receive validation and sources of emulation primarily from whites and not from blacks and the black community. This notion overlooks the "necessity (and indeed the cultural imperative) of African American people to use themselves, their culture, and their history as primary referents" (p. 43). Similarly, it ignores one crucial aspect of the forces warring for dominance and control of the consciousness of African Americans.

Smith (1995) perused the literature on black self-hatred, or internal inferiorization as he called it, and summarized it by saying that it suggests not a paucity of evidence of black internalization of inferiority, but that the evidence is inconclusive or that it is ambiguous, with a substantial amount of misinterpretation. Moreover, as many have stated before him, there is no one-to-one correspondence between individual self-esteem and group identity. In deviation from some of the critiques of the self-hatred literature, he states that although the methodological shortcomings reduce the value of the studies pointing to black self-hatred, there is sufficient evidence to suggest that "in the past and probably today *some* blacks have internalized attitudes of group inferiority and self-hatred" (p. 91). With data that have certain acknowledged limitations, Smith asserts that there seems to be a certain racial ambivalence among some elements of the African American community with respect to racial identification and its associated concepts in this post–civil rights era. Presumably, he is referring to identity and not self-esteem as I am using the term, but the same observation may be made of self-esteem.

A Secondary Analysis of Pertinent Data

Some of the above issues and problems are examined with national samples of African American adults, collected by the Program for the Study of Black Americans, the National Survey of Black Americans (NSBA).[1] Two such samples will be used. The first is a national probability household survey of 2,107 black Americans, 18 years and older, collected in 1979–80. The second is an extension of the survey with three additional waves of data collected. The data were collected again in 1979–80, 1985–86 (a telephone survey), 1988 and 1991–92. Both samples were collected using all-black male and female professional interviewers, trained and supervised by the Survey Research Center at the University of Michigan (Jackson & Gurin, 1987; Torres, 1992).

Before launching into a more detailed examination of the questions raised and the problems I have uncovered, both old and new, and before systematically bringing data to bear on some of the questions I have posed at the end of the previous chapter, it will be useful to provide a conceptualization of the term *self-esteem*. Indeed, part of the confusion that exists in the literature may be traced to using different definitions (theoretical or operational) and different concept names often with the same definitions. Since this is a secondary analysis, I am limited to the available data. These data contain Rosenberg's scale of self-esteem, which also happens to be among the most popular of the self-esteem scales. Rosenberg and Simmons (1971) conceived of self-esteem as an individual's positive or negative response to the self. The self includes the person as known to the person, through, for example, his or her cognitions and emotional reactions. According to Rosenberg and Simmons, the negative representation of self-esteem is viewed as self-hatred, self-contempt, or self-rejection. Another point worth mentioning is that when high self-esteem exists, it does not necessarily reflect the feeling that a person considers himself or herself better than other people, but it does suggest that the person views himself or herself as no less than other persons. Low self-esteem suggests that an individual considers himself or herself to be unworthy, inadequate, or otherwise lacking as an individual.

Although I am most interested in the global feeling of self-worth, or the generalized sense of self-worth as distinct from the more particular or specific aspect of the phenomenon, I acknowledge that self-esteem is associated with many other related concepts of self-esteem (e.g., self-evaluation, self-satisfaction, self-confidence). The distinction between global self-esteem and specific self-esteem (or evaluation of one aspect of the self) is important. In one of his later writings, Rosenberg et al. (1995) marshaled evidence that suggested that global self-esteem is more closely related to psychological well-being, whereas specific self-esteem is more closely related to behavior.

Although many studies of self-esteem have used the experimental, observational, or case study method, a substantial number have also used survey-based methods. The Rosenberg self-esteem scale has been used primarily in survey settings. On a 4-point scale that ranged from "almost always true" to "never true," the scale was comprised of the items listed in Table 3.1.

Kohn and Schooler (1969) showed that the Rosenberg self-esteem scale was comprised of two components, self-confidence and self-depreciation. In later research, using structural equation modeling, they confirmed that in this two-component model, self-confidence (positively worded items) and self-depreciation (negatively worded items) provided a better fit to the data than the single general component model (Rosenberg et al., 1995). Based on their exploratory factor analysis, Hughes and Demo (1989) reported two factors of the original Rosenberg scale, one representing the positively worded items, the other representing the negatively worded items. In their research, they recoded the negative items, so that all of them were in the positive direction and then summed to form a scale.

Table 3.1. The Rosenberg Global Self-Esteem Scale

1) I am a useful person to have around.
2) I'm a person of worth.
3) As a person I do a good job these days.
4) I feel my life is not very useful.
5) I feel I do not have much to be proud of.
6) I feel that I can't do anything right.

The Dimensionality of the Global Self-Esteem Scale

In pursuing the many research questions, I operationalized Rosenberg's self-esteem scale in the way suggested by Kohn and Schooler (1969, 1983) by conceiving of this self-esteem scale as representative of two aspects of global self-esteem. Whereas Kohn and Schooler conceived of these two dimensions as self-confidence and self-deprecation, with the first three items in Table 3.1 constituting self-confidence and the last three items constituting self-depreciation, I recoded the last three items in a positive direction and conceived of these items as a different way of assessing self-esteem. That is, I treated the issue as primarily a methodological one.[2]

The approach I used is similar to Hughes and Demo's (1989). They acknowledge that there appear to be two dimensions of Rosenberg's self-esteem scale which they attribute to negative wording, a methodological issue. Hence, they change the direction of the wording of the scale and sum all six items together. On the other hand, I also recoded these items in a positive direction, but I did not sum them with the other three items, at least not in this portion of this analysis. I maintained two separate scales, both conceived to represent self-esteem. Before I can feel confident that indeed there are two components, I must subject the model to an empirical test (see Appendix A).

Social Structure and Self-Esteem

Parenthetically, when I performed a difference of means test on these two scale means, the difference was not statistically significant. This suggests that whether global self-esteem is assessed by means of negatively or positively worded items, the responses are essentially the same (at time 1, 1979–80).

An issue often hinted at, but rarely accounted for, pertains to the influence of important sociodemographic or social structural variables on self-esteem or sense of worth. Focusing on black adults, some literature suggests that social class may be an important criterion variable (Gecas & Schwalbe, 1983; Rosenberg & Pearlin, 1978; Smith, 1995). Using regression techniques with the same set of data used in this analysis, Hughes and Demo (1989) performed one of the few extensive analyses of various background variables and self-esteem. A few other background variables such as personal income, education, and gender (male) all had weak, yet statistically significant, influences on the six-item summed scale of self-esteem.

I did a multiple-group analysis of the two self-esteem constructs across what I considered to be important background variables. Although self-esteem may be high for African Americans collectively, it might operate at a different level for those of different ages, those of different incomes, those of different education levels, and those of different genders. A number of scholars have noted that class cleavages are reflected in most of the sample surveys of black attitudes toward themselves in the post–civil rights era. This occurs despite the fact that most African Americans show relatively few cleavages in terms of identity with their racial community (Wilson, 1978, 1987; Smith, 1995), yet they may differ significantly with respect to their sense of self or individual assessment.

I used a two-step approach to explore these possible differences. First, I had to determine whether the measures mean the same thing across the social structural groups. This is the multiple-group analysis or the examination of factorial invariance. It may turn out that the items that represent the self-esteem constructs have different meanings within different groupings. If this is the case, comparing the means across these groups is not advisable. If there are no differences at a certain level of the hierarchical process, then I will be on more solid methodological grounds to examine the differences in means.

My initial task was to test the hypotheses for the comparison of key parameters across the different subgroups. I examined three different hierarchical specifications for each background variable. The first specification (model 1) tests whether the λ parameters or factor loadings were the same across the subgroup categories. This may be translated into the question of whether the items have the same meaning to the respondents. The second specification (model 2) tested the hypothesis of whether the errors in the indictors, $\theta\delta$, were the same for each category. This may be translated into the question of whether the items have equal reliabilities across the different categories. Finally, in the third specification (model 3), I tested the additional question of whether errors in the equations were the same, ϕ. Following generally accepted conventions, equality of the factor loadings is sufficient to consider the scale to have the same interpretation across the different categories of the variable (see Appendix B).

With data collected over time, I was able to answer many questions, which until now were only assumed. An extremely important theme that ran through the presentation of this research problem speaks to the level of self-esteem and the dynamic nature of this phenomenon. I have already indicated that at one point in time (1979–80) the mean level of self-esteem, both forms, was above average. Much of the literature refers to certain historical periods that are thought to have profound influence on the self-concept of African Americans. Some have talked about two major periods compatible with fairly recent dramatic changes that took place in American society—the civil rights era and the post—civil rights era. For example, Cross (1985, 1991) reviews articles on the black self-concept by separating them into two time periods: 1939–60, which he called the "Negro self-hatred period," and 1968–80, the "nigrescence period." During the former period, the notion that Africans suffered from distorting self-hatred was the consensus of those in academic and lay circles. Cross goes on to say that two events strengthened this position: the U.S. Supreme Court's *Brown v. Board of Education* decision of 1954, and the publication in 1955 of Kenneth Clark's *Prejudice and Your Child*. The latter period, nigrescence, was separated into two phases: (1) the civil rights stage, from approximately 1954 to the death of Martin Luther King, with some civil rights activity extending through the mid-1970s, and the (2) Black Power stage, approximately 1968 to the mid-1970s. He states that "personality and self-concept studies conducted with Blacks between 1968 and the late 1970s were often designed to capture the nature and extent of black identity change" (p. 41). In other words, black identity change was associated with the black power phase, which affirmed the evolution of a "new" black identity.

The data that will be used here were collected during the post–civil rights era (1979 on); thus, they are well suited to respond to a question posed by Smith (1995) which deals with the issues of the present and of change over time. He wondered aloud, what is the status of the self-esteem (or internal inferiorization) and the black identity of blacks? Or, to paraphrase, how enduring are the effects of the Black Power movement, as it was a major force in trying to provide Africans with a greater sense of self, on the self-concept of Africans?

I will direct attention to answering this question with respect to the self-esteem construct. In the next chapter, I explore the question relative to group identity. Table 3.2 and Figure 3.1 present the means for the two self-esteem scales at four points in time.

Looking at this table, I can see that with an average of 2, all of the means are above average, suggesting that black self-esteem does not appear to be problematic. In concrete terms, the majority of people said they had above average self-worth or self-pride. This applied for both self-esteem scales, although there is a very small difference in favor of the positively worded scale for comparable time periods. Also, it may be noted that although the difference is small, the means for data collected in 1985–86 are the lowest for both scales. The trend of the data is such that, with the exception of the telephone survey (1985–86), the means tend to become slightly smaller over time.

Table 3.2. Means of the Self-Esteem Scales at Four Time Points

YEAR	1979–1980	1987–1988	1988–1989	1991–1992
Self-esteem (positively worded)	3.61	3.52	3.54	3.52
Self-esteem (negatively worded)	3.56	3.37	3.49	3.50

Source: National Study of Black Americans Panel Study, four waves.

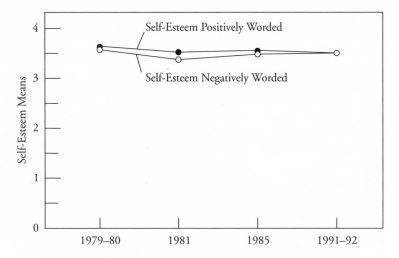

Figure 3.1. Means of the Self-Esteem Scales at Four Time Points

A measurement issue of importance is the reliability of the scale over time. I address the more interesting issue of stability over time in a later chapter. At this point, I want to know the internal consistency of the scales over time as represented by the Cronbach alpha measure. Table 3.3 and Figure 3.2 present those findings.

Table 3.3 indicates that for the self-esteem scale (positively worded) the reliability estimates tend to be low, with the highest reaching only 0.65. There did not, however, seem to be an observable trend to the estimate of this scale. There was an 11-point difference in the lowest estimate and the highest estimate for the negatively worded self-esteem scale. The internal consistency measures were low to moderate, yet substantially higher than the positively worded self-esteem scale. The lowest reliability estimate was 0.65 and the highest was 0.76. The reliability for this scale tended to increase over

**Table 3.3. Reliability of the Self-Esteem
Measures at Four Time Points**

YEAR	1979–1980	1987–1988	1988–1989	1991–1992
Self-esteem (positive wording)	0.60	0.54	0.65	0.55
Self-esteem (negative wording)	0.65	0.67	0.76	0.75

Source: National Study of Black Americans Panel Study, four waves.

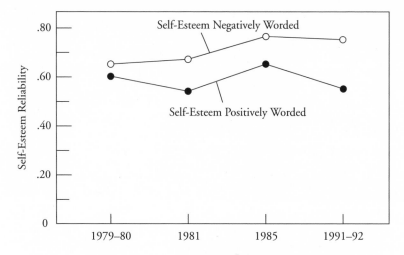

Figure 3.2. Reliability of the Self-Esteem Measures at Four Time Points

time. The haunting question that emerged from this table is: Why would the reliability of the self-esteem scale for negatively worded items be greater than the reliability for the positively worded self-esteem scale? Stated more neutrally, why would there be a substantial difference between the reliabilities for the two scales? Any attempt to answer that question would require in-depth analysis that would take us too far afield. Suffice it to say, I will be mindful of the differential reliability when I interpret the analysis drawn from the different scales at different times.

In Summary

I began this chapter by clarifying the definitional confusion that has led to considerable interpretational confusion. Recognizing the different aspects of the concept of self-esteem, and the variety of ways that it has been dealt with in the literature, I provided my own definition. Rather than trying to fashion my own idea of self-esteem, I was limited to some degree by the nature of my subsequent analyses, secondary to the operationalization of the self-esteem concept. My use of self-esteem was nonspecific, reflecting an individual's sense of self-worth. Referring to this as global self-esteem, consistent with some of the research literature, I further distinguished it from what is called specific self-esteem. I tried to make the point that any observations or findings I obtained were confined in general to my definition and operationalization of the concept of self-esteem. As a departure from much of the past literature, I operationalized the global self-esteem self-concept in terms of two related dimensions—one three-item scale comprised of positively worded items, and another three-item scale comprised of negatively worded items. One group of scholars had conceived of these two dimensions as representative of self-confidence and self-deprecation; however, I treat these items as simply different ways of measuring global self-esteem and coding the negatively worded items in a direction indicating greater self-esteem. This was instructive as it revealed that people responded to the scales differently, and thus more attention needs to be paid to the dimensionality of the commonly employed self-esteem scale. For example, it was found that the means were higher for the items that were negatively worded in the original, and that the reliability of the scale with the negatively worded items in the original was higher as well.

I surveyed some of the theories and conceptualizations that have been put forth to try to predict and explain the self-esteem of African Americans. With few exceptions, the theoretical literature posits that African Americans will have lower self-esteem when compared to whites, or with a noncomparative focus, that African Americans would have low self-esteem. As the theoretical literature was expressing one view of reality which had initial empirical support, more careful analysis revealed that the conclusions drawn from the data were often unwarranted, or there were misrepresentations of the findings, or a host of other conceptual and methodological problems. Much of the recent empirical literature (post-1968), however, has been adamant in presenting the African American as possessing a strong sense of worth (Cross, 1991). In an attempt at reconciliation, many theorists have tried to present an alternative conception of this self-concept among African Americans. In some instances, the new conceptualizations took African Americans as an exception to their theorizing but maintained the core of their theories. Others attempted to develop specific theories to handle these unexpected outcomes, without questioning the assumptions in past theorizing. Still others took the opportunity to argue that the confusion is only symptomatic of larger problems in conceptualizing the psychology of African Americans, suggesting a whole new approach to studying Africans. That approach must in some way incorporate the continuing struggle that African Americans have engaged in to maintain a positive sense of self and the group despite all odds.

Embracing this position, I referred to these struggles, the prolonged bouts of contestations, in terms of the omnipresence of the double consciousness. While this conceptualization does suggest that the adaptation of African Americans to threats to their sense of self will be dynamic, it also suggests that in the aggregate, African Americans will maintain a strong sense of the self and the group. One keeps in mind that the level of the consciousness battle is greater or lesser for different segments of the population, and that different segments of the population will be better equipped to cope and create alternatives. Thus, class or position in the social structure should also influence the sense of self.

Unlike most past studies, I used two national studies, one cross-sectional and the other longitudinal. Thus, I was better able to more faithfully explore the dynamic nature of self-esteem and its generalizability. Moreover, the data sets were large enough for me to test some of the assumptions concerning the influence of social structural variables, which included class, in this self-concept.

I feel confident in saying the following (1) African Americans tend to have high self-esteem or sense of worth. (2) This sense of self-worth varies within some education groups and within some income groups and to a small degree within age groups. If I assume that class, in a gradational sense, includes education and income, then it may be said that those of a higher class tend to have greater self-esteem. Crucially, in each category, however, the self-worth is above average. (3) The self-esteem scale is generally reliable but quite low. (4) The self-esteem scale, negatively worded in the original, is more reliable than its positively worded counterpart. This is the case at four different points in time.

I now turn my attention to the another aspect of the self-concept, group identity. I explore a similar set of questions, using the same data set. Since group identity and self-esteem have been often used interchangeably to tap the self-worth of African Americans, it is important to tease out some of the implications of this practice from past research and to put forth an alternative conceptualization of this construct for present and future investigations.

CHAPTER 4

Some Issues, Questions, and Problems Surrounding the Black Self-Concept: Group Identity

The basic tenet of black consciousness is that the black man
must reject all value systems that seek to make him a foreigner
in the country of his birth and reduce his basic human dignity.
—STEVE BIKO

I have provided support for the position that, collectively, African Americans have a positive sense of self-worth. This condition is essentially the same across different age groups, and, for the most part, the same for males and females. The exception is that males have a more positive sense of self when one evaluates their self-esteem by the negatively worded scale. While those who have more education and those with greater income tend to have a higher self-esteem, even those with the lowest income and the least education demonstrate a high sense of self-worth. In this chapter, we investigate similar issues but with respect to group identity

Although the African American may have his or her self-worth intact, does this translate into identifying with the group? The importance of group identity has been noted by many scholars and activists. It is an element of an individual's overall self-concept. The central idea is that having a favorable, or at least untainted, view of the group is crucial to any attempts to bring about social change. Phinney (1990) argues that the nature and substance of the attitudes individuals have toward their group are of particular importance to the psychological well-being of culturally, economically, and socially oppressed groups.

A number of scholars have maintained that self-worth and group identity are highly related. In fact, in some conceptualizations, the distinction is considered meaningless. Many others accepting the veracity of the distinction

85

maintain that African Americans may have high self-worth, but have hostility and contempt for Africans as a group. That is, the individual may have no problems with the "I" (the self), but serious reservations about the "We" (the group). Some have even said that frequently when African Americans exhibited low self-esteem, it was because the measure they used focused on the individuals' feelings about the group. To use Cross's (1991) distinction, the assessment of "personal identity" was confused with "reference group orientation." With respect to the latter, he says that it entails feelings of being wanted, accepted, appreciated, and affiliated, with strong ties to black people, black culture, and the general black condition.

Taking the strategy used to investigate self-worth, I will attempt to clarify the use of the term *group identity* or related terms in the literature as well as my own use of the term *group identity*. Such a wide range of concepts falls under the rubric of group identity. As in the case of self-esteem, there may be many different concept names used to label the same social phenomenon. Some commonly used concept names are: racial esteem, black identity, black autonomy, black militancy, black consciousness, and African consciousness. Under the general heading of reference group orientation, Cross (1991) specified several subcategories, which include group identity, racial identity, racial awareness, racial ideology, race evaluation, race esteem, and racial self-identification. This general category applied to Africans in the United States provides information about one's cultural frame and one's worldview. With little elaboration, three associated categories were thought to represents blacks' attitudes toward different aspects of race relations: (1) black cultural and political consciousness, (2) black alienation from white society, and (3) attitudes related to militancy (National Research Council, 1989).

While categorizing and labeling different aspects of what we call group identity has been problematic, its definition has also loomed as a source of confusion. As there is no commonly held concept name for this aspect of the self-concept, there are also no agreed-upon definitions of the phenomenon. In some instances, no theoretical definition is given at all; however, there are several insightful exceptions. Identity has been conceptualized as a component of an individual's overall self-concept. It incorporates several personal attitudes, feelings, characteristics, and behaviors, and the identification with a larger group of people who share those characteristics. If an African American, at an early stage, is enveloped by a support system that is both positive and black-oriented, then a strong sense of this identity is likely to be manifested. It is exemplified in an awareness of and attachment to an African cultural base, a keen desire to ensure the collective survival of African people and their institutions, and the participation in struggles to thwart any force that jeopardizes the continuity of one's people and oneself (for a full development of these ideas, see Kambon, 1992; Nobles, 1986; White & Parham, 1990).

Using the concept name *ethnic identity*, Phinney (1990, pp. 500–501) supplies a litany of definitions given by various scholars to capture the essence of ethnic identity. These definitions include: the part of an individual's self-concept that derives from his or her knowledge of his or her membership in a social group and the significance attached to the membership; the sense of shared values and attitudes; the awareness of behaviors, values, and the history of a particular group. Porter and Washington (1979) define racial self-esteem as how the individual feels about the self as black or about his or her group identity. Hughes and Demo (1989) interpreted this as the extent to which black people possess positive characteristics and do not possess negative characteristics. Gurin, Miller, and Gurin (1980) defined racial identification as the sense and the feelings associated with being part of a status group. Borrowing from this definition, Broman, Neighbors, and Jackson (1988) defined racial group identification as the feeling of closeness to those holding similar ideas, feelings, and thoughts.

Apart from the variety of theoretical definitions used to describe various ideas of group identity, the operational definitions are equally diverse. This has led to many inconsistent findings and predictions (Broman, Neighbors, & Jackson, 1988). The theoretical and empirical literature, therefore, would be better served by careful attention to the meaning and measurement of the variously identified constructs of group identity. With this proviso in mind, I now turn to some of the major theoretical conceptions and orientations that have been presented to describe, predict, and explain group identity. While overlap exists, the many theoretical orientations are associated with specific disciplines and, as in the case of the theoretical orientation formulation to address issues pertaining to the self-esteem, many of the theorists operating in their respective disciplines are unaware of other relevant conceptual orientations in other disciplines (Gecas, 1982; Rosenberg, 1985b).

Theoretical Conceptions and Orientations

Phinney (1990) identified three dynamic theoretical orientations spanning many disciplines and subfields that were thought to change over time and context. As mentioned earlier, these are social identity theory, acculturation and cultural conflict, and identity formation.

Social Identity Theory

Across disciplines, social identity theory is clearly the most prominent. It posits that an individual's social identity is a result of the knowledge he or she has of belonging to a group and the value, positive or negative, he or she attaches to being a member of that group. Taylor and Moghaddam (1994) point to two primary features of social identity: (1) group membership is seen from the perspective of the individual, and (2) that membership is assigned value. Social identity theory focuses mainly on the desire to maintain a positive group identity. It contends that when faced with a challenge to their social identity, people will sustain a positive social identity by identifying or creating favorable comparisons between their own group or groups and out-group or out-groups (Crocker & Luhtanen, 1990). Merely being a member of the group provides an individual with a sense of belonging that contributes to a positive self-concept, but being a member of an ethnic group represents a special case (Phinney, 1990, 1991). That is, if the dominant group looks upon an ethnic group with low esteem, the potential exists for members of that ethnic group to have a negative social identity. (This is the situation that until recently has applied to African Americans.) Citing Tajfel (1978) and several other scholars, Phinney (1990) says that those from a low-status, or a stigmatized or inferiorized, group have many ways to respond to this situation. For example, they may just leave the group by "passing"; however, this strategy is fraught with many psychological pitfalls and is unavailable to many people. An alternative is to engender pride in the group. One way of doing this is to redefine what is considered of little value or worth. Another approach is to stress the uniqueness of one group. Social identity theory also has relevance to the problem of an individual existing in two different groups, one overshadowing the other, but it does not suggest ways to resolve the problem.

Acculturation

Two models reflect the conceptualization of acculturation: the bipolar model and the two-dimensional model (Phinney, 1990). The former assumes that a strong ethnic identity is impossible for those who embrace mainstream society, and acculturation leads to a reduced ethnic identity. Conversely, the two-dimensional process is a linear model, whereby the relationship with the traditional culture and the mainstream may be independent. Thus, a member of a dominated group can have either a strong or a weak iden-tification with both his or her own culture and the mainstream culture. Also, a strong identity does not invariably lead to low involvement with the dominant culture. The major issue within this theoretical orientation pertains to the potential cultural conflict that may result and its possible psychological outcomes.

Ethnic Identity Formation

This conceptualization, according to Phinney (1990), examines ethnic iden-tity developmentally and at the individual level. A well-known developmental model—nigrescence—was proposed by Cross (1991, p. 190), which attempts to account for black consciousness (or various identity stages). In its modified and most recent version, African American racial identity frequently goes through four distinct psychological stages: (1) the preencounter stage portrays the identity to be modified; (2) the encounter stage isolates the points to which the individual feels the desire to change; (3) the immersion-emersion stage presents the vortex of the change; (4) internalization and internalization commitment occur. These last two stages describe the habituation and the internalization of the new identity. As an additional, recently incorporated component, it is possible for an individual to pass through the aforementioned stages more than once, depending on new encounters or challenges.

Porter and Washington (1979, 1989, 1993) have identified a quite different set of theoretical orientations used to assess the group identity of African Americans. These orientations overlap those they presented as explanations for self-esteem or personal identity. They suggested three prominent theoretical orientations—relative deprivation, alienation, and the role of subculture—all of which suggested high group identity. Relying on their more current and succinct statement of these orientations, they presented relative deprivation theory as based on the assumption that considerable socioeconomic change led to increased expectations and a change in reference groups. Comparing themselves with European Americans, where African Americans were said not to fare well, led them to become disgruntled and militant. This resulted in the development of racial militancy, which in turn led to high group identity.

The alienation theoretical orientation posits that due to feelings of powerlessness and isolation, alienation among black lower-income groups leads to an attachment to black identity movements. This orientation had wide currency among sociologists and social psychologists in the late 1960s and the early 1970s. In the theoretical orientation of the black subculture, during the black consciousness movement of the late 1960s, individuals became socialized directly into in-group identification and black pride, which was created and maintained in various institutions in the African American community (Porter & Washington, 1993). This present articulation of black identity is simply a different manifestation of an ongoing process.

The Empirical Literature

I will briefly discuss only a portion of the voluminous literature that is most pertinent to this inquiry. The rather strong position argues that because of the different conceptualizations, definitions, and measures that have been provided in the study of ethnic identity, empirical findings lack cross-study comparability and, not surprising, the findings are not consistent. Despite the many reservations, it is possible to make sense out of the literature, the picture it depicts, and the ways to refine that picture.

Several researchers have referred to the absence of reliable measures. Many of the consequences of ethnic identity have not been rigorously investigated, or ethnic identity as a process that leads to different outcomes has received comparatively little attention. The lack of familiarity with the different literatures, both theoretical and empirical, across disciplines has left a major void and has resulted in confusion in terms of the methods of investigation, the data requirements, and research design. For example, research using survey data rarely permits a separation of the effect of ethnic identity and social and psychological orientations. In a different vein, much of the disparity in findings may be due to the limited nature of most samples. Usually they are not nationally representative samples (Broman, Neighbors, & Jackson, 1988), and the samples are usually not composed of adults, but of children or adolescents (Cross, 1991; Hughes & Demo, 1989). On the theoretical level, there is little integration of theories formulated in different fields or disciplines, although this could be quite beneficial. As an example, the sociological theories tend to overlook the connection between social and psychological forces, whereas psychological theories tend to overlook intervening personality processes that operate in the development of group identity (Porter & Washington, 1979). A recurring theme in the literature on group identity, and something I referred to earlier, is the wide variance in theoretical and operational definitions, which often leads to conflicting and paradoxical findings. In the earlier literature on black identity, a favorite concept used to represent black group identity was racial militancy or black militancy, and this term was defined and operationalized in various ways. Broman, Neighbors, and Jackson (1988) indicated that when black identity was measured by an individual's susceptibility to using violence to achieve human rights, the results showed that African Americans of a lower socioeconomic status had stronger group identity. Conversely, when militancy was measured by an individual's favorable attitudes toward African Americans, another set of results found Africans of a higher socioeconomic status to have stronger group identity.

An Examination of the Evidence

As for self-esteem among African Americans, Cross (1985, 1991) has provided thorough and thoughtful literature reviews concerning group identity. Just as the pre-1968 studies generally showed African Americans suffering from lack of group identity, the post-1968 studies (1968–80) showed African Americans generally secure in their group identity. In a more recent literature review, Porter and Washington (1993) also observed that the available research indicates that most African Americans have high group identity, and that while differences across certain classes have been reported, such differences have been inconsistent.

Broman, Neighbors, and Jackson (1988), using a national sample of African American adults (the National Survey of Black Americans) and with an interest in the relationship of social structural variables and group identity, found that group identity (a combination of closeness to the masses and closeness to the elites) was strongest among older African Americans and African Americans with less education but greater income. Moreover, across all the demographic variables (age, gender, education, income, urbanicity, and region), the mean level for group identity was high and well above average, with a range of 3 or more on a 4-point scale. Thus, it is reasonable to say that the results show that most African Americans have a strong group identity.

Analyzing data collected in 1979–80 from two national surveys, it was found that most African Americans place substantial importance on black identity, which was referred to as group cultural identity. This identity also represented interrelated qualities. Group cohesion, striving and endurance, and perceived need to perpetuate these qualities were interpreted as important attributes of the notion of cultural identity (National Research Council, 1989).

In the 1940s, Clark and Clark conducted various studies of the development of group identity and racial preferences of African American children. They reported that black children tended to exhibit hatred of being black and generally accepted their inferior status. This conclusion was quite disturbing and led to controversy and debate (see Cross, 1985, 1991; Nobles, 1973). In another national survey, conducted in 1980, the Clarks again raised controversy with their findings. This time the sample of interest was African American adults, but the overriding research question that they were pursuing was the same: What do African Americans think of themselves? They reported that despite the elimination of blatant signs of racial rejection, and the existence of the Black Power movement through the 1960s and the 1970s, the majority of African Americans still had not developed a group identity or "racial acceptance." They noted, however, that differences within categories of education and income groups existed, with black college graduates and those with higher income being less adversely affected by racial rejection.

Since the overall conclusion is at variance with several other national surveys conducted about the same time and with studies using adults, some distinctive features about this survey may shed light on the reasons for the possible differences. Unlike many other national studies, which were household interviews, this was a telephone survey, perhaps with attendant lower response. Pointing out the difficulties of answering delicate personal questions, researchers decided not to use more direct questions, as they were misleading and for the most part invoke various forms of bias to an undetermined degree. They used an indirect approach instead. With this type question, they attempted to determine the black self-concept concept by approaching the problem based on what African Americans respondents thought other African Americans thought about themselves. This approach assumes that the concept that African Americans have of other African Americans is a reflection of the conception the individual African American has of himself or herself and of his or her race.

Dimensionality of Group Identity and Class Concerns[1]

Three major theoretical positions have relevance in explaining how African Americans holding various stations, statuses, and stigmas will relate to and be committed to the group. These theoretical positions or arguments have been identified as intergroup polarization, group interest, and group conflict theories. Jackson, McCullough, Gurin, and Broman (1981, pp. 240–241) described these theories in terms of their assumptions and predictions. Intergroup polarization theory, they say, states that with increased economic diversity among African Americans there arise different levels of attachment to the group. Thus, an individual's self-interest becomes attached more to other, non-African group loyalties (i.e., white middle class) or simply to self-interest. Given the changes occurring in the economic fortunes of various segments of the African American community, it is assumed that this will lead to a divergence which, in turn, will lead to increased conflict among these elements. The basis of such a conflict is that the African American upper and middle classes will increasingly embrace the idea that they share a common fate with the non-African upper-middle and middle classes.

Jackson and associates go on to describe both group interest and group conflict theories as predicting that the nature of the forces operating against African Americans will help them recognize that they have a common fate and this understanding will lead to a greater solidarity and commonality of beliefs. All three theories operate within a similar dynamic process. For African Americans, these theories note the importance of mobility being hampered by subordinate group status as defined by racial group membership. Moreover, to the degree that individual and economic mobility ensues, intragroup polarization should exist, and members of the group become less tied to their racially subordinate group. As I present these theories or positions, I am aware that all three theories may be in operation and exhibit considerable explanatory power. Specifically, it is likely that as a collective African Americans may have a strong sense of attachment to the group, based on some of the issues concerning group identity, yet differ across relevant measures of class or location in the social structure.

Moreover, it may be that the differences across class designations may not be in the direction often suggested by the intragroup polarization theory. For example, some empirical literature has shown, using one of the many manifestations of group identity, that socioeconomic status had no appreciable relationship with several pertinent measures of group identity (Allen, Dawson, & Brown, 1989).

Again, using the cross-sectional survey data, the National Survey of Black Americans, my colleagues and I attempted to address a number of shortcomings in the recent literature. Allen, Thornton, and Watkins (1992) examined the representations of the self-concept among African Americans, and we formulated a model of an African American racial belief system based on schema theory (Markus, 1977).

Figure 4.1 presents a proposed model of an African American racial belief system. Using the conventions suggested by Joreskog and Sorbom (1984), η represents the dimensions or the factors. λ represents the factor loadings or the coefficients of the indicators regressed on the unobserved dimensions. One of the indictors (the first one for each factor) was constrained to 1 to provide a metric for the factor. The z s indicate errors in equations, and ψs are the covariances of the ζs. By correlating these error variances, we assumed that the variances left unexplained in these constructs are due to common antecedents. The ζs indicate errors associated with the observed indicators.

A basic question has been entertained by many astute social observers: How well do we as a society incorporate people into our national whole from diverse racial and cultural backgrounds? The dominant perspective on these issues has been based upon the assimilationist model. It was believed that over time, an improving American society would bring about uniform systems of education, communication, economics, and politics which would, in turn, reduce older, more traditional distinctions among people. It was believed that ethnic and racial divisions would wither and be replaced eventually by class consciousness, something considered to be acceptable. Indeed, there is a common perception that American society has become markedly more open to cultural and racial heterogeneity over the past century, especially since the turbulent, change-inducing 1960s.

These changes were thought to be more graphically manifested in the improving position of the African American. Economic advances since the 1960s have led to a rising chorus of those who predict that as African Americans increasingly enter the middle class, the significance of race will yield to that of class. Nevertheless, this belief is not without its critics and detractors. Others suggest that only certain segments of the community have achieved parity, with significant portions of the African American community falling farther into economic oblivion. Still others argue that African Americans have not made relative progress, but instead, as a group have fallen even farther behind whites.

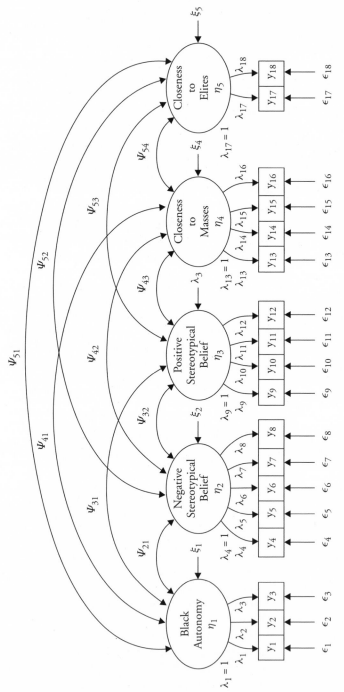

Figure 4.1. Schematic Respresentation of an African American Racial Belief System

Much of the aforementioned debate has revolved around the effect this economic progress has had on racial solidarity within African American communities. Many observers have focused on the effect increased social status has had on the worldviews of the more successful segments of the African American community. A key underlying assumption in this argument, based on Weber's definition of social class, is that life chances and worldviews flow from market positions and social status (Landry, 1987; Wilson, 1980). Thus, class or status position leads to a set of subjective experiences that cross even racial boundaries.

We maintained that an African American racial belief system is a multi-dimensional construct (with group identity being only one of those dimensions) and that each·dimension is based on one of the cognitive schemata. In our conceptualization, we assumed that the African American racial belief system is composed of multiple cognitive schemata that are distinctive yet interrelated cognitive constructs. The degree of intensity of these constructs varies across individuals and categories within the African American population. We began with a model to explain the development of five important sets of attitudes in the African American adult population. We used the following concept names: positive stereotypical beliefs, negative stereotypical beliefs, black autonomy, closeness to elite groups, and closeness to mass groups. Each of these constructs has at some time been used by a researcher to represent group identity (or black identity, racial group identity, or racial self-esteem). For example, Hughes and Demo (1989) used the concept name of racial self-esteem and the indicators we included under the names of negative and positive stereotypes. Broman, Neighbors, and Jackson (1988) used the concept name of racial group identification and included those indicators we used under the headings of closeness to the masses and closeness to the elites.

In this study, we first examined the validity of the existence of an African American racial belief system. Within that context, we investigated the influence of social status position on the holding of an African American racial belief system. We explored the relative importance of race and class among African Americans by investigating the effect of income and education variables on an African American racial belief system. The questions we raised were: Is there a significant psychological divide based on class position? Are there social class differences in how African Americans view their racial experience?

Unlike much of the previous literature, we systematically defined each of these dimensions. Closeness to the masses was defined as the emotional bonds to one's racial group, growing out of the perception that African Americans share a similar fate. Similarly, we defined closeness to elites as the extent to which an individual acknowledges that his or her political self-worth and that of the group can best be served by supporting African American leaders.

Two other related dimensions—positive and negative stereotypical beliefs—were based on Tajfel's (1981) thesis that individuals tend to assign positive attributes to their group and to reject negative ones. An individual who is continually treated on the basis of race is likely to assign either negative or positive values to his or her racial group. These two dimensions of racial consciousness suggest that African Americans find themselves facing a decision to accept positive group attributes and to reject stereotyping and debasing imagery of the group portrayed by the dominating culture.

The fifth dimension—black autonomy (called black identity in another study, Allen & Hatchett, 1986)—was defined as signifying the distinctive cultural and racial identity of African Americans. Black autonomy was conceived as an ideological position which suggests that African Americans should build political and social institutions based on the cultural values and interests of the group. Each of these five dimensions was represented by multiple indicators. The items are presented in Tables 4.1 and 4.2.

In examining the issues surrounding factorial invariance and differences in factor means, the sample was stratified on personal income and on education. For personal income, there were four categories: (1) less than $5,000, (2) $5,000–9,999, (3) $10,000–19,999, and (4) $20,000 and over. For education, there were three categories: (1) less than high school, (2) high school, and (3) greater than high school. The model in Figure 4.1 (a confirmatory factor analysis model) was used to test our hypotheses. It was estimated with the LISREL VI program (Joreskog & Sorbom, 1984), an analytical technique for testing simultaneous structural equations.

Our analytical strategy was composed of three related parts that reflected our research questions. First, we tested the hypotheses associated with the dimensionality of our model. This constituted our measurement model. Here, we were interested in the extent to which the five constructs of an African American racial identity provided a good fit to the data and whether these dimensions were correlated (negatively or positively) as proposed. Second, contingent on the outcome of the initial results, we examined the extent to which these constructs have the same meaning and perhaps measurement across education and income. This is the examination of factorial invariance. Third, assuming that the factors or dimensions had the same meaning across educational and income groups, we focused on the level of difference across income and education with respect to an African American racial belief system.

Results

Dimensionality of an African American Racial Belief System

The constructs were of varying levels of reliability. The black autonomy construct was at the low end of acceptable reliability. The overall model fits

Table 4.1. Items from the African American
Racial Belief System with Reliability Estimates

Scale	*Composite Reliability*
Negative Stereotypical Beliefs[a]	0.81
1. Most blacks are lazy.	
2. Most blacks neglect their families.	
3. Most blacks are lying and trifling.	
4. Most blacks give up easily.	
5. Most blacks are weak.	
Positive Stereotypical Beliefs[b]	0.66
1. Blacks are hard working.	
2. Blacks do for others.	
3. Blacks are honest.	
4. Blacks are strong.	
Black Autonomy[c]	0.54
1. Blacks should study an African language.	
2. Blacks should shop in black-owned stores whenever possible.	
3. Black parents should give their children African names.	
Closeness to Black Masses[d]	0.66
1. How close do you feel to poor blacks?	
2. How close do you feel to religious and churchgoing blacks?	
3. How close do you feel to middle-class blacks?	
4. How close do you feel to older blacks?	
Closeness to Black Elites[e]	0.80
1. How close do you feel to black elected officials?	
2. How close do you feel to professionals (e.g., doctors and lawyers)?	

[a,b] Both of these scales were expressed on a 4-point "very true–not very true at all" format.
[c] This scale was expressed on 5-point, agree–disagree format.
[d,e] Both of these scales were expressed on a 4-point "very close–not very close at all" format.

suggest that the proposed five-factor model of an African American racial belief system fit the data well based on the most relevant goodness-of-fit measures. Moreover, the factor loadings for each dimension were statistically significant and the magnitude of the loadings was moderate to large on each of their respective constructs. Finally, the constructs were correlated and in the expected direction. All the constructs were positively correlated, except for negative stereotyping of African Americans. As expected, it was negatively correlated with all the other constructs.

Factor Invariance or Multiple-Group Analysis

Using the convention that invariance across factor loadings denotes a minimum fit and one that suggests that the scale has the same interpretation

Table 4.2. Correlations Between
Racial Belief System Schemata

	Black Autonomy	Closeness to Black Masses	Closeness to Black Elites	Positive Stereotype	Negative Stereotype
Full Sample					
Black Autonomy	1.00				
Closeness to Black Masses	0.22	1.00			
Closeness to Black Elites	0.27	0.56	1.00		
Positive Stereotype	0.18	0.29	0.23	1.00	
Negative Stereotype	0.04	0.07	0.13	−0.10	1.00

Source: National Study of Black Americans.
Adapted from Allen et al. (1989) *American Political Science Review, 83,* 421–42.

across our education and income variables, we embarked on the analysis. Starting with the factorial invariance of income categories, we found that there is a similarity across income groups in how they relate to an African American belief system. The African American racial belief system (all five dimensions) is equally reliable and valid across income groups.

In comparison to income, the structural invariance does not extend as far. That is, there is structural invariance over fewer parameters. For education, the structural invariance ends at the invariance of factor loading. However, even in the case of education, the different dimensions of the African American racial belief system have the same meanings across the different education levels (see Appendix C, Part A).

Structured Mean Differences

We established that people across several education and income groups interpreted the five dimensions of an African American racial belief system in essentially the same way. Thus, we were prepared to find out whether there were mean differences across these income and education groups for our multidimensional belief system.

The omnibus test of the structure means across income levels indicated that there were differences. The task, then, was to determine where the differences resided. This omnibus test indicated differences across income groups for at least one of our racial belief system constructs. We investigated the location of this difference or differences. No mean differences were found for income categories for the black autonomy construct, positive stereotypic beliefs, and closeness to masses. The different income groups tend to respond to these three constructs similarly. For the negative stereotypic construct and for closeness to elite groups, however, we found that there were statistically significant mean differences. Those who earned up to $5,000 a year were more likely to hold negative stereotypes concerning African Americans as compared to those who made from $10,000 to $19,999 a year. Also, those who earned $5,000 or less hold more negative views of Africans as compared to those who make $20,000 or more. Additionally, those who make $5,000 to $9,999 were more likely than those who earned from $10,000 to $19,999 to feel closer to the elite groups. Interestingly, there were no statistically significant mean differences between the highest income group and the $5,000 to $9,999 income group and this high-income group and the next highest on this closeness construct.

One may glean from these data that, generally, those with less income are more likely to embrace the negative stereotypes about African Americans. Somewhat surprisingly, those with less income were more likely to feel a greater closeness to black politicians and professionals (the black elite). Just as interesting is the lack of difference found across income groups with respect to feeling closer to the masses, embracing black autonomy, or holding positive stereotypic views. The omnibus tests of the structured means across educational levels again indicated that there were mean differences for at least one of our racial belief system constructs. When we examined the different pairs of means for each construct across the three education groups, relationships were instructive. For the black autonomy construct and the positive stereotypical belief construct, as was shown in the case of income, there were no mean differences.

Each education group exhibited the same level of black autonomy and a sense of positive stereotypes toward African Americans. For the negative stereotype construct and the two closeness constructs (masses and elites), there were mean differences. More specifically, the pattern of mean differences for the negative stereotype construct was such that for those with the least education and those with the most education (greater than high school), a statistically significant difference was found. The least educated group tended to hold stronger negative stereotypes than the most educated group. Further, a marked mean difference was found for those with a high school education and those with more than a high school education, such that those with a high school education held stronger negative stereotypical views. The mean difference for those with less than high school and those with high school education was very small and did not reach statistical significance.

The pattern of mean differences for the closeness to masses construct revealed that all the means compared were statistically significant. The less than high school group exhibited greater closeness to the masses than the high school group and the greater than high school group. It is interesting to note that individuals in the greater than high school group showed not only less closeness to the masses but also less closeness to the elite groups in the

African American community. Thus, the lesser educated African American has a greater closeness to the masses and the elites, yet tends to embrace more negative stereotypes about African Americans.

If we look at the influence of both income and education on the various dimensions of an African American racial belief system, the aforementioned theoretical arguments all hold some sway. First, African Americans were essentially positive toward the group; however, there were some class differences (as represented by education and income). The differences, however, were not always compatible with the predictions derived from intragroup polarization theory. The patterns of these differences were such that the higher income groups had a less negative view of the group and were less likely to feel an attachment to elites. Additionally, the less educated tended to have a greater closeness to the masses and the elites and also tended to be more negative toward the group.

These findings speak to the complexity and multidimensionality of group identity, or the African American racial belief system as the term was used in this study. Although African Americans tended to embrace an African American racial belief system and to be above average in embracing these constructs, there were some class differences. The pattern suggested that those of a lower-class status, who tended to be the most negative about African Americans, also had a higher attachment to the black masses and black elites.

It is revealing to not only highlight the class differences, but also to point to areas in which such differences do not exist. Across the various notions of class, we found that African Americans did not differ with respect to the acknowledgment of a distinctive cultural and racial identity of African Americans which should empower them into concrete group action (black autonomy), and they did not differ in assigning positive attributes to their group (positive stereotyping). It may be said that education or income did not matter in how African Americans related to being African American and the positive attributes assigned to the group. However, it is those of the lower-income categories and lower educational levels who tended to be more negative toward the group yet closer to elites, and, for education only, closer to the masses (see Appendix C, Part B).

Closeness to the Masses and Closeness to the Elites

In the subsequent analysis, I explore, in detail, two dimensions of our proposed African American racial belief system: closeness to the masses and closeness to elite groups. These constructs will represent what I mean by group identity; thus, it is useful to highlight what has been gleaned from the findings on these constructs. First, both constructs are valid and reliable dimensions of our African American racial belief system. Second, those from different income categories respond to the elites differently. The pattern suggests that, generally, those who earn the least are the most likely to feel closer to elite groups as compared to several of the other income categories. Third, those from different education categories respond to the closeness construct differently. The pattern suggests that the more educated tend to show less closeness to the masses and the elites. As a last comment, and of specific relevance to our definition of group identity, the separation of the closeness construct into elite and masses revealed important findings, otherwise overlooked when the closeness items were summed into one construct.

Given the complexity and the copiousness of the findings, we have summarized these relationships in Table 4.3.

Conclusions

These findings highlight the importance of specifying which dimension of the African American racial belief system, or group identity, to analyze in terms of its antecedents and consequences. As we have shown, while there are different interrelated dimensions of an African American racial belief system, often they are influenced by different social structural forces. With an awareness of these differences, the confusion and conflicting interpretations that have engulfed this research area might be dramatically reduced. In short, it is hoped that these findings contribute to the process of obtaining theoretical and operational clarity.

Longitudinal Data (Four Points in Time)

Using the panel data provided by National Sample of Black Americans (NSBA), the same analysis was done for the self-esteem constructs. As I mentioned earlier, these data were collected in the post–civil rights era, a time when group identity was hypothesized to have increased. Just as in the case of the self-esteem construct, we will focus on closeness to the

Table 4.3. Summary of the Relationships between Class and Group Identity

	Black Autonomy	Positive Stereotype	Negative Stereotype	Closeness to Masses	Closeness to Elites
Income	no difference	no difference	lower income more negative	no difference	lower income closer to elites
Education	no difference	no difference	less education more negative	less education greater closeness	less education greater closeness

masses and closeness to elites, and the dynamic nature of this phenomenon. Using the first wave of this panel design and a construct similar to the one I used, Broman, Neighbors, and Jackson (1988) reported that the mean level of their group identity construct was high, suggesting that African Americans collectively have a high group identity. Although the panel sample is substantially smaller, I again see that the mean level of closeness to the masses is also above average, as one would undoubtedly expect unless the reduction in the sample size biased the estimates.

As the Black Power movement began in the 1960s and still exists in varying degrees today, it encouraged black consciousness or identification with the black collective. Given the assumed dynamic nature of this phenomenon, the question was raised as to whether identity was consistent over time. Table 4.4 can shed light on this matter.

Several interesting relationships may be observed in this table. With the midpoint being 2 on both scales, African American identification with the masses and the elites was above this point. For closeness to the masses, the mean level is very similar over this thirteen-year period. The mean level of closeness to elites is also similar over time, with the mean level being slightly higher in 1987–88. In comparison, African Americans identify more closely with the masses as compared to the elites, and this difference is statistically different at each time period. When again comparing the findings to the three above theoretical positions, the findings seem to deviate from those predictions. For example, all three arguments say that group identity is dynamic and always changing, that is, becoming more positive. The results show that while identity remains high, it does not seem to change appreciably, at least not in the thirteen-year period that I have examined. When I focused on the reliability of these scales, I again saw consistent relationships. Figure 4.2 and Table 4.5 present these findings.

Figure 4.3 shows that the reliability estimates (alpha coefficients) are low to moderate for both group identify scales. Moreover, these estimates do not change very much over time. For closeness to the masses, the minimum reliability is 0.71 and the maximum is 0.75. For closeness to the elites, the minimum is 0.78 and the maximum is 0.80. In comparison, the reliability

Table 4.4. Means of the Group Identity Scales at Four Time Points

YEAR	1979–1980	1987–1988	1988–1989	1991–1992
Closeness to Masses	3.57	3.57	3.53	3.57
Closeness to Elites	2.84	3.08	2.98	2.95

Source: National Study of Black Americans Panel Study, four waves.

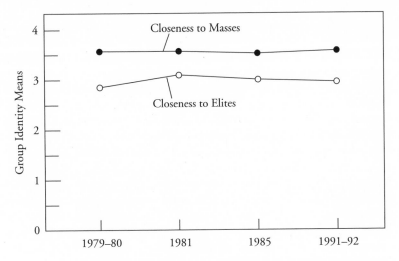

Figure 4.2. Means of the Group Identity Scales at Four Time Points

Table 4.5. Reliability of the Group Identity Scales at Four Time Points

YEAR	1979–1980	1987–1988	1988–1989	1991–1992
Closeness to the Masses	0.71	0.73	0.76	0.75
Closeness to the Elites	0.79	0.78	0.79	0.80

Source: National Study of Black Americans Panel Data, four waves. Estimates are alpha coefficients.

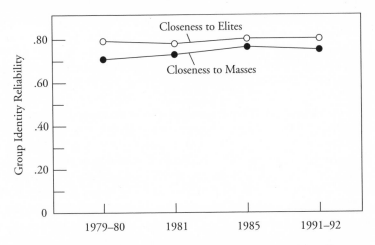

Figure 4.3. Reliability of the Group Identity Scales at Four Time Points

of the closeness to elite scale is slightly higher over time than the closeness to the masses scale, and higher estimates obtained at each time point.

The majority of the research I examined, the literature reviews I have consulted, and my own work indicate that African Americans have a strong attachment to the group. Most of this work noted that past theoretical literature had held that African Americans were purveyors of group enmity, and only during the post–civil rights era did that change. Indeed, some of the empirical work supports this perspective as well, but much of it is flawed. One recent national telephone survey by the Clarks (1980), done about the same time as the national survey study that formed the basis of my own study, reported findings contrary to my own work and the work of several other researchers. Since the work by the Clarks did not provide much information on the nature of their sample or how the data were collected beyond the basic minimum, it is difficult to assess in any detail the reasons that may account for the differences. The most obvious reasons, appear to be that (1) the Clarks' study was a telephone survey, with its attendant lower response rate and demographic biases; (2) they used various single-item measures to determine group identity, which raises the question of item reliability; and (3) related to that (and presumably to minimize the biases associated with a respondent answering sensitive or ego-defensive questions), they asked respondents through indirect "quasi projective" questioning or by asking African Americans what other African Americans think of themselves. More important, this study highlights the importance of being theoretically and methodologically precise and making clear what idea of black identity is being assessed and how it is being assessed. Otherwise, the confusion that visited much of past literature will perpetuate itself.

In this work, I went considerably further than in previous studies. After discussing several reasons for the discrepancy in some of the past research, primarily conceptual and methodological clarity, I then attempted to take these shortcomings into account in my work. Embodied in two studies I performed, I provided meaning and measurement to the notion of group identity by offering operational and theoretical definitions. In my analysis, I first made sure that the respondents across relevant demographic indicators, education and income, gave the same interpretations of the items reflecting black identity; thus, I was able to examine whether the mean differences could be interpreted as due to differences in response to our construct of group identity. Further, we were able to pinpoint within the different categories of these demographic variables the location of the largest differences. Finally, I was able to observe how the two-dimensional conception of group identity (closeness to the masses and closeness to elites) changed over an extended period, namely, thirteen years. Importantly, I found that, collectively, Africans Americans show a greater identification with the masses (i.e., those people that in the aggregate make up the majority of the African American population) than with the elites (those with an identifiable professional status), although they substantially identify with both groups. It is also interesting to note that it is the people with lower education, rather than the educational elite, who feel closer to the elites in general.

From a theoretical perspective, I interpret my findings as being consistent with the framework which posits that the African American community in the aggregate is involved in a constant struggle to maintain a sense of the group despite the many onslaughts, that is, the strong African community perspective as represented by DuBois's concept of double consciousness. In tune with this perspective, it is those of a lower status within the African American community who are most adversely affected by the onslaught as reflected in basic class differences.

It should be kept in mind that there is a gap between the theoretical conception of class—or more specifically, masses and elites—and its operationalization in this study. In conceptual terms, we thought of "masses" as being composed of the majority of African Americans who are members of the working class. We acknowledge that this designation incorporates those with substantial resources and those with very little. We conceived of the elites as being on the high end of the working class, in a material sense, but with considerably more status. These are the professionals. Thus, in one sense one might think of the categorization of masses and elites as essentially the classification of nonprofessional and professional or high status and non-high status. The operationalization of the two concepts focuses on people's *perceptions* of certain groups in the African American community. The underlying assumption is that African Americans make certain distinctions with respect to certain groupings in their community, and one of the most meaningful distinctions is between professionals and nonprofessionals or those with high status and those without high status. Furthermore, these perceptions have discernible antecedents and lead to certain identifiable outcomes. Hereafter, when the concept names *masses* and *elites* are used, they are informed by the above thinking.

With the overwhelming information suggesting that African Americans have a strong sense of self-worth and that they have an equally strong attachment to the group, I explore the relationship between these two self-concepts over time in the next chapter.

CHAPTER 5

What Identity Is Worth:
The Interrelationship Explored

I believe in pride of race and lineage and self: In
pride of self so deep as to scorn injustice to other selves.
—W. E. B. DuBois

During this research journey, I have provided the historical foundation for the interest in the concept of self among African Americans along with the dominant themes in the research literature that have tried to address the many issues growing out of that interest. With a focus on two prominent self-concepts, self-esteem and group identity, I examined the theoretical orientations and empirical literature that have a bearing on these two self-concepts. In doing this, my attempt was to clarify the many confusing issues and myriad problems associated with these concepts. The research literature for the two self-concepts showed considerable overlap; however, there are also marked differences in theories used to explain the phenomenon, in research designs employed, and in research questions posed. Thus, I performed separate inquiries into each construct and, by doing this, I was able to arrive at some verifying conclusions, some rather surprising findings, and some areas in need of greater attention.

Concerning self-worth, in brief, I provided evidence for the position that African Americans have a strong feeling of self-pride and that this sense of pride extends over time and is shared to different degrees by various class elements in the African American community, depending upon the measure of pride observed. Concerning class, those of a higher class possess a stronger sense of self-worth.

Likewise, African Americans demonstrate a strong attachment to the African American collective, which is manifested over time. Class position (education and income) influences this attachment to some degree. For example, those of lower income tend to feel closer to elites, but there are no appreciable differences between income groups in terms of closeness to the masses. On the other hand, the lesser educated African American adults are more likely to have a greater closeness to the masses, but those with the most education showed less closeness to the elites as compared to the other education groups. In short, all of these relationships must be interpreted in light of the fact that African Americans of different class standings have a strong attachment to self and to the group. However, in a comparison of categories, there were differences. Contrary to the case for self-esteem, those with a lower class standing had a stronger attachment to the group. Although a number of hypotheses have suggested a positive relationship between these two self-concepts, little research has been conducted. At this point, and due partly to data limitations, the available evidence has not provided convincing answers to the questions of whether there is an association between the two concepts, such that one leads to the other, or whether there is reciprocal causation. In this chapter, using data collected over four points in time, I present information to shed light on these issues. Moreover, I address the issue of the stability of these constructs over time and their other measurement properties.

Self-esteem is produced by microprocesses in the African American community, which may help shield it from institutional inequality. On the other hand, group identity is partly produced by cultural and interpersonal processes within the African American community. It is also produced by institutional inequality through many structural forces and the perception that white supremacy militates against the achievements of African Americans (Hughes & Demo, 1989). It is then reasonable to assume a relationship between these two constructs. What is quite striking about the past studies is that few have examined this relationship empirically, but many have touted its importance. Usually, it is assumed that a relationship exists between self-esteem and group identity. In some instances, one construct is used as a substitute for the other. In concrete terms, the findings of group identity studies often form the basis for inferences about self-esteem and vice versa (Cross, 1991). Further, some have predicted that not only are these two constructs associated but that one leads to the other. That is, group identity leads to self-worth (e.g., Porter & Washington, 1979). This idea was said to be derived from social identity theory and elaborations thereof (Crocker & Major, 1989; Phinney, 1990; Phinney & Onwughalu, 1996).

Crocker and Luhtanen (1990, p. 60) stated that

> Social identity theory posits that individuals are motivated to achieve or maintain a high level of self-esteem. However, whereas other perspectives focus on maintaining a positive personal identity (i.e., personal self-esteem), social identity theory is primarily concerned with the motivation to maintain a positive social identity (i.e., collective self-esteem). The theory proposes that when confronted with a threat to their social

identity, people maintain a positive social identity by identifying or creating favorable comparisons between their own group(s) and outgroup(s). Thus, individuals will discriminate against or derogate outgroup members relative to the ingroup to create a favorable comparison between their own group and the outgroup. These comparisons result in positive social identity, or high collective self-esteem.

Although one may not embrace the theoretical linkages between personal identity (self-esteem) and collective identity (group identity), the theoretical statement remains the same: positive group identity produces positive self-esteem.

Cross (1991) also indicated that the theoretical underpinning for the study of the black self-concept has had its tradition in the work of Kurt Lewin, but he frames the issues as representing a positive linear correlation between self-esteem and group identity, without specifying a causal order. In the early work on the black self-concept (1939–60s), Cross notes that while the positive relationship was often specified it had "seldom, if ever, been explored empirically, let alone confirmed." He said that in the early 1970s, however, a noticeable shift took place that included studies that examined both self-esteem and group identity. He studied empirical studies between 1939 and 1987 and found forty-five studies that investigated the correlation between personal identity (which includes self-esteem) and reference group orientation (which includes group identity). He reported that the majority of the studies reported no relationship between the two constructs, but a substantial number did. From this "mixed bag," he proceeded to do further analysis and found that the purported positive relationship withered under closer scrutiny. He concluded that the null hypothesis (i.e., the hypothesis of no relationship) had stronger support.

Oyserman, Gant, and Ager (1995) used a concept called "ethgender" to explain how African Americans interweave gender and race or ethnicity . They say that African Americans create a gendered identity schema because they (1) understand the self a member of a group; (2) provide meaning and organization to past and present racism and consequences; and (3) organize information about personal activities and the meaning attached to it by African American males and females.

An interesting conceptualization of the relationship between the sense of self and group evaluation, referred to earlier, was proffered by Nobles (1973). Without specifying causal direction, he further assumed that a positive relationship exists between notions of the self and notions of the group or the "I" (self) and the "We" (the group). He maintained that the interaction an individual has as a member of a specific group is a crucial referent for the self. Although employing a sample of black youths and testing several implications of Nobles's work, Wright (1985) reported a strong relationship between group identity and self-esteem.

Implicit in the prediction derived from social identity theory that the greater the group identity, the stronger the self-esteem, is the possibility of reciprocal causality. Phinney (1990) captured the essence of the problem when she posed the following questions: Does a strong identification with one's ethnic group promote positive self-concept or self-esteem? Or, conversely, is identification with an ethnic group that is held in low regard by the dominant group likely to lower one's self-esteem? Further, is it possible to hold negative views about one's own group and yet feel good about oneself?

The conceptual problem with reciprocal causation (sometimes called mutual causation) resides in the meaning and validity of the reciprocal paths, and longitudinal models are needed to make definitive conclusions about the direction of causation between two variables. Rosenberg, Schooler, and Schoenbach (1989) pointed to the importance of exploring the reciprocal relationship between self-concepts. While the data requirements for doing reciprocal analysis are greater, the advantages are pronounced. Rosenberg, Schooler, and Schoenbach (1989) noted that doing reciprocal analysis would afford the opportunity (1) to examine whether self-esteem and group identity influence the other significantly and equally; (2) to examine whether each variable has a significant effect on the other but that one has a greater magnitude than the other; (3) to detect whether it is one of the variables that influences the other, that is, the relationship is in one direction; and (4) to assess the directionality of the effect which may be different, with one effect being positive and the other negative. Such a countervailing effect assumes that the relationship is not spurious. Another important advantage is whether these relationships remain the same or whether they change over time. As I have previously noted, most past theorizing assumes or states explicitly that the self-concept is dynamic and subject to change over time. Although this is a common refrain, few investigations have been performed to determine the nature of this relationship.

In this chapter, I accomplish two tasks. First, I test the hypotheses derived from social identity theory concerning the relationship between self-esteem and group identity. My analysis will be fairly extensive, as I explore the relationship of two versions of self-esteem (self-worth with a positively worded scale and with a negatively worded scale) with our two versions of group identity (closeness to the masses and closeness to the elites). Second, and related to that, I examine the dynamic nature of the self-concept by concentrating on a heretofore neglected aspect of the self. Namely, I examine the degree to which these self-concepts change over time as well as the issue of the directionality of the self-concepts.

I use the same panel data (NSBA) used earlier. As an accumulation of all the previous analyses, Figure 5.1 contains the overall model that I test.[1]

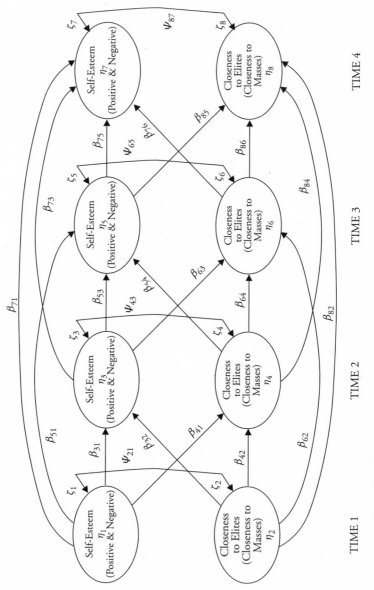

Figure 5.1. Schematic Representation of Self-Esteem and Group Identity at Four Time Points

Self-Esteem (Positively Worded)
and Closeness to the Elites

Before examining all the theoretical and empirical implications of Figure 5.1, my first task is to answer the question pertaining to the assumed correlation between self-esteem and group identity. I will start with one dimension of the self-esteem construct and one dimension of the group identity construct, namely, self-esteem positively worded and group identity as manifested in the closeness to the elites. Table 5.1 provides the correlations of our self-concepts over four time periods. The underlined values indicate the correlations of self-esteem and closeness to elites at each time period.

As may be observed, self-esteem at time 1 and closeness to elites at time 1 show a small correlation that is statistically significant. All the other correlations are substantially smaller and statistically nonsignificant.

Taking up the question of reciprocity as shown in Figure 5.2, many interesting relationships emerge. Looking at the overall fit measures, this model provides an excellent fit as represented by the various X^2 measures and other fit measures. For example, X^2 was 1.64, with 2 df, p = 44;

Table 5.1. Correlation Between Positive Self-Esteem and Closeness to Elites

	Self-Esteem (1)	Close-ness to Elites (2)	Self-Esteem (3)	Close-ness to Elites (4)	Self-Esteem (5)	Close-ness to Elites (6)	Self-Esteem (7)	Close-ness to Elites (8)
Self-Esteem (1) (pos)	1.00							
Closeness to Elites (2)	0.17*	1.00						
Self-Esteem (3) (pos)	0.15	0.01	1.00					
Closeness to Elites (4)	0.12	0.41	0.04	1.00				
Self-Esteem (5) (pos)	0.21	0.04	0.32	0.024	1.00			
Closeness to Elites (6)	0.07	0.49	0.00	0.591	0.03	1.00		
Self-Esteem (7) (pos)	0.24	−0.03	0.36	−0.021	0.41	−0.01	1.00	
Closeness to Elites (8)	0.09	0.44	−0.03	0.517	0.02	0.61	−0.01	1.00

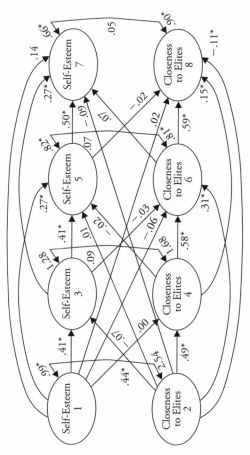

Figure 5.2. Positive Self-Esteem and Closeness to Elites

the CFI was 1.00 Substantively, self-esteem was stable at four time points (the reliability coefficients range from 0.41 to 0.50). All were statistically significant. Similarly, but with great magnitude, the construct of closeness to elites was also stable over time. The values ranged from 0.49 to 0.59; again, all the values were statistically significant. Concerning the question of reciprocity, the findings indicated at four points in time reveal that self-esteem (positively worded) does not have a statistically significant influence on closeness to elites. On the other hand, closeness to the elites does not have a statistically significant influence on self-esteem over four points in time. In short, neither construct produced the other.

Self-Esteem (Positively Worded) and Closeness to the Masses

Table 5.2 and Figure 5.3 provide the correlations over four time periods for self-esteem (positively worded) and closeness to the masses. Compared to

Table 5.2. Correlation Between Positive Self-Esteem and Closeness to Masses

	Self-Esteem (1)	Close-ness to Masses (2)	Self-Esteem (3)	Close-ness to Masses (4)	Self-Esteem (5)	Close-ness to Masses (6)	Self-Esteem (7)	Close-ness to Masses (8)
Self-Esteem (1) (pos)	1.00							
Closeness to Masses (2)	0.24*	1.00						
Self-Esteem (3) (pos)	0.18	0.02	1.00					
Closeness to Masses (4)	0.07	0.39	0.08*	1.00				
Self-Esteem (5) (pos)	0.24	0.04	0.31	0.04	1.00			
Closeness to Masses (6)	0.09	0.45	0.64	0.54	0.03	1.00		
Self-Esteem (7) (pos)	0.23	0.00	0.34	−0.00	0.41	−0.00	1.00	
Closeness to Masses (8)	0.13	0.36	0.09	0.47	0.06	0.49	−0.08*	1.00

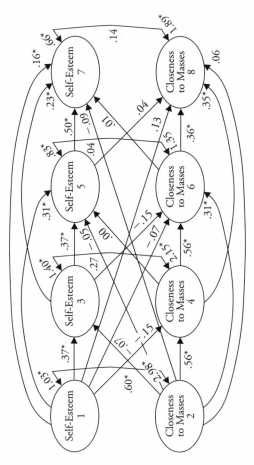

Figure 5.3. Positive Self-Esteem and Closeness to Masses

the previous output, it shows a contrasting picture of the self-esteem and group identity relationship.

Looking at the underlined values, I see that three of the four are statistically significant. Two of the three, however, are small, with the third being moderate. Nonetheless, there is evidence which suggests that self-esteem and closeness to the masses are positively related.

I now move to an investigation of our two constructs within the context of our omnibus figure. The overall model fit is excellent ($X^2 = 0.91$, df $= 2$, p $= 0.63$, CFI $= 1.00$). Thus, I can analyze the components of the model. The results show that self-esteem is fairly stable over time, that each estimate is statistically significant, and that the estimates range, in time order, from 0.37 to 0.52. Stability seemed to increase over time. For closeness to the masses, the stability coefficients were all statistically significant. They ranged in value, in time order, from 0.56 to 0.36. Stability decreased over time. Again, there was no evidence that either of the constructs produced the other.

Self-Esteem (Negatively Worded) and Closeness to the Elites

Table 5.3 and Figure 5.4 present a few confusing findings. The underlined values show the estimates to be statistically significant. But what is somewhat surprising is that I found both estimates to be negative—self-esteem and closeness to elites at time 2, and self-esteem and closeness to elites at time 4.

The overall fit measures suggest an excellent fit, $X^2 = 1.11$, with 2 df and p $= 0.57$. The CFI was 1.00. For the self-esteem construct (negatively worded), the stability coefficients were significant, but they varied substantially in magnitude. In order of appearance, the stability coefficients were 0.42, 0.61, and 0.26.

The structural portion of the model indicates that self-esteem and closeness to the elites had countervailing effects. From time 1 to time 2, having greater self-esteem resulted in a greater closeness to the elites. Conversely, feeling closer to the elites led to having lower self-esteem. From time 2 to time 3, I find a quite different relationship. Here self-esteem had no relationship with closeness to the elites; however, feeling close to the elites resulted in having greater self-esteem (the exact opposite of the relationship found at time 1 to time 2). At times 3 and 4, I again find that the negative relationship of closeness to elites and self-esteem prevails. That is, the greater the closeness to the elites, the less the self-esteem. At this time interval, however, self-esteem had no effect on closeness to elites.

Table 5.3. Correlation Between Negative
Self-Esteem and Closeness to Masses

	Self-Esteem (1)	Close-ness to Masses (2)	Self-Esteem (3)	Close-ness to Masses (4)	Self-Esteem (5)	Close-ness to Masses (6)	Self-Esteem (7)	Close-ness to Masses (8)
Self-Esteem (1) (pos)	1.00							
Closeness to Masses (2)	0.09*	1.00						
Self-Esteem (3) (pos)	0.21	−0.09	1.00					
Closeness to Masses (4)	0.08	0.40	−0.05	1.00				
Self-Esteem (5) (pos)	0.27	0.00	0.48	0.03	1.00			
Closeness to Masses (6)	0.01	0.45	−0.04	0.56	0.04	1.00		
Self-Esteem (7) (pos)	0.264	−0.00	0.42	0.00	0.42	−0.03	1.00	
Closeness to Masses (8)	0.039	0.36	−0.01	0.50	0.08	0.51	0.05	1.00

Self-Esteem (Negatively Worded)
and Closeness to the Masses

Table 5.4 and Figure 5.5 show that there was only one statistically significant relationship among the four underlined values (at time1), and that the magnitude of the relationship was small.

As with all the other models, this one was also found to provide a good fit. The X^2 was 0.13, with 2 df and p = 0.94. The CFI was 1.00. For the self-esteem construct, the stability coefficients were all statistically significant. These values were 0.42, 0.59, and 0.26, respectively. The latter coefficient was fairly small. The stability coefficients for the closeness to the masses construct were also statistically significant. They tended to be larger than those found for the self-esteem coefficient. Those values were 0.54, 0.59, and 0.36, respectively. The latter coefficient was again the smallest. It is worth noting that those who felt closest to the masses were more likely to

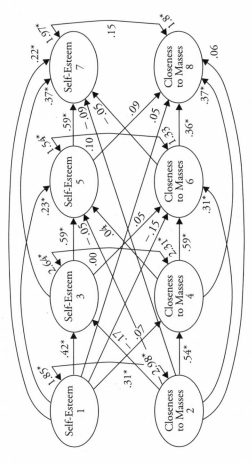

Figure 5.4. Negative Self-Esteem and Closeness to Masses

Table 5.4. Correlation Between Negative Self-Esteem and Closeness to Elites

	Self-Esteem (1)	Closeness to Elites (2)	Self-Esteem (3)	Closeness to Elites (4)	Self-Esteem (5)	Closeness to Elites (6)	Self-Esteem (7)	Closeness to Elites (8)
Self-Esteem (1) (pos)	1.00							
Closeness to Elites (2)	0.06	1.00						
Self-Esteem (3) (pos)	0.22	−0.15	1.00					
Closeness to Elites (4)	0.12	0.41	−0.14	1.00				
Self-Esteem (5) (pos)	0.28	−0.07	0.48	0.00	1.00			
Closeness to Elites (6)	0.07	0.49	−0.15	0.59	−0.00	1.00		
Self-Esteem (7) (pos)	0.27	−0.13	0.43	−0.08	0.41	−0.15	1.00	
Closeness to Elites (8)	0.10	0.44	−0.13	0.52	0.00	0.61	−0.08*	1.00

have lower self-esteem (negatively worded) initially. This relationship did not persist over time nor were any other significant relationships found for these two constructs.

In Summary

Given the abundance of the information provided in this analysis, it would be useful to bring it together in some kind of coherent whole. As an extension of the previous theorizing and empirical work, I was able to demonstrate that the African Americans' self-esteem and closeness to the masses and to the elites was stable over time yet that change also occurred. While the stability coefficients fluctuated depending on the construct under investigation, and the magnitude of these coefficients varied depending on the time period observed, these constructs areremarkably stable given the thirteen-year period of the observation. The correlations of the self-esteem

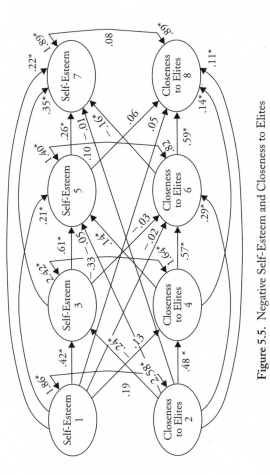

Figure 5.5. Negative Self-Esteem and Closeness to Elites

constructs and the group identity constructs varied considerably. Each of the self-esteem constructs was correlated with each of the group identity constructs at least at one time point. For example, self-esteem (positively worded) correlated positively with closeness to elites at time 1 only. It correlated positively at three points with closeness to the masses (times 1, 2, and 4). Self-esteem (negatively worded) correlated positively with closeness to the masses at time 1, but in stark contrast to all the other patterns shown, self-esteem (negatively worded) correlated negatively with closeness to the elites at time 2 and time 4.

To the question of whether there is a positive correlation between self-esteem and group identity, I must respond with a resounding sometimes. Overall, however, I must say that even when the correlations are positive and statistically significant, the magnitude of the relationships is usually small. This relationship corresponds to that reported by Cross (1991).

Concerning the directionality of the effects of the self-constructs, I found no discernible pattern. For the self-esteem (positively worded) construct and the two closeness constructs, none of the reciprocal relationships was statistically significant. For the self-esteem construct (negatively worded) and closeness to the masses, I found that there were also no reciprocal relationships; however, with this same self-esteem and closeness to elites, I found a perplexing relationship. Those with higher self-esteem (negatively worded) at time 1 tended to feel closer to the elites at time 2; however, this self-esteem construct did not influence closeness to the elites at any other time. Those who felt close to the elites at time 1 were less likely to have stronger self-esteem at time 2. (This is an instance of a countervailing effect.) Further, those who felt close to the elites at time 2 were more likely to have greater self-esteem. But at time 3, again, those who felt close to the elites were less likely to have high self-esteem at time 4.

I entertained the possibility that the results of the analysis on reciprocity were a possible harbinger of the biases introduced by the limitations of the sample, and that these may have differentially influenced our results. The analyses I performed suggest that the bias may not be serious, but it is still something that needs to be pursued further. What seems to be in order is a more detailed analysis of the sample characteristics.

Sample Characteristics

A national sample of African Americans was used to perform the multiple-group analysis. The sample referred to as the National Survey of Black Americans (NSBA) is a nationally representative cross-sectional data set of African Americans 18 years old and older living in the continental United States. The response rate was approximately 69 percent. A comparison of the NSBA sample with the U.S. Census Bureau data showed that the former contains slightly older, slightly less Western, and more female respondents. As compared to the Census Bureau data, educational achievement of the respondents is similar in the NSBA data, but family incomes are slightly higher. Broman, Neighbors, and Jackson (1988) reported that the missing respondents are more likely to have low education and low income. No differences were revealed, however, on the measures of group identity.

The strongest predictor of nonresponse was whether the respondent or his or her family were homeowners, followed by a variable correlated with it, the condition of the living unit (as assessed by the interviewer).

Most relevant to this inquiry, it is important that the two social structural variables that are of particular interest to us, income and education (two prominent indicators of the gradational conception of class), seem to have had an effect on the response rate (Torres, 1992; Wolford & Torres, 1994). I do not know, however, whether this resulted in a nonrepresentative sample or whether it had a demonstrable effect on the results. For this reason, and in the spirit of extension and replication, I decided to take the information I gathered from this extensive analysis and use it as the basis of theory construction and hypotheses testing. The results are presented in the next chapter.

PART III

THEORY CONSTRUCTION

CHAPTER 6

Another Look
From Another Angle:
A Move Toward Theory

There is no road to the universal except through the particular.
—W. E. B. DuBois

In this chapter, I formulate a tentative theory, one that is informed by past theorizing and the insights garnered from past research, and by some of the contemporary perspectives that have been formulated to explain the self-concept of African Americans.[1] I attempt to compile the relevant assumptions from a wide variety of sources, with an emphasis on those formulations that are testable. Moreover, the major thrust of the theory or theory fragment is to explain the antecedents that produce the sense of self and a sense of group. The predicted outcomes of the self-concept will also be explored, both to extend the scope of the theory and, primarily, to validate my conceptualization of the self-concept and to test the proposed hypotheses using exploratory data. This endeavor may be usefully conceived of as the process of theory construction.

Given the many positive aspects of the data upon which my analysis is based, I rely heavily on the findings derived from the rich data sources used in the previous chapters. I synthesize the thinking from many sources, with an emphasis on transcending their shortcomings and incorporating their insights, wisdom, and revelations. By examining surface structures, one can gain some helpful knowledge; however, one of the major values of taking a scientific approach is that one can penetrate to deeper structures and see things that are not immediately obvious. This entire endeavor is an attempt to probe the deep structure of the self-concept of African people. A considerable amount of what we think we know of the African self-concept is based on many faulty assumptions and inadequate methodological and epistemological conceptions (Myers, 1998).

To improve our understanding, I first present the major assumptions undergirding the literature on the self-concept. These are the assumptions that have been thought to be relevant across cultures. Second, I present the assumptions that are particularly pertinent to African Americans. I provide a rationale for treating African Americans as being influenced by forces quite different from those affecting non-African Americans. This entails an articulation of the thinking of many different scholars who have looked at the question from many different ideological and philosophical perspectives. Third, from these different assumptions, I formulate different hypotheses and a rationale for each. This involves tapping into several theories of varying levels of formality to act as the theoretical linkages for the hypotheses. The hypotheses predict the antecedents and, in limited instances, the outcomes of the self-concept. Finally, operating from an extended set of assumptions and with additional self-concepts drawn from these assumptions, I present an alternative representation of the African American self-concept. This approach leads to a new conceptualization of the self-concept.

Global Assumptions

While I argue that an extensive set of assumptions is required to address the experiences of African Americans, I find that researchers have used several general assumptions to characterize the experiences of the self across cultures. Drawing from many sources (e.g., Kambon, 1992; Myers, 1993; Nobles, 1986, 1992; Triandis, 1994), I conclude that the relevant general assumptions are as follows:

1. The self-concept is the cognitive component of the psychological process known as the self.
2. Individuals possess many self-concepts.
3. The self-concept is situation-specific. That is, self-concepts tend to operate in specific situations producing particular self-conceptions.
4. The self-concept is a highly complex, evolving entity, offering different components of its totality for investigation. Sometimes the structure of these components is studied, and sometimes the focus is on the broad dimensions of the self-concept, such as self-esteem, identity, and self-confidence.

Operational Assumptions

Throughout this analysis, as is often the case with any investigation of the self-concept of African Americans, there is a set of assumptions that are evident, if not always made explicit. Some recent theorizing has addressed the general issue of the self-concept as having two dimensions—Western and non-Western. The work of Markus and Kitayama (1991, 1994) is instructive in this regard. They have noted that Western or European American theories of the self argue essentially that people are independent, bounded, autonomous entities who must strive to remain unencumbered by their ties to various groups and entities. The individual is thought to be fundamentally removed from the group and to be an independent entity. This conception of the self is evident in almost all social institutions in the United States. Further, social science embraces some aspect of this conception as reflected in the notion that the person is "a rational, self-interested actor, and on occasions [has] a desire not to be defined by others, and a deep-seated wariness, in some instances even a fear, of the influence of the generalized other, of the social and of the collective" (Markus & Kitayama, 1994, p. 568).

In this view, the individual lives in opposition to the collective. Most contemporary thinking on the self characterizes the healthy self as one who is impervious to outside social intrusions (Gaines & Reed, 1995; Markus & Kitayama, 1991; Nobles, 1992; Tyler, Kramer, & John, 1999). Moreover, social behavior is often fashioned as inimical to individual behavior and acts as a force that compromises individual behavior (Markus & Kitayama, 1994). The enduring contemporary model of the self is asocial (Akbar, 1984; Kambon, 1992; Oyserman & Markus, 1993).

Criticism of this conception of self has been long, loud, and lavish. Shweder and Bourne (1982), for example, stated that people coming from different cultural backgrounds or societies exhibit distinct worldviews and that these worldviews influence cognitive functioning. While some aspects of the self may be universal, other aspects may be specific to certain cultures (Markus & Kitayama, 1991). The fundamental American conception of the self may be reflective of whites or Western Europeans. Markus and Kitayama contend that this conception is representative of white, middle-class men with Western European backgrounds, but it may be much less characteristic of other cultural groups, and even less descriptive of white Western European women in general.[2] Recent work exploring the self in other cultures, especially African American, has yielded relationships between the self and the collective quite different from those deemed representative of European Americans, male or female (Kambon, 1992).

Many scholars have distinguished the idea of conceptualizing the self-concept of African Americans from the standard conceptions of self most prominent in the United States. Nobles (1992) posits that the African conception of the self, unlike that exhibited for the European American, emphasizes the survival of the group and the feeling of oneness with nature. From such guiding principles, he argues, a sense of cooperation and collective responsibility emerges. He goes on to say that the modalities consistent with the African worldview are "commonality," "groupness," and "similarity." Akbar (1995) refers to the African self-conception as an unqualified collective phenomenon that acknowledges the uniqueness of the individual self as a component of the collective.

Elaborating on the African in the diaspora, Nobles (1973) identifies the African worldview as embodied in the statement: *I am because we are, and because we are, therefore, I am*. He contends that there is no real distinction between one's self and one's people, that one's self-identity and the identity of one's people is always a people's and are not merely interdependent or interrelated, but identical. He refers to this as the "extended self." Unlike the Western concept of the self, the African worldview finds it difficult to make a distinction between the self, or the "I," and one's people, or the "we."

In support of his attributing an African worldview to peoples of African descent living in the United States, Nobles refers to the writings of such scholars as DuBois (1903, 1964) and Herkovits (1958). This list could also include several other prominent scholars who have done more recent work in this area, such as Akbar (1995), Diop (1991), Hilliard (1995), Holloway (1990), and Thompson (1984). While these scholars have differed in terms of emphasis, they argue for the existence of a substantial number of cultural retentions from Africa. This overall African worldview, an integral part of the life of African Americans, is mostly unconscious, frequently disguised, and often disfigured (Kambon, 1992). Undoubtedly, Africans in the diaspora and, to a lesser degree, generally, Africans on the continent, have been informed by a basically European construction of reality, or what has sometimes been called the Westernization of human consciousness. This European conception overlooks the collective, social, and spiritual sense of the African conception of self (Kambon, 1992; Nobles, 1992).

As I suggested earlier, several scholars have questioned the usefulness of the European conception of self and have presented a recent alternative to it, the essence of which is (Markus & Kitayama, 1994) as follows:

The self is an interdependent entity, the self is not separate from the collective.

The self is inherently social, with primacy given to the relationship between self and others.

The self becomes whole only through interaction with others. There is no self without the collective.

This alternative is compatible in several fundamental ways with the assumptions underlying the African worldview put forth by many African American scholars (Myers, 1998). Within this worldview emphasis is placed on the survival of the group and the individuals as part of the natural rhythm of nature. The fundamental assumptions of the African worldview are:

The self cannot be thoroughly analyzed into parts separated and isolated from the context of the whole.

The self is a collective and social phenomenon.

Like all human thought and practice the self is socially rooted and thus most meaningfully understood within a given context.

The African self is exemplified not only in cognitive but also in emotional and spiritual components.

Humans are fundamentally spiritual entities whose physical forms are only reflections of a material expression of their true spiritual essence.

The African holds a nonindividualistic, dualistic approach to the self (i.e., the incorporation within the self, the "I" and the "we"). The duality is more a consequence of divisions within the group and in an individual's notions about his or her relationship to others.

All aspects of nature, including consciousness, are interrelated and interdependent, resulting in a communal phenomenology—commonality, corporateness, groupness, cooperation, collective responsibility (Nobles, 1991b, p. 298).

In formulating a more holistic view of Africans, it is crucial to understand also that aspects of their being transcend the external impositions over which they have little control and attempt to mold a healthy self. Here, I am referring to the culturally, philosophically, and spiritually distinct elements among African Americans in the United States that make them distinct from other groups. It is from this basic understanding that I examine the African in the United States. This examination takes into account the woeful experiences of chattel slavery, but also keenly notes those aspects of African life that allow Africans in various locations to withstand onslaughts and to fashion a self that holds on to conceptions of the world grounded in African culture. This process is reflective of the double consciousness or duality, that is, being "builders of an economic infrastructure, yet dispossessed of its fruit; creators of one of its truly original native cultures, in story and song, yet culturally demeaned and maligned; faithful adherents to the nation's basic ideals and values, yet shunned, abused, and stigmatized as if an alien people" (Holt, 1990, p. 303). According to some researchers, this double consciousness also arises from Africans' attempts to achieve the American Dream (National Research Council, 1989) or from tensions between pride and shame in self (Gaines & Reed, 1994).

The concept has similarly been framed as a hypothesis about resilience in the face of major challenges, which led DuBois to speak of Africans in the

United States as a proud people. A crucial aspect of the double consciousness concept, however, is that the African part of the equation has not been fully developed. I contend that the more an African American develops this element, the more he or she will get in tune with his or her self, and the greater will be both individual and group health. This idea is reflected in the earlier quote from Malcolm X (1990), "Show me a person who hates Africa, and I will show you a person who hates himself" (p. 85). Not only is one's sense of self connected to the collective, the collective is defined in broad, encompassing terms, that is, the extent to which the origin of most Africans' understanding of and attitude toward Africa is positive will determine the extent to which the individual will be positive toward himself or herself. Alternatively, as Malcolm X put it, "You can't hate your origin and not end up hating yourself. You can't hate Africa and not hate yourself" (p. 85).

The interesting question for many African Americans is, what constitutes the American Dream, or, at least, which aspects of the Dream they are seeking. If the Dream merely means having a fairly comfortable living with the associated trappings, then it may not require major psychic confrontations. Conversely, if following the Dream means striving to acquire substantial wealth and perhaps influence, if not power, then within the context of contemporary America this will usually require that major choices be made. These choices often entail distancing oneself from the group and functioning for one's own separate advancement or, in short, embracing an approach more attuned to individualism as distinct from collectivism. This may involve accepting a view of nature that may be at odds with an individual's own perspective, and will, therefore, likely produce identity tensions.

One might assume that these individuals will exhibit a greater acceptance of those aspects of mainstream American culture so as to reach their goal of the American Dream, meaning greater assimilation. One might also assume that this group would tend to be of a higher socioeconomic status, either as a consequence of their compromises or as a strategy to maintain their status.

Tensions also exist for the individual who has a strong attachment to Africa and African Americans. If this person is steeped in African culture or more generally has an African worldview, he or she will be under pressure to modify or compromise his or her position. An African worldview that includes, for example, an emphasis on the collective and the spiritual, would conflict with the individualistic and the materialistic view that characterizes the European worldview and predominates among those in power in the United States. Given the unequal power relationship between the dominating European American group and the African American group, it would be difficult for members of the latter group to maintain an alternative African conception of reality.

Individuals who are attuned to an African worldview may strengthen this tendency to the extent that their actions or their conceptions challenge the dominant European worldview. Such persons would tend to be more collectivist in orientation and to foster a stronger sense of group identity, either as a consequence of their initial position or as a result of the response to their position by the dominant group. One might assume that these individuals would not be of high socioeconomic status, but yet might hold greater status in the community and perhaps be more highly educated.

Akbar's (1995) ideas concerning grafted knowledge and real knowledge illuminate the self-concept of African Americans. Just as DuBois's double consciousness may be used as an organizing scheme to explore the self-concept of oppressed people, in a related manner Akbar's idea of real and grafted knowledge might be used to explore transformations among oppressed people. Akbar noted that his concept of human transformation was intended to have relevance to the healing of oppressed people of African descent specifically, but also may gain significance as a key to the heightening the spiritually oppressed humanity in general. He sees "grafted" knowledge as a form of knowledge that presents an incomplete and distorted picture of nature's processes but claims to be the entire picture. It is seen as interfering with this transformation. "Grafted knowledge" gives a retarded image of the human being and human capabilities, and views human life in terms of its physical manifestations. Many Americans hold this view, tending to be enamored by material life and to define themselves in those terms, often at the expense of other aspects of self—spiritual, moral, and mental.

Finding themselves encased in a deforming, alienating, and alienated context, African Americans often confuse actuality with potentiality and established order with eternal order (Karenga, 1982). Nonetheless, African Americans have managed to fashion a favorable image of themselves and their group not individually but with the support of the black community collectively. This is what has been referred to in the literature, in more restricted terms, as the "supportive black community thesis" or theory (Porter & Washington, 1979, 1993).

Hypotheses

I maintain that much past theorizing operates from inappropriate assumptions, or what Akbar called grafted knowledge. Nonetheless, earlier researchers have generated considerable data and subsequent theorizing that exposed their shortcomings. Making certain modifications in the theorizing and incorporating alternative assumptions, I was able to provide a consistent set of findings that were compatible with the findings reported by Cross (1985, 1991) and Porter and Washington (1993). For example, I found that African Americans have a strong sense of black identity and self-esteem. Additionally, these two constructs were remarkably stable over a relatively long period (thirteen years). I was not able to confirm some of the assumptions that emerged from an African-centered perspective. The data requirements were not met, since the African-centered assumption is that the self cannot be distinguished from the collective, and that any measurement instrument that makes such a distinction violates the assumption of the "I" and "we" being inseparable.

Noting the need for a culturally specific instrument to assess the various areas of African American life, the creators of the Baldwin and Bell (1985) scale based it on an "Africentric" theory of black personality. The theory posits that the core component of the African American personality reflects the conscious expression of the "oneness of being"—a communal phenomenology that is thought to characterize the fundamental self-extension orientation of African people. The theory's fundamental operating principle is that the social reality in the United States constitutes its owns values and standards undergirding black behavior. This "Africentric" social reality therefore projects a normalcy referent for black behavior that is independent of Euro-American culture and Western racism (Baldwin & Bell, 1985, p. 62). Baldwin and Bell recognize, however, that there is an interplay between individual personality attributes and social and environmental elements that partly shape the individual self. They go on to say that this normalcy behavior has essentially positive outcomes, under natural conditions, and is proactive as opposed to merely reactive to negative and adverse environments. That is, this conception of the self has a normalcy referent for black behavior, namely, actions in the service of the "needs and social priority of the African American community" (p. 62).

The major dimension of their self-consciousness construct is exemplified in: (1) an awareness of collective consciousness (or black identity) and African heritage; (2) the recognition of a need for institutions to foster such things as values and practices that affirm African life; (3) involvement in activities that celebrate African dignity, worth, and integrity; and (4) participation in actions that resist onslaughts on the development and survival of African people.

Operating from a set of alternative assumptions presented above, I formulated the following hypotheses. The first three hypotheses have been examined with a national survey of African Americans, so they are being replicated in the form of a new set of data. The first hypothesis refers to the group identity construct (closeness to the masses and to the elites, ethnic identity). The second hypothesis makes the distinction between self and group and suggests that these two constructs are associated. The third hypothesis makes a comparison between the racial-specific group identity dimensions and the presumably nonracial self-esteem constructs. In short, it says that the attachment to the group is even more pronounced than individual self-worth. The fourth hypothesis grows out of the conception of self as represented by the African-centered conceptions of self. This normative construct of self reflects the collectivism and cooperation that, in contrast to European American culture, is hypothesized to have a notable existence in the African American community. The final hypothesis suggests that the different African-centered conceptions—one race-oriented and one race-neutral—are positively interrelated. This relationship, although not stated in the hypothesis, is assumed to be more strongly associated than the non-African-centered notions of group identity.

African Americans have a strong sense of the group.

African Americans have a strong sense of the self.

African Americans have a strong ethnic identity.

African Americans have a strong African self-consciousness.

The various self-conceptions are associated for African Americans.

Antecedents of the Self-Concept

The self-concept comes into being with a certain shape and form based on a certain social structure, institutional arrangement (e.g., economy, family), and culture. Here, I attempt to provide some of the major social environments, socialization processes, and institutional processes most conducive to the self-concept. Different factors and processes often influence different reflections of the self. For example, as noted earlier, those processes that influence the nonracial conception of self may overlap less or have less influence than those factors that influence an individual's attachment to the group. These, in turn, may be quite different from those that influence a particular worldview as represented by the more philosophically based African self-concept. In short, the antecedent factors have varied tremendously depending upon the self-concept under consideration. Given the range of constructs that I have been entertaining under the rubric of the self-concept, the most prominent and most consistent across the various self-concepts are religiosity, communication, age, and class. Several of these influences are actually categories of specific variables.

Class Issues

The setting for my discussion of class surrounds recent dramatic changes in the economic conditions of the United States. Poverty and income inequality in the 1990s, even with highly divergent definitions, were high by historical standards (Danzinger & Gottschalk, 1993, 1995). While the economic contours are generally quite complex, they are magnified when exploring the economic standing of African Americans. For example, several social commentators have underscored the rising inequality of earnings between African Americans and European Americans, and they have also pointed out with great consistency the gap between earnings of various groupings in the African American community. The most distressing aspect of this economic situation, many have said, is that there is a segment of the African American community that has been variously defined but is often labeled as an "underclass," a segment at the periphery of the economy. Conceptually, the underclass is universal, cutting across racial and regional lines; however, many scholars implicitly link the concept operationally to race and residence. This practice ignores the fact that among blacks, poverty is greatest not in urban areas but in the rural South (Smith, 1995, p. 115). Further, it has been noted that the present definition of underclass has moved from a general reference to poverty that included whites to an emphasis on the behavioral, cultural, and moral characteristics of the black urban poor (Lott, 1992).

Among the criticisms leveled at the concept of the underclass, one of the most fundamental is that the term is imprecise and vague in meaning (see, for example, Boston, 1988; Jones, 1992; Lawson, 1992). With respect to the underclass being a new phenomenon, Jones (1992) takes a sorely neglected historical analysis. He states that if the "underclass" refers to African people who are uneducated, unskilled, unemployed, and often underemployed, living in unrelieved poverty and engulfed in a culture conditioned by these abject conditions with little chance of upward mobility, then the term denotes nothing new. He argues that the creation of an underclass is a "logical, perhaps even necessary, outgrowth of American political economy conditioned by white racism" (p. 53), and that there is still an economic crisis that exists in the African American community that needs immediate attention.

What influence might these ostensibly new class configurations have on the group solidarity that has existed for some time and is a subject of much concern? Will changes in the class structure in the African American community result in a reduced sense of shared group interests across various class designations? Some shout a resounding "yes"; others confidently cry "no."

Clearly, wages of employed African Americans have risen and a higher number of African Americans hold professional, managerial, and technical jobs than ever before. Just as the black middle class has increased, however, so too has the percentage of low-status and low-income blacks. Thus, the potential for class divisions, heightened by the racial climate of the larger society, has also risen (Dawson, 1994).

An issue of paramount concern when exploring the self-concept is the extent to which class status influences an individual's sense of self, whether self-esteem, group identity, or African self-consciousness, as I have used these constructs. These issues possess added meaning when one takes into account the much discussed alleged cleavage in the African American community.

Up to this point, I have not defined the concept as I will use it. When one talks about class, one is talking about myriad different conceptualizations which often have conflicting theoretical implications (Mincy, 1995). This impression in terminology is exacerbated for African Americans, for whom the class structure suffers from major distortions as a consequence of the historical legacy of racism and exploitation (Dawson, 1994; Wright, Hachen, Costello, & Sprague, 1982; Wright, 1985).

Two of the most widely explored and employed formulations are the Weberian and Marxist. In the Marxist definition, classes are viewed in terms of their ownership relation to the means of production. This has been called the relational definition of class (Wright & Perrone, 1977). The Weberian definition of classes pertains to status groupings denoted by a common set of socioeconomic relations and life chances. This has been referred to as the gradational approach to class (Wright, 1985). Each has shortcomings related to setting boundaries (Boston, 1988).

Without question, the Weberian approach is the most commonly employed in the analysis of class in the African American community. However, it has several limitations, many of which were keenly observed by Boston (1988). He stated that the most serious problem was a misspecification of class boundary. He cited the unwarranted practice of merging the black capitalist class with the black middle class as if they were one. While the smallness of the capitalist class was the reason usually given for the merger, the practice results in major conceptual oversights. Boston argued that the separate category for the black capitalist class is important for analysis, as it is a fundamental part of contemporary racial inequality.[3] Aside from these errors, he said that there is also in the Weberian approach a faulty tendency to classify the middle class arbitrarily by income boundaries. Finally, he noted, while the term *underclass* is bandied about, it is not defined in any precise terms and "we are generally led to believe this underclass consists primarily of black female-headed households and pathological misfits" (p. 7).

Since there are many different definitions of class and problems associated with each, I thought it most feasible to use a definition often employed to explore the self-concept. Although the definition, and the rationale for it, by Boston (1988) was inspiring, I decided to forego it until I had more appropriate measures. Thus, I borrowed the definition of Wilson (1980), as did Dawson (1994) in his analysis of class and politics. Here, class is defined as individuals or a group of people who have comparable goods, services, or skills to offer for income in the labor market. As adequate indicators of the theoretical definition, two commonly employed measures were used: education and income.

A long and complicated debate marks the discussion of the relationship between class (sometimes referred to in terms of socioeconomic status) and the self-concept. Some of the literature suggests that high-status African

Americans have a high group identity. In contrast, a number of other observers have maintained that African Americans of low status have the highest levels of group identity. Concerning self-esteem, those of a higher status are typically thought to have more self-pride. Excluding self-esteem, a plethora of unreconciled, often contradictory findings is the rule for various measures of group identity. In the empirical analysis performed on a national survey sample, the picture that emerged was that the two most often employed indicators of class (income and education) influenced both the self-esteem and the group identity of African Americans. Those individuals with more education and, to an even greater degree, those with more income, were found to have a greater sense of self-pride. However, those with the lowest income and with minimal education showed a high sense of group pride. Further, those individuals with less income felt a greater closeness to the black elites. With respect to education, those with more education felt less closeness not only to the masses but also to the elites. These relationships need to be interpreted in light of the fact that the mean values of the two constructs are high. That is, most African Americans feel above average closeness to African people, to both the masses and the elites. Indeed, the African American population generally shows a greater sense of closeness to the masses. The mean differences that were reported pertained to differences among income and education groups and to a high sense of closeness. The differences were real in a statistical sense, but they were of a small magnitude and thus of little substantive significance.

Age

Age situates African Americans in a specific sociohistorical context (Demo & Hughes, 1990); that is, it is often assumed that at one historical juncture, major psychological changes took place during what is commonly called the civil rights era. Thus, social observers will refer to African Americans' sense of self and of the group in terms of pre– and post–civil rights movement. Depending on the self-concept under scrutiny, age tends to have either a profound effect, no effect at all, or a bimodal effect. For example, some theorists have argued that it is the young who are most likely to have a strong sense of self and the group. Others have argued just the opposite. For the self-concept associated with militancy or direct action, the young have the stronger tendency. When the self-concept has more to do with an emotional tie to the group, then the older tend to demonstrate a stronger feeling. Moreover, it is the older who are more likely to have a greater sense of pride. Trying to predict the influence of age in the African American community, the literature suggests, is very difficult and complex. This complexity is highlighted when one researches the young to middle-age African American. It has been duly documented that African Americans in that group are disproportionately unemployed and in dire economic and social straits (Lusane, 1991; Tonry, 1995). The question is how that group maintains a strong self-concept. If their self-concept is extreme, presumably in the negative direction, how does this influence this overall age category? Present theorizing or empirical work provides few convincing answers. However, weighing the quality of the theorizing and research, and taking into account my earlier empirical work, I hypothesize that:

Those who are younger tend to have a greater closeness to the group (the elites and the masses).

Those who are older tend to have a greater self-worth.

Those who are older are more likely to have a higher African self-consciousness.

Those who are older are more likely to have greater ethnic identity.

Those who are older are more likely to have a greater sense of black autonomy.

Two Contrasting Perspectives

Competing perspectives have identified class or race as dominating the life of African Americans. Clearly, the perspective with a longer history of adherents is the race view.

The Race Perspective

The essence of this perspective is that being African in the United States carries a certain burden beyond one's economic status, that because race continues to be a prominent social, economic, and political force in the United States, it is the major molder of African Americans' lives and determines what it means to be an African American.

On the social level, evidence has been provided which has shown that African Americans and European Americans still live in two distinct worlds. Massey and Denton (1993) described the persistent and deliberate racial segregation and related this to the ongoing poverty of African Americans. Further, the analysis of racial incidents perpetrated against African Americans showed no differentiation for class background or socialization experiences. Those living very well as well as those barely living have been victims of these racist intrusions.

On the economic level, a view that cogently captured the significance of race was submitted by Oliver and Shapiro (1995). They stated that what is often not acknowledged is that the same social system that fosters the accumulation of private wealth for many whites denies it to blacks, thus forging an intimate connection between white wealth accumulation and black poverty. "Just as blacks have had 'cumulative disadvantages,' many whites have had 'cumulative advantages.' Since wealth builds over a lifetime and is then passed along to kin, it is from our perspective an essential indicator of black economic well-being. By focusing on wealth, we discover how blacks' socioeconomic status results from a socially layered accumulation of disadvantages passed on from generation. In this sense we uncover a racial wealth tax" (pp. 5–6)

In a similar vein, Boston (1988) presented evidence that suggests that historical and current investigation of primary stages of African American development suggests that racial antagonism plays a significant role in the character of black class stratification. That is, race then and now is responsible for placing African Americans disproportionately into the lower economic classes, thus disfiguring the class structure of African Americans.

On the political level, some take the position that African American political interest is dominated by a lack of competition for the black vote by both political parties, which has led to the indiscriminate destruction of programs that were intended to help African Americans at different economic levels (Dawson, 1994).

In short, the gist of this race-first argument is that because African Americans' and European Americans' life experiences diverge so strikingly, race interest will take primacy over class interests and this understanding will manifest across economic strata.

The Class Perspective

This relatively new, competing perspective maintains that race is no longer the most determining factor in the lives of African Americans. Rather, because of the recent assumed economic polarization of African Americans, class has become more germane. A fundamental aspect of the class perspective is that most humans are extraordinarily self-interested. This nonengaging assumption leads to two typical contentious claims. First, it emphasizes the dominance of self-interest over racial orientations; it posits that even when people have racist orientations, most will downplay them if doing so furthers their interest. Second, it stresses the dominance of self-interest over morality. It posits that most people will avoid the demands of justice or morality if these demands threaten their interests (Boxill, 1992). In summarizing this class perspective, Dawson (1994) remarked that the abject economic condition of a substantial segment of the African American population, especially in comparison with the improved economic condition of large numbers of other African Americans, suggests that class will overwhelm race as a salient factor for African Americans.

Another Framework

I think that it is more useful to apply aspects of both perspectives, although I give the race perspective more weight. After all, it is the benighted concept of race that justifies the assignment of African Americans into disproportionately lower socioeconomic groups. All too often, scholars and activists have overlooked the insidious working class racism and the involvement of organized labor in maintaining the structure of occupational discrimination and exclusion (Steinberg, 1995).

The awareness of both race and class, it is argued, will allow for a greater sense of understanding, explanation, and prediction. Class is indeed a real consideration, that is, class is responsible for real hardships and limitations, but with respect to African American socioeconomic status it is largely the outcome of past racism now reinforced by present racism. These limitations form the basis for continued racial division and inequalities.

From the class perspective, I accept the difficult-to-dispute notion that most humans are heavily self-interested. I also accept the notion that one's location in the social structure affects one's perspective, although this formulation loses much of its explanatory power in the case of African Americans because of other extenuating circumstances (shared life experiences regarding being African). From the race perspective, it is argued that the nature of racism in the United States makes it in the interest of most African Americans to align themselves with the group, which suggests a group identity. That is, I am suggesting that their individual interests lie in collective action and that most African Americans share this assessment. Some suppose that an expanding new class of African Americans will weaken collective identity and action. I am in agreement with the social observers who point to the very small number of "new class" Africans and, by and large, their tenuous economic position (Boston, 1988; Dawson, 1994; Franklin, 1991; Oliver & Shapiro, 1995). Such a small new black middle class, even if most identify outside the group, which is highly doubtful, probably has little impact in dampening the nature of the African American's identification with the collective. It is important to note that many of the jobs that the new black middle class holds are those that to a large degree are earmarked for blacks and function within the framework of racial hierarchy and division. As a consequence of government policy decisions, the future of this class is susceptible to the uncertainty of politics. Since many African Americans have benefited from the growth of government jobs, they undoubtedly will be adversely influenced by the current diminution in the size and scope of the public sector (Jones, 1992; Steinberg, 1995).

Aside from those forces of exploitation and oppression that encourage greater closeness within the group, there are also certain indigenous cultural forces that encourage a closeness or a sense of shared fate, a concern for the well-being of the group or collectivity. One such force is the ethos of Africans in the United States. It was presented above in the form of an assumption and an important part of an African-centered expression of African life. Finally, my empirical findings revealed that there was a strong sense of self- and group identity within various educational and income groups, with small differences across levels of education and income for certain measures of identity. Considering the above statements, I submit the following hypotheses:

> Those who have less education feel closer to the masses and to the elites.
>
> Those with more education and greater income will have a greater sense of self-worth.

No hypotheses were offered for the relationship between class and African self-consciousness and black autonomy. Since there is such a paucity of research on this issue and limited theorizing, I am left to weigh the existing evidence and rely heavily on hunch. On the one hand, one may argue that since having an African self-consciousness, and to a much smaller degree, a sense of the importance of black independence (black autonomy), that this entails, in part, having a greater knowledge of Africa and things African and thus an individual's relationship to a higher aspect of self (e.g., sharing and collective responsibility). Since none of these things presently comprise the dominant perspective nor are they societally encouraged, it is probable that the more educated, but not necessarily the more affluent, are more likely to exhibit this form of consciousness. Conversely, one may also argue that since the African consciousness reflects an African worldview and since this view is thought to be fundamental to African Americans, whether they are conscious of its existence or not, one might assume that the African worldview would be equally distributed regardless of education or income. I assume that an African self-consciousness and ethnic identity are related positively and that nether will be influenced by class. That is, African Americans across educational and income groups will also have a strong ethnic identity and an African consciousness.

Religiosity

It is generally acknowledged that religion plays an essential role in the life of Africans in the United States and elsewhere. Aside from the most obvious physical manifestations of an abundance of places of worship in the African American community, the pervasiveness of religiosity has been duly noted and consistently documented (see Cone, 1986; Drake & Cayton, 1945; Frazier, 1974; Taylor & Chatters, 1991; West, 1982). In the spirit of clarity, I would like to indicate what I consider religion to be. Borrowing from Karenga (1982), I view religion as the thought, belief, and practice concerned with the transcendent and ultimate question of existence.

Although the church in the African American community has been at various times lagging in the struggle against oppression, it has a history of social involvement and upliftment that continues today. Karenga (1993, pp. 234–235) identified four factors that relate to its past and present relevance in the African American community. First, the church has served as a spiritual protector against the violent and destructive transgressions of slavery. Thereafter, it buttressed the racist attacks on the "dignity, relevance and self-worth" of African Americans. Second, the church acted as an agency of "social reorientation and reconstruction." It reinforced the traditional "values of marriage, family, morality and spirituality," which had been undermined during enslavement. Third, it was the place were African economic cooperation was intensely encouraged and initiated, providing "social services for free Blacks, purchasing and helping resettle enslaved Africans, and setting up business for economic development. Fourth, the church created its own educational projects, training their own ministers and teachers alike. Fifth, as an invisible spiritual community, it supported social change and struggle, providing leaders and leadership at various points in the struggle for Black liberation and a truly higher level of human life."

In previous studies, my colleagues and I (Allen, Dawson, & Brown, 1989; Dawson, Brown, & Allen, 1990) and other researchers (e.g., Ellison, 1991) hypothesized that those with a firm sense of religious commitment would also have a strong sense of racial identification and consciousness. Accordingly, we found that religiosity was a potent force in shaping African American group identity and consciousness. With the same logic used to predict a positive relationship between identity and consciousness, I assume now that religiosity will have a strong impact on one's sense of self-worth since that is one of the major activities of the church.

From the above considerations, I hypothesize that:

Those with a greater sense of religious commitment or religiosity are more likely to have a strong group identity (closeness to the masses and elites).

Those with a greater sense of religiosity are more likely to have a strong sense of self-worth.

Those with a greater sense of religiosity are more likely to have a strong sense of African self-consciousness.

Those with a greater sense of religiosity are more likely to have a strong ethnic identity.

Symbolic Social Reality

Under the rubric of symbolic social reality, I include any form of symbolic expression of objective reality such as art, literature, or media content (see

Adoni & Mane, 1984), all of which have been used to fashion the image of the African. In the current context, the mass media (television, newspapers, radio, and magazines) are clearly the most influential purveyors of information. They create and foster the objectivity of the autonomous, independent self (Kitayama & Markus, 1993; Markus & Kitayama, 1994) that is realized by the acquisition of things. The majority mass media crystallize and reinforce certain racist conceptions by changing history to accommodate the preferred image of the dominating group and by presenting pejorative images of dominated groups. They perpetuate the idea that, in the United States, only the reality of certain people is valid or worthy of consideration (Myers, 1993).

Several theoretical frameworks illuminate the influence of the mass media. One of the better known is cultivation analysis. Its proponents assert that the mass media, especially television, make specific and measurable contributions to the audience's conceptions of reality. The basic premise is that television images cultivate the dominant tendencies of a culture's beliefs, ideologies, and worldviews. The observable independent contributions of television can sometimes be relatively small. Indeed, the size of an effect is far less critical than the direction of its steady contribution. For many people, television viewing overshadows other sources of information, ideas, and consciousness. Thus, cultivation theory suggests that the more time one spends "living" in the world of television, the more likely one is to report perceptions of social reality that can be traced to (or are congruent with) television's most persistent representations of life and society (Gerbner et al., 1980, 1982; Gerbner, 1990).

The influence of television on African Americans has been conceptualized as having debilitating or dysfunctional "trace contaminants." Using an analogy from medicine, these contaminants were described as elements that are plentiful in microscopic quantity and typically are without obvious influence on the organism (Pierce, 1980). Over an extended period of time, these elements are thought to inflict serious cumulative harm on the organism. Further, Pierce states that despite superficial improvements in many portrayals of Africans, the images still carry subtle levels of social trace contaminants. While noting the increased frequency of African American portrayals, many social observers have pointed out that the roles often convey stereotypical messages. Television has been reluctant to present Africans in a wide range of settings and personalities or in a variety of social roles. Rarely have lower working class or dispossessed Africans been presented in their own cultural milieu or terms. Typically, these groups are most evident in crime and conflict stories appearing on local and national newscasts. Specifically, Gray (1995) contends that television's depiction of Africans relies substantially on the programs about family, the genre of black situation comedies, entertainment and variety programming, and the social issues tradition of Norman Lear.

Two insightful documentaries, *Color Adjustment* and *Ethnic Notions*, further buttress these observations (Riggs, 1991a,b).

The Black Media: Electronic

Black media are viewed as a filter of African Americans' information sources pertaining to the general status of African Americans as an autonomous group and their relation with the dominating society. Thus, black media should play a significant role in determining the content of the African American self.

The increase in television shows about Africans written by African Americans and often directed toward Africans, albeit small, may require a reassessment of the direction of the impact on African Americans. African American-controlled alternatives have long existed for the print media, but only recently have there been any serious African alternatives on television. It may be, as many have argued, that these new shows and new stations (e.g., Black Entertainment Television on cable) would have a more salutary effect on African Americans' self-concept, since the creators of such programs would have greater sensitivity and understanding of African American culture and aspirations. On the other hand, others have suggested that it does not matter if an African American or a non-African American was responsible for the programming; the crucial issue is that the fare presented represents, accurately and sensitively, the life of Africans. Thus, there are those who argue that a distinction be made between black-oriented (content pertaining to blacks but presented through an outsider's perspective, usually nonblack) and black television fare (written in an attempt to capture black experiences and history and usually written by an African American), while others maintain that this is a superfluous distinction since the difference in content is imperceptible.

In fact, many factors impinge on the creation of black television fare beyond the group to which the individual belongs, for example, whether the individual has a sufficient independence to produce a product that resonates with the audience or whether restrictions are placed on this endeavor. Is the fare directed essentially at African Americans, or is it basically an attempt to explain African American life and culture to non-African American audiences? If it is the latter, the conceptual distinction may not be pertinent. If it is the former, all things being equal, I would think that on average an African would be better able to represent the African image to the African, particularly given the constraints placed on non-Africans to know Africans and African culture.[4] Whether the media product is black or merely black-oriented, I assume that it has a demonstrably different effect on African Americans' self-concept than does majority television fare.

Black television has a substantially different relationship with the African American community than the black press. Unlike the black press, the black electronic media, especially television stations, are more likely to be controlled but rarely owned by African Americans. This means, in the context of contemporary America, that relatively little of the television fare is written by and directed to African Americans.

The Black Media: Print

Although television is often considered to have a more pronounced effect on various attitudes and behaviors of African Americans than it does on non-African Americans, the black print media also commanded a considerable amount of attention from African Americans.

The black press consists of a number of weekly newspapers, periodicals, and magazines directed at African American readers. What little theorizing that exists concerning the black press suggests that it is generally a positive and progressive force in the African American community. Historically, this press has received an honored place in the African American community. At particular historical periods (e.g., the antislavery period), the black print media answered the cry for independent newspapers to portray positive aspects of the group and uplifting images. It relayed the messages of self-help organizations that could instill a sense of pride and identity and black racial consciousness (Allen, Dawson, & Brown, 1989). Significantly, black print media outlets are still vehicles for galvanizing group solidarity and support. Some critics maintain, however, that the press has not fulfilled its mandate to the people. Nonetheless, the print media still influence political activists because they are in a communication network with people who are more likely to have information about how the political system can be used to foster the group's interest (Dawson, Brown, & Allen, 1991). The black press, particularly magazines, also continues to offer viable alternatives for expressing African American views and perspectives.

Empirical evidence shows that the black print media have positive influence on various measures of self- and group identity. There is considerable ideological variance in the black press, especially with respect to magazines, many of which have local circulation. For example, some print media might be classified as traditional and nontraditional, or assimilationist and nationalist. But the classification that seems to capture the essence of these media was provided by Gray (1995). When referring to the images presented of African Americans in the electronic media,[5] he identified three conceptual categories: (1) assimilation or discourse of invisibility (the marginalization of social and cultural differences); (2) pluralist or separate-but-equal discourse (commitment to universal acceptance into the transparent "normative" middle class); (3) multiculturalism or diversity (an exploration into the interiors of black lives and subjectivities from the angle of, or in terms of, the African American). These categories were not conceived as being mutually exclusive or independent; rather, they were assumed to have considerable overlap. The labels and their descriptions, however, capture their essence. These categories provide a basis for examining the relationship of different print media on the self-concept.

Many of the aforementioned concepts are assumed to relate to the attention given to the media, especially the black media; I have not specified these relationships because they are of lesser importance to my theorizing. Based on previous work, for example, more religious people are more inclined to attend to black media, both print and electronic. Further, the more educated and the higher income groups are more likely to relate to the black media, especially print.

By focusing on the explication of the mass media, both majority and black, I generated several hypotheses:

Electronic Media Hypotheses

Those who attend more to black-oriented and black television are more likely to have a greater sense of pride.

Those who attend more to black-oriented and black television are more likely to have a positive attachment to the group.

The greater the amount of time spent with nonblack electronic media (majority television), the less the self-esteem, group identity, African self-consciousness, and ethnic identity.

Print Media Hypotheses

Those who attend more to black print media are more likely to have a greater sense of pride.

Those who attend more to black print media are more likely to have a positive attachment to the group.

Those who attend more to black print media are more likely to have a strong African self-consciousness.

Those who attend more to the black print media are more likely to have a strong African-centered belief system.

The greater the exposure to nonblack newspapers, the less the self-esteem, group identity, African self-consciousness, and ethnic identity.

The greater the attention to the print media, the greater the closeness to the black elites.

Nonmedia Communication

I make the assumption that African Americans who are regularly in an environment with African Americans sharing cultural and social experiences will have the wherewithal to ward off hostile actions and pejorative images presented of African Americans; they will also develop a positive sense of self and of the group to which they belong. Thus, I hypothesize that:

> Those who are more likely to participate in black cultural activities and rituals are more likely to have a higher self-esteem, group identity, African self-consciousness, and ethnic identity.

The essence of this conceptualization is embodied in Figure 6.1, and the many arguments presented above may be summarized as follows. The broad assumption is that African Americans—despite the major internal tensions and struggles and despite enduring, and consistent, real and symbolic denigrations—have a strong sense of self and of the group. The level of this positive self-worth and group identity is influenced by several categories of

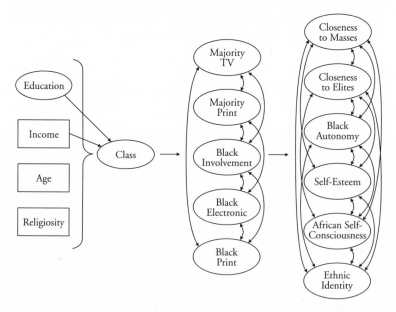

Figure 6.1. Schematic Representation of a Model of an African Self-Conception

variables: class and background characteristics and responses to the symbolic social reality. The direction and strength of influence of these variables vary, depending upon the conceptualization and measurement of the self.

I argue that those better placed in the social system tend to have a greater self-worth, but these differences are less obvious in regard to identity and African self-consciousness constructs. When examining self as a combination of self-worth and group identity (typically associated with an African-centered conceptualization), the relationship of class disappears.

Age, another background variable and an indicator of life experiences as well as a reflection of an era, has a positive effect on self-esteem and group identity, but the younger will feel a greater closeness with a wider range of African people, that is, people from various stations in life (the masses as well as the elite). The younger are more likely to associate, often through necessity, with other African Americans from nonprofessional backgrounds, but also have more admiration for the professionals and black political figures, perhaps as role models.

Religiosity is conceived as a positive force on all forms of identity. That is, the more religious are more likely to have a greater sense of self-worth, group identity, and an African-centered self-conception.

With respect to symbolic social reality, the assumption is that those who are more involved in black life (the music, literature, and the rituals) are better able to ward off the impositions on their self-conception. Thus, those who read more black literature, attend to black-oriented materials on television, and actively engage or even attend African American-initiated activities are more likely to have a greater sense of self-worth. On the other hand, those who attend more to the majority media, especially television, with its latent and manifest negative portrayals of Africans, are less likely to have a strong sense of self.

Research Design

The data were collected in Detroit among African American adults in 1996–97. The sample was selected to reflect a wide range of views on social issues. This purposive sample contained respondents from identifiable social, professional, and religious groups and was selected to reflect different ages and income groups, and a similar composition of males and females. Individuals were recruited from three major churches, one sorority, one fraternity, one community college, and a major university. Trained interviewers from the area were responsible for identifying the desired groups based on our stratification scheme. The target was to get six hundred completed interviews, but our final sample size was 551. The respondents received $10.00 for completing the interview schedule, which lasted on average about forty minutes.

The questionnaire covered such topics as self-esteem (two different scale versions), several versions of scales tapping the identity construct (general and race-specific), a number of social beliefs and opinions on individualism and collectivism, individual well-being, and a host of media attitudes and behaviors. The analysis of our sample was compared with 1996 Census data for Detroit on basic demographic variables: age, education, income, and gender. It indicated generally that there were no major discrepancies between the measures we obtained and those obtained by the Census Bureau. We did find, however, contrary to the Census data, that our sample had a larger number of males.

Measures

Self-Esteem

This scale is an abbreviated version of the Rosenberg self-esteem scale. Using a 5-point scale, the following items were used:

1. I feel that I'm a person of worth, at least on an equal plane with others.
2. I feel that I have a number of good qualities.
3. I am able to do things as well as most other people.
4. I feel I have much to be proud of.
5. I take a positive attitude toward myself.
6. Most of the time I think I am a good person.

Closeness to the Masses

This construct was measured by six indicators on a scale ranging from 1 = "not close at all" to 4 = "very close." These items were:

1. I feel close to black people who are religious.
2. I feel close to black people who are young.
3. I feel close to black people who are poor.
4. I feel close to black people who are middle class.
5. I feel close to black people who are working class.
6. I feel close to black people who are older.

Closeness to the Elites

This construct was measured by two indicators on the same scale as above. These items were:

1. I feel close to elected officials.
2. I feel close to professionals.

Black Autonomy

This construct was measured on a 5-point scale, ranging from 1 = "strongly disagree" to 5 = "strongly agree." The items were:

1. Black children should learn an African language.
2. Blacks should always vote for black candidates whenever possible.
3. Black women should not date white men.
4. Black men should not date white women.
5. Black people should shop in black-owned shops whenever possible.
6. Black parents should give their children African names.

African Self-Consciousness

I selected twenty-two of forty-two items Baldwin and Bell used to constitute the African self-consciousness scale.[6] They were considered to exemplify the different dimensions of the scale and to capture its essence. My abbreviated version of the self-consciousness scale consisted of the following items, which were originally evaluated on a 5-point agree-disagree scale:

1. I don't necessarily feel like I am also being mistreated in a situation where I see another Black person being mistreated.
2. Black people should have their own independent schools which consider their African heritage and value an important part of the curriculum.
3. Blacks in America should try harder to be American rather than practicing activities that link them up with their African cultural heritage.
4. Regardless of their interests, educational background, and social achievements, I would prefer to associate with Black people than with non-Blacks.
5. It is not such a good idea for Black students to be required to learn an African language.
6. Blacks who place the highest value on Black life (over that of other people) are reverse racists and generally evil people.
7. Black children should be taught that they are African at an early age.
8. As a good index of self-respect, Blacks in America should consider adopting traditional African names for themselves.
9. Blacks born in the United States are Black or African first, rather than American or just plain people.
10. In dealing with other Blacks, I consider myself quite different and unique from most of them.
11. I have difficulty identifying with the culture of African people.
12. It is intelligent for Blacks in America to organize to educate and to liberate themselves from white American domination.

13. There is no such thing as African culture among Blacks in America.
14. It is good for Blacks in America to wear traditional African-type clothing and hair styles if they desire to do so.
15. I feel little sense of commitment to Black people who are not close friends or relatives.
16. All Black students in Africa and America should be expected to study African culture and history as it occurs throughout the world.
17. Blacks in America who view Africa as their homeland are more intelligent than those who view America as their homeland.
18. Blacks in America should view Blacks from other countries (e.g., Ghana, Nigeria, and other countries in Africa) as foreigners rather than as their brothers and sisters.
19. Black people's concern for self-knowledge (knowledge of one's history, philosophy, culture, etc.) and self (collective) determination makes them treat white people badly.
20. The success of an individual Black person is not as important as the survival of all Black people.
21. If a good/worthwhile education could be obtained at all schools (both Black and White), I would prefer my child to attend a racially integrated school.
22. Being involved in wholesome group activities with other Blacks lifts my spirits more so than being involved in individual-oriented activities.

Ethnic Identity

These items are non-race-specific identity indicators. The author of this ethnic identity scale (Phinney, 1990) attempted to tap a more general conception of ethnic identity. The assumption is that it is a scale valid across racial groups. I used twenty questions from the scale and asked the respondent to express how well each question described him or her:[7]

1. Does not describe me at all   2. Describes me a little bit
3. Describes me moderately well   4. Describes me a lot
5. Totally describes me

1. I have spent time trying to find out more about my own ethnic group, such as its history, traditions, and customs.
2. I am active in organizations or social groups that include mostly members of my own ethnic group.
3. I have a clear sense of my ethnic background and what it means for me.
4. I like meeting and getting to know people from ethnic groups other than my own.

5. I think a lot about how my life will be affected by my ethnic group membership.
6. I am happy that I am a member of the group I belong to.
7. I sometimes feel it would be better if different ethnic groups didn't try to mix together.
8. I am not very clear about the role of my ethnicity in my life.
9. I often spend time with people from ethnic groups other than my own.
10. I really have not spent much time trying to learn more about the culture and history of my ethnic group.
11. I have a strong sense of belonging to my own ethnic group.
12. I understand pretty well what my ethnic group membership means to me, in terms of how to relate to my own group and other groups.
13. In order to learn more about my ethnic background, I have often talked to other people about my ethnic group.
14. I have a lot of pride in my ethnic group and its accomplishments.
15. I don't try to become friends with people from other ethnic groups.
16. I participate in cultural practices of my own group, such as special food, music, or customs.
17. I am involved in activities with people from other ethnic groups.
18. I feel a strong attachment toward my own ethnic group.
19. I enjoy being around people from ethnic groups other than my own.
20. I feel good about my cultural or ethnic background.

In summary, all of the constructs were coded to reflect a higher degree or a greater amount of the attribute in question. Thus, for example, the higher the score, the higher the African self-consciousness, and so on.

Basic Background Measures, Class, and Age

The following measures were used to tap three of the four fundamental background variables. Religiosity, another background measure, is subsequently examined.

1. How old are you? _____ years old.
2. Education (check highest level attended):
   1. Elementary school ____   2. Middle or junior high school ____
   3. Some high school ____   4. High school graduate ____
   5. Some college ____   6. College graduate ____   7. Graduate degree ____

3. Approximate total family income from all sources:
   1. $0–4,999____   2. $5,000–9,999 ____   3. $10,000–14,999 ____
   4. $15,000–19,999 ____   5. $20,000–29,999 ____

6. $30,000–39,999 _____   7. $40,000–49,999 _____
8. $50,000 and more _____

Measures of Religious Background

The following six measures were used to reflect religiosity.

1. How often do you attend religious services?
    1. Never   2. Once or twice a year   3. About once a month
    4. Two or three times a month   5. Every week
2. How religious would you say you are?
    1. Very much   2. Moderately   3. Somewhat   4. Not at all
3. How often do you read religious books or other religious materials?
    1. Never   2. Once or twice a year   3. About once a month
    4. Two or three times a month   5. Once a week
    6. About two or three days a week   7. Every day
4. How often do you listen to or watch religious programs?
    1. Never   2. Once or twice a year   3. About once a month
    4. Two or three times a month   5. Once a week
    6. About two or three days a week   7. Every day
5. How often do you pray?
    1. Never   2. Once or twice a year   3. About once a month
    4. Two or three times a month   5. Once a week
    6. About two or three days a week   7. Every day
6. How often do you ask someone to pray for you?
    1. Never   2. Seldom   3. Frequently   4. Very frequently

Symbolic Social Reality

I chose only a sampling of the many indicators of symbolic social reality. It was operationalized by a wide variety of indicators.

MAJORITY TELEVISION
1. How much time do you spend watching TV on an average day?
   About _____ hours

MAJORITY PRINT
1. How many days during the week do you read the newspaper?
   Never   1   2   3   4   5   6   7   days
2. How often do you read magazines?
   Never   1   2   3   4   5   6   7   days often

BLACK COMMUNICATION BEHAVIORS
The respondent indicated on a 5-point scale, where 1 ="never" and 5 = "all the time," the frequency of doing the following things or using the following media:

Black electronic
1. Watch black TV stations/shows
2. Go to black movies
3. Listen to black radio stations/programs

Black print
1. Read black newspapers/magazines
2. Read books by black authors

Black involvement
1. Attend or participate in black festivals or celebrations
2. Practice customs or traditions unique to your black heritage
3. Teach your children about black history
4. Plan or desire to visit Africa

Results

Analytical Strategy

Structural equation modeling was used to analyze the data. A general program for estimating the unknown coefficients in a set of linear structural equations (LISREL) was used (Joreskog & Sorbom, 1988). The first step in the analysis was to test for the overall model fit to see whether the general theorizing was sound. This involved the examination of the measurement aspect of the model. The second step was to estimate the many hypotheses to see whether they were confirmed. Before investigating the many relationships, it is useful to examine the descriptive statistics, for some of the hypotheses are examined with these summary measures.

The means for all the constructs indicate that African Americans have a particularly high self-esteem, ethnic identity, African self-consciousness, and closeness to the masses, in descending order of magnitude (see Table 6.1).

Table 6.1. Means for the Self-Concept

Constructs	Means
Closeness to Masses (6 items, 4-point scale)	19.53 (3.25)
Closeness to Elites (2 items, 4-point scale)	5.44 (2.72)
Black Autonomy (6 items, 5-point scale)	21.08 (3.51)
Self-Esteem (6 items, 5-point scale)	26.53 (4.42)
African Self-Consciousness (18 items, 5-point scale)	64.11 (3.56)
Ethnic Identity (12 items, 5-point scale)	45.69 (3.81)

Note: The initial value is the sum of the item means; the value in the parentheses is the average value of the scale (i.e., the sum divided by the number of item.)

While closeness to the elites shows the smallest mean, it is still above the midpoint of the scale. Thus, the hypotheses that predicted that African Americans have a high sense of the individual self and of the group, variously defined, received support. Moreover, when a difference of means test for the two closeness constructs was performed, it showed that African Americans feel closer to the masses than to the elites.

As an important initial step in the examination of the full model, an assessment of the scale reliability is in order. Using a measure of internal consistency, the Cronbach's alpha, Table 6.2 indicates that the reliability of the scales range from fair to good, with the exceptions of majority print exposure (0.57) and black involvement (0.68). This outcome increases my confidence that the obtained relationships are less influenced by the inadequacy of measurement.

It was hypothesized that the different self-concepts are related positively. Table 6.3 provides information on these associations. As can be seen, there are several moderate to large correlations, most are positive, and most are

Table 6.2. Reliability Estimates for All the Self-Constructs

Constructs	Alphas
Self-Esteem	0.90
Closeness to Masses	0.82
Closeness to Elites	0.74
Black Autonomy	0.83
African Self-Consciousness	0.88
Ethnic Identity	0.86
Majority Print	0.57
Black Involvement	0.68
Black Electronic	0.74
Black Print	0.72
Religiosity	0.82

Table 6.3. Zero-Order Correlations for the Self-Concept Scales

	1	2	3	4	5	6
Closeness to Masses (1)	—					
Closeness to Elites (2)	0.46*	—				
Black Autonomy (3)	0.04	−0.13*	—			
Self-Esteem (4)	0.22*	0.00	0.14*	—		
African Self-Consciousness (5)	0.14*	−0.25*	0.64*	0.15*	—	
Ethnic Identity (6)	0.11*	−0.13*	0.50*	0.38*	0.44*	—

*Signifies statistical significance at p < 0.05.

statistically significant. The negative relationships are also predictable. We can see that those who embrace the idea of black autonomy and those who have a high African self-consciousness and high ethnic identity are associated with those with less of a closeness to the elites. The picture that emerges is that the self-concepts have positive relationships, that both African self-consciousness and ethnic identity are strongly related to the other self-concepts, and that there is a substantial association between African self-consciousness and ethnic identity. Moreover, the strongest relationship exists between African self-consciousness and black autonomy, but ethnic identity is also strongly associated with black autonomy. The only two relationships that were not statistically significant were the relationships between closeness to the masses and black autonomy and closeness to the elites and self-esteem.

Turning to the full model, there are a variety of relevant overall measures of model fit. Each explores different aspects of model adequacy. While opinions differ as to what constitutes the best measure, I present several generally agreed-upon fit measures. First, the χ^2 is 3.92 with 8 degrees of freedom. The p value is a statistically nonsignificant 0.864, indicating that the model provides an adequate fit. Moreover, the goodness-of-fit measure was 1.00; the adjusted goodness-of-fit measure was 0.98; the comparative fit index was 1.00, and the non-normed fit index was 0.99. They all suggest that the model fit the data well. Hence, it is possible to examine the component fit measures and the hypotheses.

Figure 6.2 presents the relationships found to be statistically significant and thus sheds light on the hypotheses. Looking at the relationship between the constructs of symbolic social reality and the various self-concepts, many interesting patterns emerge. The majority media measures—majority television exposure and print media exposure—have observable effects. While they do not have an influence on the extent to which African Americans feel close to the masses and the elites, greater exposure to majority television has a negative influence on black autonomy, African self-consciousness, and self-esteem. Majority print media also had an influence on several self-concepts: they had a negative effect on self-esteem, but a positive effect on African self-consciousness. With the exception of the positive relationship between the African self-consciousness construct and majority print media, they all support the proffered hypotheses. Black involvement was positively related to four of the six self-concepts. The greater the black involvement, the greater the black autonomy, African self-consciousness, ethnic identity, and self-esteem. These relationships support the hypotheses; however, it was hypothesized that black involvement would also have a positive impact on closeness to the masses. This relationship was positive, but the critical value was only borderline (p < 0.10). These obtained statistically significant relationships were moderate to strong in magnitude. Similarly, greater exposure to black print media led to greater self-esteem, greater

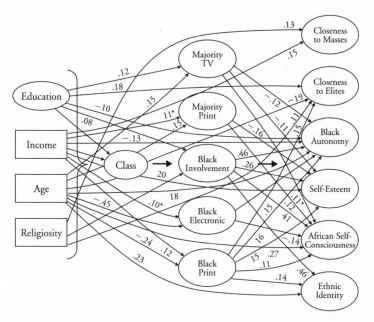

Figure 6.2. Statistically Significant Relationships
in the Model of an African Self-Conception

closeness to the elites, greater black autonomy, greater ethnic identity, and, to a lesser degree, greater African self-consciousness. All these relationships were supportive of the hypotheses. One hypothesized relationship did not reach statistical significance, namely, the relationship between black print media and closeness to the masses. The exposure to black or black-oriented electronic media (television and movies) showed surprising relationships. It had a relationship with only two of the six self-concepts, each in a negative direction. The greater the black or black-oriented electronic exposure, the less the sense of black autonomy and African self-consciousness.

Focusing on the relationships of the antecedent class and background constructs with the other constructs in the model, we can see that there are many statistically significant relationships. The two indicators representing the gradational conception of class had several statistical relationships, but often on different variables or in a different direction. Education had a positive influence on two measures of symbolic social reality: majority television exposure and, to a lesser degree, black involvement. Income had a positive influence on majority and black print media exposure. Whereas education had a positive influence on closeness to elites, it had a negative relationship with black autonomy. Contrary to prediction, education had no influence on self-esteem. On the other hand, income had a positive influence on closeness to the masses and self-esteem as predicted but, as in the case of education, a negative influence on black autonomy.

Turning to the complex age variable, the findings reveal that the older tend to watch more majority television and to read more majority print media whereas the younger tend to watch more black or black-oriented visual fare and to read more black print media. Concerning the self-concepts, the younger feel closer to both the masses and the elites, but the older tend to have a greater sense of black autonomy, greater ethnic identity, and greater African self-consciousness. These results provide substantial support to the hypotheses.

The more religious tended to have greater black involvement, but were not demonstrably different on any of the other symbolic social reality variables. Moreover, religiosity had a positive influence on closeness to the masses and closeness to elites constructs, but did not have relationships with any of the other self-concepts. I had hypothesized that religiosity would have a more extensive effect across the self-concepts.

A relatively small amount of the variance was explained in the symbolic social reality measures: 6 percent of majority television exposure, 3 percent of majority print exposure, 4 percent of black involvement, 20 percent of black-oriented electronic exposure, 7 percent of black print media. A larger amount of variance was explained for the self-concepts: 9 percent of closeness to the masses, 11 percent of closeness to the elites, 31 percent of black autonomy, 17 percent of self-esteem, 31 percent of African self-consciousness, and 33 percent of ethnic identity.

Conclusions

In this chapter, I proposed theoretically and tested empirically the extent to which African Americans have withstood the brunt of denigrating images and the onslaught of a racist society, how they manage to maintain their sense of the self and the group. Conceptualized as a dynamic process, the theory I have outlined emphasizes that African Americans' senses of self and of the group are engaged in an ongoing battle. The original formulation of this battle was presented by DuBois as "double consciousness." One of the major thrusts of double consciousness is that despite the many challenges, African Americans, because of the power of their culture and the fortitude derived from it, will in struggle have a healthy sense of self and an attachment to the group.

I developed the outline of a theory, consistent with the notion of double consciousness and its many contemporary modifications, and I identified the forces that influence the African American self, variously defined. I posited that there is a set of assumptions that inform the African American self-concept. Some of these assumptions are shared by and manifested in all groups, others apply to other oppressed groups, and still others are unique to the experiences and historical context of African American life. From these assumptions, I was able to formulate an interrelated set of hypotheses that took into account the different conceptions of self. I fashioned hypotheses for the variables conceived to influence the self. I maintained that religion, age, and class influenced how the individual feels toward the internal self and the external self, or the individual's self-esteem and group identity. Further, I argued that the symbolic social reality also has a major bearing on the self, so that those who attended more to black-oriented information and activities were substantially different in self-conception.

In broad terms, I hypothesized that those who aspire to a higher order of morality or who attach themselves to a supreme being, namely, those who are more religious, will feel a strong relationship to African American people, no matter what station in life they might hold. Age was also thought to have an inverse relationship with the self. That is, those who were older were more likely to have a stronger sense of self and a stronger sense of black consciousness, but the younger were more attached to the various elements within the African American community. Class, a complex variable, both operationally and theoretically, reflected a complex picture. The people who had a greater income were more likely to feel closer to the masses, but not to the elites, and they tended to not have an appreciably different African self-consciousness than those with less income. They did, however, have a greater sense of self-worth. The income/closeness to the mass connection is put in stark relief when considering the other element of class, education. Those who had more formal training tended to feel closer to the elites, but not to the masses. Moreover, those with more education did not have a greater sense of self-worth nor did they have a relationship with any of the other self-concepts, save black autonomy or independence, and that relationship was negative.

Many analysts have speculated about how the media, both majority and black-oriented, militate against or facilitate the self-concept. I found that those who attend to the black print media are more likely not only to think more highly of themselves, but also to hold the group in higher esteem. Relatedly, those who participate actively in black affairs are also more likely to relate positively to themselves and to the group, and to have a stronger African self-consciousness.

The major aspect of my theorizing as reflected in the proposed model was supported. Of special interest is the contention that the black media have a positive effect on the black self-concept and the majority media have a negative effect. Generally, this assumption was supported. The black print media exposure was compatible with having a strong self-concept, and the majority media exposure, especially television, militated against a strong black self-concept. This outcome provides added strength to the charge that the majority media present less than inspiring images, or, at the very least, that these images are interpreted that way. No matter the interpretation, however, the effect is the same. Another symbolic social reality category, black involvement, produces striking effects. Those who are engaged in activities and rituals initiated by blacks tend to have a greater sense of the self and the group.

A few other points are worth mentioning. First, the majority media tended to have a negative influence on the black self-concept, when it had any influence at all. There was, however, an exception. Those who read more majority print media were more likely to have a greater African self-consciousness. Second, watching more black-oriented electronic media led to less of a sense of black autonomy and African self-consciousness. Perhaps because these two self-concepts present a more normative conception of what constitutes desirable African behavior, this would conflict with the more mainstream, more supervised content of the electronic media. An intriguing alternative interpretation is that the electronic media, whether black-oriented or majority, follow a format and pursue certain content themes that operate in opposition to the fostering of a strong black self-concept, albeit the effect is stronger for majority television. All of these interpretations need to be explored. The above outcomes have profound theoretical and practical implications.

A point that was stressed throughout this study was that the different aspects of the self that are under investigation should be clarified. Within my theoretical framework, three different orientations are evident. One important distinction of concern is that between self-esteem or self-worth and group identity. While this distinction has not always been made, the concepts of self-esteem and group identity have been popular areas of research. A number of researchers (e.g., Cross, 1991) have pointed out the significance of this conceptual distinction. Others (e.g., Kambon, 1992; Nobles, 1991a,b) have argued that self-esteem and group identity are best conceptualized as different aspects of what they call an African self-consciousness. These scholars, often identifying themselves as operating from an African-centered perspective, maintain that the individual conception of self and the individual concept of the group are intertwined. That is, the African's self-conception is strongly connected with the group conception and vice versa.

A second distinction addressed in this study was between the theoretical and operational definitions of personal self-identity and group identity. Although I used the self-esteem concept in terms of self-worth in a global sense, it would be possible to use self-esteem in the sense of performance in concrete settings. Similarly, under the heading of group identity, many aspects that might have been examined, for example, black militancy, black consciousness, and black alienation, were not available. Extending this line of reasoning, how one defines the self-concept dictates the concept names one will use as well as the operationalization and, ultimately, the direction of the hypotheses. In my theorizing and model development, I remained acutely aware of this reality.

The revelation that African Americans have a strong sense of self, variously defined, is attuned to some of the more recent research; however, the mechanisms that account for this have rarely been investigated. There has been relatively little attempt at explicating the antecedents of the self-concept, especially in its many manifestations. It is instructive to point out that my conceptualization differs in fundamental ways from some of the major theorizing done in this area of research, especially by mainstream researchers. Much of the literature speaks of in-group–out-group bias as a universal. This conception maintains that there is a proclivity for individuals to regard in-group members as possessing more desirable qualities than members of out-groups. Contemporary psychological theorizing tends to treat the presumed in-group–out-group bias as " psychological realities and the sociohistorical realities of racism as merely footnotes" (Gaines & Reed, 1994, pp. 14–15). Along with several other scholars, I argue that Africans' sense of self is influenced heavily by their African heritage and is not merely a response to the hostility demonstrated toward them by European Americans. This sense of self, as I have noted, is essentially collectivist as distinct from individualist, and is informed by a sense of "we-ness" as elaborated by Nobles (1973, 1992). In short, this conceptualization has a keen awareness of culture and acknowledges individual differences among ethnic groups within the United States and undoubtedly across the world. It is decidedly historically and culturally specific, however, as argued for one conceptualization of the black self, namely, African self-consciousness, it is similar throughout the African diaspora because of the similarities in history and culture.

In summary, across self-constructs, age has powerful effects. The younger people feel closer to African Americans, but the older have a stronger sense of ethnic identity and black autonomy as well as a more African-centered consciousness. Further, the black print media tend to have a positive effect across the self-constructs. The majority media, on the other hand, tend to have a negative effect, when they have any effect at all. Class, as represented by the two indicators of education and income, has quite different effects on the different self-constructs, with its influence being entirely absent from the African self-consciousness. With direct reference to the race/class influence on the self-concept, I had argued that while race was the overriding factor, class modified this connection in most instances, and that the impact of class depended on the conception of self being explored. This interpretation received clear support. In the case of the self-concept that explores self-esteem and group identity, class has a certain importance. When the self-construct is linked to black autonomy or a sense of black independence, class garners substantial importance. Conversely, class has little significance in producing an African self-consciousness or ethnic identity. Further, it is worth considering that education and income often had quite different relationships with media behavior and self-conception. Significantly, the only self-concept that both education and class predicted—and in the same direction—was black autonomy. This negative relationship suggested that those of a higher class tend to be in opposition to the notion of independence and separateness as embodied in the black autonomy construct. Taken together, the findings reveal how important the symbolic social reality (media and nonmedia, black and nonblack) and class are in fashioning the black self-concept. This area requires great theoretical and empirical attention.

Double consciousness was the overarching theoretical framework that informed the formulation of the hypotheses, and their rationale, in the construction of a testable model. In essence, it alerts us to the challenges and impediments that confront African Americans daily. Further, it specifies in general terms the dynamics that exist and suggests that, while a struggle persists, the likelihood is that African Americans will have the fortitude to maintain a strong sense of self and the group by creating institutions or other mechanisms to sustain themselves. In one sense, this framework is a prescription to psychological survival (developing alternative institutions and conceptions) and an assessment of the success of such an endeavor at any one point in time. It describes African Americans as active participants in their own mental liberation, rather than merely passive receptacles or reactive entities. Clearly, the double consciousness framework needs to be further explicated and refined. Social observers and activists are beginning to see its usefulness as a conceptual tool. The contribution that this study has made is to tie together this framework with others into a larger system that weighs the importance of symbol systems in society, especially the mass media. I have yet to find out whether double consciousness, or the hypotheses partly derived from it, applies to the same degree to other oppressed groups, especially those experiencing major cultural impositions.

As was acknowledged in this study, the sample was relatively small and nonprobabilistic. Thus, it may not generalize to the larger African American population. It is worthy of note, however, that the patterns of the findings for the self-esteem and group identity constructs were quite similar to those found using a national probability sample. Since to my knowledge no other study has used as elaborate a model to examine the several conceptualizations of the self, I cannot comment in any detail on the extent to which this study supports past findings. This study must be considered an exercise in theory construction rather than theory testing. A test of theory must await a larger and richer data set.

CHAPTER 7

Epilogue:
The African Self From the Past,
Revelations in the Present, and
Foreshadowing of the Future

Nothing the future brings can defeat a people who have come
through three hundred years of slavery and humiliation and
privation with heads high and eyes clear and straight.
—PAUL ROBESON

The questions that have informed this inquiry pertain to the effects of systematic and continuous aggressive acts against Africans in the United States on the self-concept. With uncanny consistency, African Americans have been projected in an unfavorable light. While historically the form and the intensity of these malignant forces have changed, they nonetheless remain in existence. The larger white society has moved from considering Africans as only partial humans to granting them second-class citizenship. The struggle of Africans in the United States has been for full citizenship in the land of their birth. The forces that have militated against the realization of citizenship in the United States and the world have taken many forms, from government sanctioning to government disavowal, from societal acceptance to societal rejection.

I have argued that in order to get a better understanding of the self-concept of African Americans, one must examine the historical treatment that Africans have received over time. One cannot help but be amazed at the level of rancor and hostility such an examination discloses, and the egregious behavior one sees exhibited against Africans over an extended period of history. As I have attempted to demonstrate, the onslaught has come from many different circles, ranging from highly respected academics to borderline defectives, from the scientific community both then and now, and of course, from the political community, those varying in range of political orientation. The mode of assault against African Americans has included attempts to reduce their confidence (i.e., you are inferior, your imposed station in life is justified) and to ensure what Clarke (1994) calls "historical amnesia" (i.e., your history began on a slave ship, and becoming a good slave is among your few realistic goals). To provide a flavor of some of this thinking and the techniques used to bring these states into existence, I have quoted extensively from many historical sources and have revealed some graphic contemporary instances of racist symbolism and terminology.

Since mass communication has such a powerful influence on the conception of the world, I have undertaken a more detailed analysis of how it conveys ideas. Focusing primarily on the mass media, I have been able to show how each medium has dealt with the portrayal of the African over time. Although each medium has had its own terminology for the description of the African, the essence of the portrayals of Africans has been similar during the same time periods. Moreover, looking at the current scene, it is possible to find character portrayals rooted in the earlier depictions. As I examined some of the earlier characters presented in distorted and degrading stances, I was able to attach contemporary labels to these characters, with little hyperbole. As a consequence of the dastardly performance of the majority media toward Africans, media fare by and for Africans was developed. With a more pronounced presence in the print media (newspapers and magazines), it also was extended to included a considerable position in radio. The black media have usually operated from a comparatively small budget. Their influence, however, belies this fact. They have tried not only to undo the damage done by the majority media during their most insidious days, but also to more positively provide a view of the world from an African American perspective. Thus, these media were and still are a source of resistance and redefinition. For example, the most blatant and horrendous portrayals, allusions, and descriptions of African people have to a large degree disappeared, yet the more subtle traces still remain. Additionally, the media provide a frame for interpreting events and people often go to the media for cues and clues on how to interpret events; the black media often serve that purpose for African Americans. Presently the majority media are the main source of information about the world, if for no other reasons than that the black media are more limited in their scope and reach. The black media are consulted for the many issues that may not appear in the majority media, and also for a black perspective on many of the issues that the majority media have investigated.

Just as the black media have fostered the idea of the group, other institutions within the African American community have acted as keepers of the faith, preservers of the history, and teachers of the possible. For example, the black church has been a source of sustenance to the always challenged, frequently battered black self. Being a highly religious people,

African Americans have often taken their pains and formulated their responses and struggles within the black church. It has not only been within the edifice of the institutionalized church that this religiosity has manifested itself. Without attending church services or even being members of a church, Africans will often appeal to forces greater than themselves to assist them in times of need and to provide them with the vision necessary to transcend the multitude of problems that visit them and their people. It is the close association with the church and the dependence and responsiveness to force not materialized that have led many scholars to refer to Africans as in essence a spiritual people at their core.

It is truly baffling that after the Africans conspired to end their enslavement, there have been several opportunities to dramatically reduce the impact of the brutality of enslavement on the Africans' total being, including and perhaps especially upon their psyche. After the abolition of slavery, the African had no monetary foundation upon which to build. During this reconstruction period (DuBois, 1935), the many hopes and dreams for a more equalitarian society were quickly dashed. This has been referred to as one of four lost opportunities. Another squandered chance was during the industrial revolution, when in the growing industrial quarters, European immigrants were recruited instead of newly liberated Africans for these jobs. African Americans were systematically excluded from the industrial workforce. Again, after World War II, with the nation enlivened by the defeat of fascism and African Americans proud of the role they had played in that war effort as both soldiers and citizens, many promises made to African Americans went unfulfilled. It was essentially business as usual, with white supremacy and Jim Crow laws or the Black Codes still in force. The third lost opportunity, given the monumental changes brought about by the human rights movement, was the nation's failure to institutionalize or further develop human rights. In fact, if concerted pressure is not constantly maintained on the dominating society, the gains won in the past quickly fall under renewed attack (Steinberg, 1995).

The aforementioned observations and events have formed the context for this study of the African self, and they capture its profundity and complexity. Steinberg (1995) posed the question: If the United States has been unsuccessful in its response to the legacy of the enslavement of Africans in an "era of empire," what can be hoped for in the era of decline (the present)? It is in this era of decline that I have examined the many forces that have impinged, individually and collectively, on the African American's sense of self. My broad questions have been: How do African Americans manage to withstand the many attacks on the group to which they are members and relatedly their conception of self? What are some of the things that influence self-esteem and influence black identity, or more generally, the African Americans' sense of self? Are these influences the same? Does class make any difference in determining one's sense of self? Does self-esteem or group identity change appreciably over time? What are some of the things that influence an African-centered conception of the self? How does an African-centered approach to the study of self differ from a non-African-centered approach? How do the mass media influence the different self-concepts, and do the black media have differential effects on these self-concepts?

DuBois's double consciousness and its extension were the umbrella perspectives used to predict and explain the outcomes for self-esteem, group identity, and the African self-consciousness. Often touted as an important yet underused perspective, I tried to show how it might be usefully employed. It was invoked for all of the social phenomena under investigation, but other, more specific theories were also employed in the examination of each of the different self-concepts. This double consciousness focuses on the resilience and strength of Africans in the face of many attempts to treat them as inferiors. The theme is that Africans in the aggregate remain proud individuals, attached to their group despite oppressive forces. Moreover, this tenacity grows out of their sociohistorical realities of racism or white supremacy and certain cultural differences concerning epistemology and axiology between African Americans and European Americans. This perspective holds that African ideas concerning the self may fluctuate as a consequence of the intensity of the oppositional forces, and by extension, these forces will affect different elements in the African American community more intensely than others.

The Construction of a Theory

Informed by the empirical findings and directed by some of the recent philosophical and theoretical formulations, I synthesized the information in an attempt to formulate a theory. Given the foundation from which my findings derived and the interpretations made, I thought it useful to compile the insights obtained and explore some of the questions raised by this study. The emphasis was placed on identifying additional and associated research questions. Several theoretical formulations have been used to predict and explain the black self-concept; however, none of them alone has been adequate to the task.

On the philosophical level, I embrace the position that those Africans in the United States who resist the dominant or dominating culture tend to be more collectivist (as distinct from individualistic) and more spiritual (as distinct from material) in orientation. These different elements, along with other related elements, constitute what has been called an African worldview (Akbar, 1995; Kambon, 1992; Nobles, 1992). Also consistent with the African worldview is commonality, groupness, and similarity. Importantly, this African worldview fosters the idea that people are part of the natural rhythm of nature and that the closer a person gets to understanding nature, the closer he or she gets to gaining self-knowledge, to gaining "natural knowledge" as opposed to "grafted knowledge." If we build on images found in the natural world, it is possible to know the essence of our real form and to realize that "human beings have powerful, but untapped potential that has been obscured by false and erroneous messages about the true human nature" (Akbar, 1995, p. iv).

The African in the United States is inundated with a system of reality grounded in Europe, one which precludes the realization of an African concept of self that is grounded in the collective, social, and spiritual sense, sometimes called the "extended self" (Nobles, 1992). Thus, two distinct philosophical systems are vying for space in the same black body. Since the European conception has been presented as the only viable and meaningful conception of the world and since this often is a negation of the African conception, African Americans can experience conceptual conflict if they attempt to deny their African grounding or to accept uncritically the European philosophical tradition of the African self. This is one way to characterize the "double consciousness" that has acted as the organizing scheme of this study. Thus, while acknowledging the elements of the African consciousness that have grown out of contact with the European, it is the African in African Americans that has seldom been acknowledged, and as a consequence has been the source of contestation for the healthy black self. In this theory, the importance of the conception of the black self that was not only born out of the oppression or domination endured, but that which remained with Africans despite the attempts to impose another worldview on them.

On the theoretical level, it was assumed that because many African Americans have alternative conceptions and many have been able to hold on to African-based traditions and to use them as the foundation of their strength, as DuBois suggests in many of his writings, this would have profound and predictable effects on their concept of self. Many implications were drawn from viewing the state of nature in fundamentally different ways from the majority and putting forth this idea in the form of testable hypotheses. The theory emphasized the antecedents or processes that impinge on the African American conception of self. When outcomes of the black self were explored it was done so to validate the different constructs of the self. This conceptualization focused on two major categories of variables, namely, communication (especially majority media and the black media) and a variety of social structural variables (including the basic demographic variables, the gradational conception of class, and religiosity). In broad terms, the theoretical model posited that one's location in the social structure, one's spiritual foundation, and the kind of information an individual is exposed to will substantially influence his or her sense of self and the group. The model also assumes that the culture of the African fosters a collective commitment and a belief in the inherent worth of the individual. One, therefore, may look at the model as reflecting the extent to which the culturally derived "extended self" is maintained, elevated, or reduced. This, I maintain, is an ongoing and ever-present struggle.

A Theory of the African Double Consciousness

In this theory, I incorporated two major conceptions of the black self. One conception maintains that the individual self can be separated from the group self, and is reflected in the idea of self-worth and group or black identity. The other conception contends that the individual self cannot be separated from the group self. Therefore, taking into account the worldview attributed to Africans in the diaspora, one realizes oneself only through the group, the collective. This idea is exemplified in the previously cited statement: *I am because we are.* This is commonly called the African-centered perspective, or one in which African people can understand the universe by beginning from the center of their personal experience and extending outward to embody all of humanity (Akbar, 1995). From these two understandings, a number of hypotheses were generated, some of which were substantially different from those assumed for the other conceptions of the self.

On the empirical level, the part of the model that includes a separation between self-esteem and group identity, or, more generally, a self that is race-neutral and one that is race-related, fits the data well. This was shown in the two studies using the longitudinal data and the study using the more focused exploratory data. Thus, the theory seemed to predict and explain fairly well. The second and more extended aspect of the model, which encompassed the African-centered aspect of the self, also revealed an adequate correspondence of the data and the theory. This model, however, was tested with a nonprobability sample. These data, however, had a wider assortment of explanatory variables and a broad range of self-concepts under investigation.

As partial replication of an earlier study, my findings gave additional weight to the previous conclusions that African Americans have a strong sense of self and an equally strong group solidarity. And while African Americans of all classes have high self-esteem, it is higher among those who are better located in the social structure (i.e., those with higher income, and in one study, those with higher education). Also, those who are older seem to have a slightly greater self-conception. Moreover, the various measures of black identity are all high, and as shown before, it is the African's closeness to the African American community (masses and elites) that reflects the class differences—and in the same direction found in the previous study.

The working class (those with less education and lower income) tends to show greater group solidarity.

The Black Self Extended and Other Constructs of Self

In this theorizing, the African-centered perspective of the self was thought to operate in ways similar to the non-African-centered perspective, but also to show distinct differences. Clearly, the former perspective incorporates some of the major assumptions surrounding the non-African-centered perspective, but it also entails a host of other assumptions, many of which are derived from the idea that the self and the group cannot be meaningfully separated. With that in mind, I briefly summarize the major assumptions of the African-centered extended self conception, before turning to the more explicit and more typical conception of the self-concept of African Americans.

The Extended Self

Building on past research and the present empirical study, an attempt was made to construct a theory which incorporated the many disparate elements that have been assumed to influence several concepts of the African American self. With a concern toward building a theory, I compiled a set of relevant assumptions derived from the African-centered self. Using measures representing the "extended self" concept (the combination of the individual self and the group self), African Americans were hypothesized to have a strong African self-consciousness that is not moderated by class. I posited that across class, African Americans possess a consciousness that supports the collective and the idea of collective responsibility, emphasizes the spiritual, and feels a strong attachment to Africa. Further, age was posited to influence this sense of consciousness, with the older African Americans having a greater sense of the collectivity. Finally, I maintained that the nature of the symbolic social reality influences the African self-consciousness, and that different media produce different effects on African self-consciousness. Involvement in black activities and rituals produces this type of consciousness, and I further contended that the black media, especially the print media, would encourage an African self-consciousness. Conversely, the majority media would tend to negate this form of self-consciousness.

As expected, the class relationship was absent, while the existence of an age effect was not. I found that those who were younger were more likely to embrace this kind of consciousness that emphasizes human transformation from what presently exists for most African Americans. And those religiously inclined exemplified an African self-consciousness. Relatedly, the category of symbolic social reality was revealing. The involvement with black activities resulted in a strong self-consciousness. Whereas black print media had a positive impact on self-consciousness, black electronic exposure had an unexpected negative impact. The direction of majority media effect was the same. That is, the majority print media had an unexpected positive effect, whereas, as expected, the majority electronic media had a negative effect on African self-consciousness.

Broadly speaking, there is support for the argument that class, at least in a gradational sense, does not have an influence on the African-centered notion of self. Across education and income there is an attachment to Africa, things African, and a sense of self. Having a religious base and being older also produce this consciousness. The print media and electronic media have an impact on self-consciousness, with the print media, both black and majority, having a positive influence and the electronic media, both black and majority, having a negative influence. Could it be that there are certain elements within or attributes of the print media that generally influence the self-consciousness in the positive direction, whereas the reverse is true for the electronic media? Perhaps these media influence consciousness in the same direction, but the causal mechanisms in operation are quite different. Indeed, there is a litany of alternative explanations, and it is tempting to speculate on what this means, but it would probably be more judicious to suggest that these outcomes warrant further consideration, both conceptual and empirical.

Other Conceptions of Self: The Personal Self and Group Identity Distinction

I now turn to the predictors or antecedents of the non-African-centered conception of self-concept, which include the constructs of self-esteem and ethnic identity (two non-race-referenced constructs), and black autonomy and closeness to the black masses and elites, three group identity constructs, with a reference to being black. Operating from a more limited set of assumptions, I argued that religiosity looms as very important. Those more attuned to the black church and their more spiritual side were predicted to have a higher sense of self, a greater attachment to the collective (the masses and the elites), and a greater African self-consciousness. Level of education was assumed to have a positive influence on many on the self-constructs, especially self-esteem. Income was posited to have a positive influence on self-esteem and a positive influence on the group identity constructs. Age was again expected to have complex relationships with the various self-concepts. While age was assumed to have powerful positive influences on the self-concepts, the direction of the influence was considered to be contingent on the self-concept under investigation. Further, these individuals were predicted to avail themselves more of black media, especially to information exhibiting a black perspective or interpretation of social reality.

African Americans who attend to black media more frequently were reasoned to have a stronger personal self and group identity. That is, they were posited to have a higher self-esteem, a greater sense of the collective, and a more developed ethnic identity. Conversely, those who attend more to the majority media were predicted to have a weaker sense of self and less of an attachment to African Americans. In short, the majority media were argued to have a debilitating effect on African Americans' sense of self, whereas those who attend more to the black media were thought to be influenced in the opposite way. In light of the presumed advancements made by the majority media in the quantity and quality of black presentation and representation, the basis of this idea is looked upon with skepticism. As I suggested in my theorizing, the majority media present conceptions of the world that to a substantial degree are at odds with the conception of the world held by many African Americans. Also, more subtle cues exist in the media concerning the way African Americans act and behave, and these portrayals are not generally flattering. They exist both in entertainment fare and in the news.

What is clear from the preliminary analysis is that the media have powerful effects on the black self-concept. The direction of the media influence is also clear: majority media tend to militate against a black self-concept, whereas black media tend to foster a strong black concept. More specifically, the black print media have significant influence on nearly all the self-concepts: they produced a stronger endorsement of the idea of black autonomy, and generated greater self-esteem, a stronger ethnic identity, and a greater attachment to black professionals and politicians. A puzzling outcome, however, was that it did not generate an attachment to the masses. Significantly, the majority print media reduce blacks' self-esteem, whereas the black print media tend to increase it. The majority electronic media militated against endorsing black autonomy and self-esteem. Also quite striking is the positive impact that the participation in black festivities and rituals has on the black self-concept. Those who participate in these activities exhibit a stronger self-esteem. Although the other communication processes are strong, the concept of black participation exhibits the strongest effect on the largest number of self-constructs.

The effect of education indicated that those with more education were more attuned to the elites and less attuned to ideas surrounding black political and social independence (black autonomy). Income, on the other hand, showed contrasting effects: those with greater income felt a greater closeness to the masses and felt better about themselves; however, they too were less likely to embrace the ideas associated with black autonomy. Those who tended to be religious were more likely to embrace the entire black community—the masses as well as the elites. In that sense they may be said to have greater black identity. This relationship is consistent with the theorizing; however, I expect religiosity to have additional effects on the other self-concepts. With the difficult-to-interpret concept called age, I found (as predicted) that those who were older were more likely to embrace an idea of black autonomy and to feel a greater ethnic identity. However, it was the younger, as predicted, who felt a greater closeness to the elites (professionals and politicians).

Together, the relationships I found for the non-African-centered self-concept are revealing. Since there are several (five) measures of the non-African-centered conception of self, and only one African-centered construct, it is difficult and unwieldy to make comparisons, except on the general level. The similarities revolve first and foremost around the positive impact of black participation, as this is a variable that influenced almost all the constructs, both those with and those without a race referent. In contrast, whereas the two indicators of class had major influences on most of the self-constructs, it had none on possessing an African self-consciousness. Just as in the case for self-consciousness, the older African Americans were more inclined to embrace the sense of black autonomy and ethnic identity, but it was the younger who felt a greater closeness to the elites.

Most of the relationships I found were supportive of my theorizing. The influence of symbolic social reality, black involvement, and mass media exposure showed pronounced confirming relationships.

When conducting empirically based research it is necessary to pay considerable attention to the quality of the measures employed. This was done throughout this study. Issues pertaining to reliability and validity and more generally measurement were addressed in detail. Acknowledging that the many concepts used in this study are difficult or impossible to measure objectively (Bollen & Paxton, 1998), as is the case for social science in general, I was forced to rely on subjective assessments. Typically, these assessments contain measurement error, both systematic (or nonrandom) and random, which can create interpretive problems. By using structural equation modeling (i.e., the LISREL model) for a substantial portion of my analysis, I was able to take into account both random and systematic error. I was able to show, with minor deviations, that the scales used in all the empirical investigations were reliable (had internal consistency) and stable (were reliable over time). Reliability being a prerequisite for validity, I was then able to show substantial nomological validity (as a dimension of construct validity). This form of validity provides information on the validity of measures of a concept when the concept is part of a larger theory. Nomological validity is difficult to establish because the predictions are incorporated within a context of other predictions and the focal prediction and may depend on other variables in the theory or may be qualified by them (Bagozzi, 1994). Establishing these many forms of reliability and a high degree of nomological validity as was done in this study is rare indeed. Nonetheless, it would be useful to acquire a wider range of measures (e.g., behavioral measures) gathered from various designs (e.g., ethnographic) and subject them to the same rigorous assessment. Clearly, our understanding would be enhanced.

While it is possible to examine the self-concept with many different kinds of measures, I have focused on the self-report attitudinal measures. Many of them were subjected to rigorous psychometric testing. I have not used the various behavioral measures or what have sometimes been called unobtrusive or indirect measures in my own studies. These measures can be quite useful in revealing information otherwise difficult to obtain. Although the studies using these types of measures were reviewed and included as part of the rationale for some of the hypotheses, they were not part of the litany of measures used in this study. The review of the literature using these measures revealed that just like the other types of measures, they yielded several conflicting results and had many of the same measurement shortcomings. Several excellent reviews of these measures have been conducted, pointing to their strengths and weaknesses (see, for example, Baldwin, Brown, & Hopkins, 1991; Cross, 1991; Rosenberg, 1981, 1986, 1995).

Because a portrayal of the African self is an essentially empirically based endeavor, the data used become crucial. It must be kept in mind their limitations for the purpose at hand. While extremely rich in terms of the range and number of variables it contains, quite commendable with respect to methodology and sampling, and unparalleled in its design, a national panel design of African Americans puts certain restrictions on our ability to fully answer some appealing questions. Since we have argued that it is important to take into account the social and historical conditions when interpreting the African self-concept, our data were gathered shortly after the dynamic, change-inducing 1960s, that is, in the late 1970s. It has been argued that the civil rights and Black Power movements combined in the 1960s to create a relatively high degree of race consciousness and group solidarity, which effects are thought to persist today. Thus, it may be assumed that our sample population may think more in terms of group solidarity and self-worth as compared to those individuals from earlier years. Thus, strictly speaking, if we accept the importance of historical era, any outcome for the self-concept of these African Americans may not be the same as that from previous periods.

Conclusions

I began this investigation by setting forth the framework for studying the African American self-concept. I argued that the organization of human relations between African Americans and the larger society and the African Americans' sense of self within the larger society were formulated during the horrendous period of human bondage—that peculiar institution called slavery—during which even the basic humanity of the African was denied. This slavery was sanctioned by the Constitution and existed for nearly a hundred years—with formal, legally anctioned, caste restrictions. During and after slavery, many institutions and organizations harnessed their energy to prevent African Americans from attaining their basic civil and human rights. As I attempted to show, the culture industry (e.g., the media, both electronic and print) took an active part over time in fostering distorted, grotesque, and thoroughly repulsive images of the African. Such a practice continued well into the 1960s, when consistent and uncompromising challenge led to certain modifications, although as of yet there has not been complete elimination of this system of oppression and racial discrimination.

With the many attacks on the Africans' sense of humanity, many have wondered how they have managed to withstand the assaults and even prosper. DuBois, while stating that the dominating society looks upon Africans with amused contempt and pity, and acts in ways to ensure a dehumanized individual, pointed to the strength of the response to the onslaught. He alluded to the elements in the culture that were used to sustain the people in the face of this omnipresent challenge. His ideas on the essence of African people in the American context, as embodied in the principle of double consciousness, were included in my entire analysis of the black self, and were more formally presented in my subsequent attempt at theory construction. I embraced the idea that the self-conception of Africans is influenced not only by the many external hostile forces, but also, and perhaps more significantly, by the internal dynamics that are intrinsic to African culture. That is, it is culture that softens the blow and orchestrates an alternative response, that draws upon assumptions and viewpoints which are still intact after a long historical tradition that preceded the ravages of enslavement.

Unlike DuBois's perspective, much of the early examination of the African American self-concept made the fundamental assumption that Africans as oppressed people would be withering under self-hatred and simmering with opposition to their own group. Much of the early literature appeared to support this view, especially when children were the subjects under investigation. But when many of these studies are closely scrutinized, they often have an abundance of methodological and design problems which make any inferences risky. Most of the present conceptions and the more recent, better executed empirical studies provide a quite different picture. The majority of them suggest that Africans tend to have a high assessment of themselves and their group, examined either separately or in comparison to European Americans. Many of these empirical studies suffered from certain shortcomings, for example, inadequate measures and low generalizability.

Drawing upon more recent cross-sectional and panel-level national studies, I was able to extend the understanding of previous studies. Many of the pressing issues that were only speculations or many of the inadequately examined hypotheses were subjected to a more rigorous treatment. My overall analysis complemented and further underscored DuBois's idea that despite the struggle, African Americans are positively disposed to the group and experience substantial self-worth. Little support was shown for the speculation that self-esteem and group identity have a causal relationship. These self-constructions remain strong over an extended period of time. That is, despite the many elements and events that might diminish that sense of the self and the group, it remains stable, without major fluctuation. This latter point is particularly telling when one considers that for a large percentage of African Americans, life has become more difficult; yet their sense of self-worth, in the aggregate (global self-esteem), has not been diminished and their sense of group unity or solidarity has even increased slightly.

Because of the strong intuitive and experiential bias held by many people concerning the idea that Africans in the United States are suffering from low self-esteem and group identity, many people find it puzzling that several serious research endeavors have found the opposite. In an attempt to make sense out of these seemingly counterintuitive results, a number of ideas or suggestions for further inquiry have been presented. The most cogent among them are as follows. First, although the self-concept of Africans may be high when attitudinal measures are the primary indicators, a more expanded use of behavioral measures (e.g., color preference, language use, and mate selection) may provide a different picture. Second, using experimental manipulations of preferred objects in the environment, as opposed to naturalistic survey methodology, one would be better able to ascertain the individual's self-esteem and the extent to which he or she identifies with the group. With data collected over time using this design, it may also be possible to talk with greater certainty about the directional relationship between self-esteem and group identity. Third, given the sensitive and provocative nature of the subject matter, the traditional and more popular methods (e.g., survey or experiment) yield less accurate and valid information. The demand characteristics or reactive nature of these methods may impede a fully accurate assessment of the self-concept. Fourth, while not denying the existence of the relationships, attention should be directed at the minority that indeed have low self-esteem and group identity. Their numbers may be comparatively small, but their societal impact may be very visible and pronounced. A specific group that may be a target for study might be those who are nonfunctioning members of the larger society, sometimes called the 'underclass.'

It is worthy of note that the aforementioned ideas essentially call for an extension of or broader scope for this area of research. I would agree with that position but would emphasize that it in no way negates the present findings or interpretations.

Theoretically, I tried to bring clarity to the neglected issues concerning class and the self-concept of African Americans. Class operates in different directions depending on the self-concept. The better placed African Americans have a greater sense of self-worth, while those not so well placed have a greater sense of group solidarity. It is tempting to read quite a bit into this relationship. For example, it might be argued that despite the many societal processes that might militate against having a strong self-esteem, if through hard work, luck, or some other external circumstance, an individual manages to attain a certain status, this translates into feeling good about himself or herself and his or her worth as an individual. The struggles may have indicated how worthwhile that individual is or how he or she succeeded against the odds. It is important to keep in mind that even the lower-status people have above average self-worth (statistically speaking), giving credence to the notion that class may not be of major importance in determining self-worth, despite its statistical significance. Conversely, the people who have a lower status, who are the majority, have a stronger solidarity, which may suggest that they realize the importance of the group in attaining goals. This may be interpreted as indicating that people who have not particularly reached what may be considered a successful status in society have an attachment to more than themselves. That is, they endorse more of a collective responsibility. Again, one must be mindful that no matter the class, the sense of group solidarity is high.

To sum up, African Americans across all classes seem to embrace a worldview that is more collective, less competitive, more group-oriented, less material, and as such quite distinct from the well-documented European American worldview.

As I have acknowledged throughout, there are many conceptions of the black self, or more generally the African worldview, and many fundamental ways of explaining its existence. Some theories, certainly the majority, pinpoint the formulation and perpetuation of the African self as arising in response to external rather than internal forces. The stress is on an individual's attempt to rise above the racial and related class oppression. In their extreme form these theories present the African self as reactive.

An increasingly entertained alternative conceptualization of the African self focuses on the "natural" and "normal" condition of African psychological functioning and behavior, independent of white domination or racial oppression. The African is seen as striving for self-affirmation, self-determination, and self-fulfillment. The African self is characterized as arising from the natural requirements of one's own being, one's essence. It is pro-active and affirmative, geared toward optimization (Kambon, 1992, p. 37). The operationalization of this perspective is embodied in the African self-consciousness scale. Other theoretical and measurement possibilities, however, have been suggested and appear to have promise (see, for example, Akbar, 1995, and Myers, 1993, 1998a,b). It is the more normative conceptions of the self, which put emphasis on human transformation, that tend to indicate that

African people must move away from merely surviving in an oftentimes hostile environment, toward a further crystallization and elaboration of an African worldview, which has sheltered them from abuse and which promises to uplift Africans to greater material and spiritual heights. Those who have this conception of the African self are more likely to view African people as presently having less of an African self-consciousness. They are more likely to express how far African Americans have moved away from their core, their center, to borrow foreign representations of the world and of themselves. These scholars, many times also activists, refer to ways and means of Africans realizing a greater sense of their culture, history, and actions. They stress how with such a consciousness Africans will be better able to move back on the stage as active participants in world decision making.

I contend that the more recent basis for the discrepancy in how the state of the African self is perceived among many scholars has a great deal to do with how they conceive of the African self. For example, much of the recent work with a less normative, more traditional conception of the African self tends to see a strong and healthy African. Thinking of the self in global terms as represented by the self-esteem scale I used in this study, clearly there is substantial support. But as many skeptical observers have noted, it does not seem likely that African Americans' self-esteem is not significantly and adversely affected by a number of contemporary circumstances. They in fact contend that there are many instances of a diminished self-worth in the African American community, particularly among the young. Indeed there is a basis for their skepticism. Thus, I think an explanation is in order.

First, the condition of a lower self-worth may exist more prominently among the young, particularly adolescents, although recent work suggests that this may not be the case. Nonetheless, it may be that it is those younger people locked in the worse material conditions who exhibit lower self-worth. Also, some forms of black self-hatred may indeed be internalized, as some have suggested, but may be signified by more aggressive tendencies or behaviors, especially among African American males. This is clearly worthy of investigation. Informed by this perspective, it is most likely that such information would be more accurately captured using clinical techniques as part of a more wholistic approach, which is beyond this investigation. Second, the survey method used to obtain the data may not have been sensitive enough to reach the most dispossessed, and, while it may have many useful features (e.g., representativeness), it has not been used effectively to reach certain populations within the African American communities. While their numbers may be comparatively small, this social impact is quite large. Their situation is one that requires more conceptual and practical attention. By not examining in detail this significant group, it is possible to arrive at a partial understanding of the black self-concept. Third, it may be that if self-esteem or black identity were conceptualized differently, hence measured differently, a different picture might be evidenced. Instead of focusing on self-esteem as self-worth in a global sense, it might be equally useful to conceptualize self-esteem in concrete terms as competence or performance in various areas of endeavor. Instead of focusing on black identity essentially in feelings toward the group, this construct might have a more cognitive or behavioral components with associated measures.

With a different emphasis, there are those working from a more normative perspective, who, while acknowledging the strength of African Americans, maintain that in order to move beyond indignation and reaction, African Americans must attain a perspective or consciousness that will facilitate group advancement and transformation, which they do not presently possess. So within this perspective, African Americans are lacking in African self-consciousness. To them, many African Americans have not resolved the problem posed by many African American scholar-activists and insightfully articulated by Malcolm X, who argued that there is an unavoidable and intimate connection between the love of Africa and things African, and the love of self.

Compatible with my theorizing was the finding that those who are more religiously oriented are more given to valuing the spiritual and are more self-confident and supportive of the African American community. Further, those who are consumers of the black media, especially print offerings, which generally foster a more genuine and hopeful portrayal of African people, tend to exhibit a greater sense of self-worth and group identity. The black media seem to live up to their reputation as a positive force in the African American community.

As part of this investigation, group identity was separated from self-esteem and the antecedents of both of these constructs were explored. Within the African-centered framework, the separation is unwarranted. Using the construct that emerges from this framework, religiosity and attention to black media fare carry particular importance. They both have strong influences on the existence of this form of consciousness.

Although this conceptualization focused primarily on African Americans, the assumption was that the theory would apply to Africans in the diaspora. Because of historically similar experiences and because of the strength and commonality of expressions of the African heritage, I assume that the theory proposed also would have applicability in these settings. I think the categories of variables proposed in the African double consciousness perspective are relevant, although the magnitude of their influence would vary depending upon the particular history and specific form of oppression. Further, the African-centered conception and operationalization of the self-concept grows out of that awareness. Therefore, I assume that it would have widespread relevance. I also assume that the more traditional conception of the black self-concept will have relevance, but to a lesser degree. One cannot help but be struck by the extent to which the African is relegated to a lower status, to varying degrees, across the globe and to observe the similar means used to engage in the struggles for social justice and human transformation. Lastly, the scope of this theory undoubtedly has relevance for non-African historically oppressed groups, particularly those oppressed at not only the economic but also at the social, political, and cultural levels.

I was able to show that although past and present impediments and unwholesome characterizations of Africans still exist, these besieged people have managed to remain without a broken spirit or a shattered self. The theory proposed to explain this outcome points to the awesome challenges confronting African Americans, but it also suggests that certain internal dynamics in the African American community historically honed and contemporaneously polished have allowed it to soften the many transgressions. The charge now, however, is to not only to shore up those mechanisms of defense, but to fashion an African self that more actively defines itself out of its own history, culture, and desired future.

The decision to study African Americans was based on the understanding that it is imperative that such a study be informed by their own historical experiences and in accord with their own reference points. This does not, however, reduce the significance of studying other groups. It points to the relevance of studying a group unique in the level of attack directed toward its humanity; however, it might also provide insights about other spiritually oppressed humanity (Akbar, 1995).

I have only penetrated the surface of an in-depth exploration into the African self, with an emphasis on its present state. More attention needs to be directed toward its future aspirations and to the possible uplifting transformations that remain to be made. As one struggling to be an activist-scholar, I would like to pursue, develop, and implement further strategies that maximize human self-consciousness based on this inquiry. After defining the many elements that influence the black self, I would like to combine them to fashion a more wholesome we-ness. In making this statement, I acknowledge that the impetus for such transformations will come from the masses of the people themselves. I hope to be one of the facilitators in this process, one who could participate in achieving the highest good, a true public servant.

The *Book of Ptah Hotep* provides an inspiring example:

> Be generous as long as you live. What goes into the storehouse
> should come out. For bread is made to be shared. Those whose
> bellies are empty turn into accusers, and those who are deprived
> become opponents. See that none such as these are your neighbors.
> Generosity is a memorial to those who show it, long after they have
> departed.

APPENDIXES

APPENDIX A

The Cross-Sectional Study

Figure A.1 graphically depicts the model I proposed.[1] Employing structural equation modeling techniques (Joreskog & Sorbom, 1989), I arrived at overall fit measures which suggest that this model fits the data well.[2] Table A.1 shows that the χ^2 is 13.02, with 6 df. This value was statistically significant at the p = 0.04 level. Since χ^2 is influenced by sample size (and I have a large sample), I gave more weight to other overall fit measures and the component fit measure. All of the other overall fit measures also suggest a good fit. For example, the goodness-of-fit index (GFI) was 1.00, the adjusted goodness-of-fit index (AGFI) was 0.99, and the comparative fit index (CFI) was 1.00.

Looking at the factor loadings, I found that they were statistically significant, fairly uniform in value (each of a substantial magnitude), and, thus, seemed to be reflective of their respective constructs (see Table A.2).

Since I obtained a good fitting model at the overall level and component fit level, I was able to move to a further investigation of this model. As a first step, I examined the means for both self-esteem constructs to see whether the means were different across these two factors. I was addressing the question whether African Americans as a group have low self-esteem. There is the question of what constitutes high or low self-esteem. I took the straightforward position that (using a 4-point scale) if the mean was above

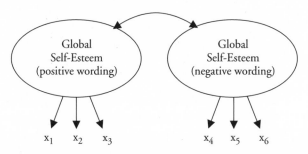

Figure A.1. Conceptual Representation of a Model of Global Self-Esteem

181

Table A.1. Goodness-of-Fit for the Self-Esteem Model

Summary Measures	Estimates
χ^2	13.02
df	6
p	0.04
χ^2/df	2.17
Goodness-of-Fit Index (GFI)	1.00
Adjusted Goodness-of-Fit Index (AGFI)	0.99
Normed Fit Index	0.99
Non-Normed Fit Index	0.99
Comparative Fit Index (CFI)	1.00

Source: National Study of Black Americans (1979–80).

Table A.2. Completely Standardized Coefficients of the Self-Esteem Model

Parameters	Estimates
x_1	0.52
x_2	0.86
x_3	0.64
x_4	0.62
x_5	0.64
x_6	0.80

Source: National Study of Black Americans (1979–80).

2, then this would be indicative of high self-esteem. Any value lower than 2 would constitute low self-esteem.

Keeping in mind that the range of the two self-esteem scales is 1 = "almost always true" to 4 = "never true," I found the mean to be 3.59 for the positively worded scale and 3.48 for the negatively worded scale. With the items coded so that a higher score indicated greater self-esteem, the findings indicated that Africans, as a collective, have above average self-esteem or self-worth. The reliabilities (as internal consistencies) of these scales were 0.64 for self-esteem, positively worded, and 0.68 for self-esteem, negatively worded.

APPENDIX B

Tests Across the Social Structural Variables

Education

Education and Positively Worded Self-Esteem

Model 1 shows that χ^2 is statistically nonsignificant ($\chi^2 = 9.04$, with 6 degrees of freedom, p $= 0.17$) and the other measure of fit, the comparative fit index (CFI), is 1.00. Less promising findings exist for models 2 and 3, but both show a statistically significant χ^2, with statistically significant incremental χ^2s. The CFIs for both models, however, indicate an adequate fit.

Education and Negatively Worded Self-Esteem

For all of the models, the χ^2 is statistically significant, suggesting a poor fit. Moreover, only the CFI for model 1 is considered high. All the incremental χ^2s were large and significant. Overall, with the possible exception of model 1, there appeared to be a noticeable difference between model 2 and model 3 across education levels. The items had different reliabilities and explained a differential amount of variance across education levels. A cautious stance toward these findings would be to say that the negatively worded self-esteem items had the same meaning across education groups, but do not seem to have equal reliabilities across these groups. (See Table B.1.)

Age and Positively Worded Self-Esteem

The hypothesis of equal factor loadings cannot be rejected based on the chi-square measure (χ^2/df (4) $= 4.46$, p $= 0.35$). Further, the CFI (1.00) also suggests an excellent fit. Therefore, it appeared that my proposed model fits the data across the different age groups and that the items in the positive self-esteem scale have the same meaning. Moving farther up the hierarchy, the picture became unclear. Model 2 poses the question of equal reliability. When I look at model 2, which also constrains $\Theta\delta$ to be equal, both χ^2-based measures, the χ^2 measure and the incremental χ^2, suggest that the model did not fit well. However, the comparative fit index suggested a good

Table B.1. Test of Generalizability of the Confirmatory
Factor Model for the Self-Esteem Constructs by Education

		Positive				*Negative*	
χ^2	*CFI*	*Test of Hypo.*	χ^2	*CFI*	*Test of Hypo.*
Model 1 Invariance	$\chi^2_{(4)} = 9.04$	1.00 p = 0.17		$\chi^2_{(4)} = 24.91$	0.98 p = 3.5	
Model 2 Invariance	$\chi^2_{(10)} = 44.05$	0.99 p = 0.00	36.01/6 df	$\chi^2_{(10)} = 172$	0.84 p = 0.07	47.09/6 df
Model 3 Invariance	$\chi^2_{(12)} = 64.61$	0.99 p = 0.11	19.56/2 df	$\chi^2_{(12)} = 2.96$	0.72 p = 0.00	124/2 df

fit. The full model (model 3), which adds the equality constraints for the parameters representing error in the equation, showed that the χ^2 barely reached significance, and that the incremental χ^2 and the CFI indicated that the model fits well. So in addition to the items appearing to have the same meaning across age groups, they also seemed to have equal reliability across these groups.

Age and Negatively Worded Self-Esteem

I again found that the hypothesis of equal factor loadings cannot be rejected. The χ^2 is 0.81, with 4 df, p = 0.94. The CFI is 1.00. Also, model 2 provides a nonsignificant χ^2, unlike what was found for the positively worded self-esteem scale. The CFI was 0.99, but the incremental χ^2 suggested a less than adequate improvement in model fit over model 1. The final model showed that while it was statistically significant, the other two measures reflected a good fit (CFI = 0.99, incremental χ^2 = 0.98). (See Table B.2.)

Gender

Gender and Positively Worded Self-Esteem

Model 1 shows a nonsignificant $\chi^2 = 0.12$ (df = 2, p = 0.94), with a large CFI of 1.00. The positive side of models 2 and 3 is that the CFI is adequate (0.98 and 0.97, respectively), but the χ^2s were significant and the incremental χ^2s are also significant. At the very least, it is possible to say that males and females seemed to attribute the same meaning to the positively worded self-esteem items.

Table B.2. Test of Generalizability of the Confirmatory Factor Model for the Self-Esteem Constructs by Age

	Positive			Negative		
	χ^2	CFI	Test of Hypo.	χ^2	CFI	Test of Hypo.
Model 1 Invariance	$\chi^2_{(4)} = 4.46$	1.00 p = 3.5	1.00	$\chi^2_{(4)} = 0.81$	1.00 p = 0.94	
Model 2 Invariance	$\chi^2_{(10)} = 17.07$	0.99 p = 0.07	12.51/6 df	$\chi^2_{(10)} = 18.40$	0.99 p = 0.05	17.59/6 df
Model 3 Invariance	$\chi^2_{(12)} = 18.06$	0.99 p = 0.11	1.19/2 df	$\chi^2_{(12)} = 19.26$	0.99 p = 0.08	124/2 df

Gender and Negatively Worded Self-Esteem

The same pattern shown for the positively worded self-esteem scale exists for the negatively worded self-esteem scale. Thus, the same interpretations were made. The clearest picture to emerge is with respect to model 1. Males and females shared the same interpretation of negatively worded self-esteem. Model 2 and model 3 gave some indications of a good fit (CFI = 0.98 for both models), but the χ^2 indicated that the fit was less than adequate. Thus, I cannot state unequivocally that the scale had equal reliability for both males and females. (See Table B.3.)

Table B.3. Test of Generalizability of the Confirmatory Factor Model for the Self-Esteem Constructs by Gender

	Positive			Negative		
	χ^2	CFI	Test of Hypo.	χ^2	CFI	Test of Hypo.
Model 1 Invariance	$\chi^2_{(2)} = 12$	1.00 p = 0.94		$\chi^2_{(2)} = 1.98$	1.00 p = 0.37	
Model 2 Invariance	$\chi^2_{(5)} = 16.78$	0.98 p = 0.00	15.74/3 df	$\chi^2_{(5)} = 23.22$	0.98 p = 0.00	21.24/3 df
Model 3 Invariance	$\chi^2_{(6)} = 24.73$	0.99 p = 0.00	7.95/1 df	$\chi^2_{(6)} = 26.33$	0.98 p = 0.00	3.11/1 df

Table B.4. Test of Generalizability of the Confirmatory Factor Model for the Self-Esteem Constructs by Income

	Positive			Negative		
	χ^2	CFI	Test of Hypo.	χ^2	CFI	Test of Hypo.
Model 1 Invariance	$\chi^2_{(6)} = 7.72$	1.00 p = 0.26		$\chi^2_{(6)} = 12.03$	0.99 p = 0.06	
Model 2 Invariance	$\chi^2_{(15)} = 31.98$	0.99 p = 0.01	36.01/9 df	$\chi^2_{(15)} = 131.60$	0.87 p = 0.00	119.57/9 df
Model 3 Invariance	$\chi^2_{(18)} = 51.16$	0.99 p = 0.00	19.56/3 df	$\chi^2_{(18)} = 176.60$	0.76 p = 0.00	480.00/3 df

Income

Income and Positively Worded Self-Esteem

Model 1 and model 2 both showed statistically nonsignificant χ^2 X^2 and very good CFIs. However, for model 2, the incremental χ^2 is statistically significant. The findings showed that the meaning attributed to and the reliability of the positively worded items were the same across income groups. There were greater discrepancies in model 3, thus I can say that it did not provide a good fit.

Income and Negatively Worded Self-Esteem

Only model 1 provided a good fit to the data. The various income groups also seemed to share the same meaning for the negatively worded self-esteem items.

To summarize, if I placed substantial importance on the χ^2 measure, I may say that these items had the same meaning for the respondents. However, it appears that for some of the scales, the reliability varies across some of the different social structural groups. By allowing the χ^2 to be one of the major measures of the validity of our model, I overlooked certain points. First, I know that χ^2 is heavily influenced by sample size. It tends to increase with sample size. Given our N of 2,107, which is considered fairly large in most quarters, even very small differences in model fit are detectable.

Many would argue in such an instance that the χ^2 should be given less weight than measures that are not influenced by sample size. The CFI is one such measure. At the present, it is considered the single best overall fit measure (Bagozzi & Baumgartner, 1994). If I rely more heavily on the CFI, I may say that all across both aspects of the self-esteem construct, the respondents share the same meaning and the scales are equally reliable across social structural groupings. (See Table B.4.)

Test of the Factor Means

I have thus far shown that the psychometric properties of the self-esteem scales are adequate and generalize across age, gender, income, and, to a large degree, education. Across different important social structural variables, people seem to at least attribute the same meaning to positively and negatively worded self-esteem items. These items seem to have the same reliability across the different groups. This does not imply that the means will be equal across these categories. I have yet to examine possible mean differences. Following convention, any test of the difference between means assumes at least across pertinent variables that the people under investigation share the same meaning for outcome variables. Succinctly stated, any test of the difference between means assumes at least invariance of factor loadings (Bollen, 1989; Liang et al., 1989).

I used techniques elaborated on by Joreskog and Sorbom (1989, pp. 245–253) to test for differences in means. The findings are presented in Tables B.5 and B.6.

Table B.5. Comparisons of Factor Means for Self-Esteem Constructs by Social Structural Variables

	Social Structural Variables	Positive Self-Esteem	Negative Self-Esteem
Education	a. Less than H.S.	(a,b*)	—
	b. High School	—	(a,b)
	c. Some Colleges	—	(a,c), (b,c)
	d. College and more	(a,d), (b,d), (c,d)	(a,d), (b,d)
Age	a. Young (17–34)	—	—
	b. Middle (35–54)	—	—
	c. Old (55 and over)	(a,c)	—
Income	a. < 5000		
	b. 5 < 10,000	(a,b)	(a,b)
	c. 10 < 20,000	(a,b)	(a,c)
	d. over 20,000	(a,d)	(a,d), (b,d)
Gender	a. Male	—	—
	b. Female	—	—

*The second letter indicates the grater magnitude.

Table B.6 Summary of the Relationships Between
Self-Esteem and Social Structural Variables

	Self-Esteem (positively worded)	Self-Esteem (negatively worded)
Education	more education, greater self-esteem	more education, greater self-esteem
Age	older, greater self-esteem	no difference
Gender	no difference	no difference
Income	more income, greater self-esteem	more income, greater self-esteem

Note: Longitudinal data (4 points in time).

For education, those with a college education or greater have higher self-esteem than those with less education—those with high school education and those with some college. Those with less than high school education have a higher self-esteem than those with a high school diploma. These findings applied to the positively worded self-esteem scale.

A slightly different pattern was evident for the different education categories on the negatively worded self-esteem scale. Those with college education or more have greater self-esteem than those with less than a high school education, those with a high school education, and those with a high school diploma. Those with some college have greater self-worth than those with a high school diploma and those with less than a high school education. And those with a high school education had greater self-esteem than those with less than high school education.

Looking at the differences among age groups for the positively worded self-esteem scale, I found that those 55 and over have greater self-esteem than the younger adults (17–34). No age differences were found for the negatively worded self-esteem scale.

For gender, there were no statistically significant differences on either of the self-esteem scales; however, for the self-esteem scale, negatively worded, the relationship came close to being significant, with males showing greater self-esteem.

For income, those with the highest income (greater than $20,000) had greater self-esteem than those with very little income (less than $5,000). Those with the next to the highest income ($10,000–$20,000) had a greater self-esteem than those with very little income. Finally, those with an income of from $5,000 to $10,000 had a greater self-esteem than those with the lowest income. These findings apply to the positively worded scale.

When I looked at the mean differences for income and the negatively worded self-esteem scale, I found very similar relationships. There is only one addition: in the highest income group, there was a greater sense of self-worth as compared to those with the next to the lowest income ($5,000–$10,000).

Wolford and Torres (1994) performed the most systematic and extensive analysis of these panel data to date. They noted that the atypical time frame of the panel data presented a formidable challenge. The first wave of the study was a household interview conducted during 1979 and 1980, which was not originally designed as a panel study and thus only sparse recontact information was obtained. The second wave of data was conducted eight years later (in 1987 and 1988) by telephone interviews. As anticipated with the scant information and the long hiatus between the first and second studies, there was considerable attrition. One year later, a third wave was collected. The fourth and final wave was collected three years later.

The analysis done by Wolford and Torres indicated the demographic variables that typically predict attrition in panel data—region urbanicity, gender, and age—had an effect on the response rate. The only exception was for the variable region. Nonetheless, these variables played a substantially lesser role in predicting responses across waves than other characteristics of the individual. Age showed a nonlinear relationship to nonresponse, with middle-aged respondents most likely to respond to later waves. Also, level of education was associated with nonresponse in the first two interviews, but not in the third. Those with higher education were more likely to respond. Similarly, the response rate for personal income was nonlinear. Those with incomes near the median were more likely to respond.

The strongest predictor of nonresponse was whether the respondent or his or her family owned their own home, followed by a variable correlated with it, the condition of living unit (as noted by the interviewer).

My own preliminary analysis of the data indicated that for the social structural variables of interest to us, the effective sample size is large enough to perform a multigroup analysis. That is, the effective sample size appears acceptable for the social structural variables. (See Table B.7.)

Table B.7 National Panel Survey of Black Americans—Response Rate

	N	% of Wave 1	Response Rate
Wave 1 (1979–80)	2107	NA	67.0%
Wave 2 (1987–88)	935	46.6%	46.6%
Wave 3 (1988–1989)	779	39.1%	84.3%
Wave 4 (1991–92)	652	33.4%	83.6%

Source: Wolford and Torres (1994).

APPENDIX C
Factorial Invariance and Structured Means

The results have been divided into two sections (Part A and Part B) which correspond to the two comparisons—income and education—that were made within the broad analysis strategies of factorial invariance and tests of factor means. Factorial invariance was examined as follows. First, we assessed the goodness-of-fit of the proposed model for comparisons across the education and income groups. Because at the time of this analysis there was no one measure that was considered to be the best, we used several measures to evaluate these models. We also examined differences in factorial structures across these comparisons. Lastly, we evaluated the hypotheses that accounted for any observed differences within these comparisons. Since factorial invariance is a matter of degree, we extended this conventional strategy of evaluating the invariance of the factor loadings by exploring mean structures. A critical assumption in testing for mean differences is that the measurement and structure of the underlying constructs are equivalent across groups (Bejar,1980; Byrnes, Shavelson, & Muthen,1989; Drasgow & Kanfer, 1985).

A structural equation version of MANOVA was used to test mean differences (see Bagozzi & Yi, 1989; Kuhnel, 1988). First, we performed an omnibus test and tests of means. The omnibus test of equality of means was performed by fixing $\gamma^{(1)} = \gamma^{(2)} = \gamma^{(3)} = \gamma^{(4)}$ for the income groups and $\gamma^{(1)} = \gamma^{(2)} = \gamma^{(3)}$ for the education groups and comparing the obtained chi-square goodness-of-fit to the χ^2 values revealed for the respective full models making no equality constraints. The omnibus test examines the multivariate null hypothesis of equality in means of the dependent variables across groups against the alternative hypothesis that one or more of the means differ across groups. If a significant χ^2 difference test results, then it is appropriate to examine each dependent variable to find out where such differences exist.

PART A

Factorial Invariance

Income Differences

The initial goodness-of-fit measure we used was the χ^2, which signifies the probability that the observed covariance matrices could have been generated by the hypothesized model. The smaller the χ^2, the better the overall fit. As χ^2 is sensitive to sample size, it is not recommended as the most desirable measure when the sample size is large. As an extension of the χ^2 and a recommended correction for the sample size problem, χ^2 / df, was used. A χ^2 / df in the vicinity of 3 or less is considered to be an acceptable fit (Carmines & McIver, 1981). Looking at Table C.1, the χ^2 values in the first column are all statistically significant. The χ^2 /df for all the models, except the null, ranged from 1.96 to 2.10. These values give a more positive indication of the fit of all the models.

The third measure of fit came from significance tests of the χ^2 differences under the various equivalence constraints. Table C.1 lists these results under the heading labeled "Incremental χ^2." The findings indicated that assuming the equivalence of the factor loadings across income groups, the χ^2 increased

Table C.1 Goodness-of-Fit of Models for Racial Belief System with Various Equivalence Constraints Across Income Levels

Likelihood χ^2	df	χ^2/df^a	Incremental χ^2 χ^2	df	Bentler-Bonett Index	Corrected Normed Index	Hoelter's CN
Null Model (Model 1)							
8412.43	612	13.75					171.37
Model with No Equivalence Constraints (Model 2)							
1048.51	500	2.09			0.88	0.93	1113.17
Model with Equivalence Constraints on λ_y (Model 3)							
1105.54	539	2.05	57.03	39	0.87	0.93	1134.95
Model with Equivalence Constraints on λ_y, ψ (Model 4)							
1163.15	584	1.99	57.61	45	0.86	0.93	1164.30
Model with Equivalence Constraints on λ_y, ψ, 0ε (Model 5)							
1249.70	638	1.96	86.55	54	0.85	0.921	1178.24

[a]Likelihood ratios are significant at $p < 0.001$.
Adapted from *National Journal of Sociology* (1991) 6 (2), 157–186.

by 57.03 with 39 degrees of freedom. This value is statistically nonsignificant, thus indicating an adequate fit.

The remaining entries in the incremental column show the differences in χ^2 when additional equivalency constraints are added to the model that preceded it. For instance, relative to model 2, which assumed the equivalence of the factor loadings, the additional assumption of equivalence of ψ substantially increased the χ^2 relative to the increase in the degrees of freedom. The largest increment in χ^2 relative to its degrees of freedom occurred in model 5, where the assumption of equivalence in measurement error was added to model 4. However, even here the difference was not statistically significant. That is, for a very rigorous test of invariance (equivalence of measurement error), there does not seem to be a difference across income groups on this measure. Similar to the likelihood ratio, this incremental χ^2 test is also very sensitive to sample size.

Another index of goodness-of-fit was developed by Bentler and Bonett (1980). Their measure, called the normed fit index, ranges from 0 to 1. It shows the improvement achieved by a proposed theoretical specification over the null model, which assumes no causal linkages among the variables. As revealed in Table C.1, this index for the proposed models ranged from 0.851 to 0.875, which indicated a borderline fit.

Yet another goodness-of-fit index is presented which is a correction of the Bentler and Bonett normed index. It was developed by Bollen (1989) and is referred to here as the corrected normed index. It corrects for the influence of sample size and degrees of freedom on the normed index. Table C.3 shows the corrected normed index to have values ranging from 0.921 to 0.930. These values show very little difference across models and represent good fits.

Income equivalence was highlighted, however, by an additional index of fit, Hoelter's Critical N, or CN (Hoelter, 1983). CN estimates the sample size for which a model is statistically acceptable. Hoelter maintained that with two groups, CN values of 800 or above (200× the number of groups) suggest that a model adequately reproduces an observed covariance structure. The CNs for models 2 through 5 ranged from 1113.13 to 1178.24.

Collectively, the measures of fit indicate that the proposed model has an adequate fit across income. In short, there do not appear to be any major income differences in the proposed model. With respect to the measurement properties, the results indicate that the constructs and indicators are identical across income groups and that the eighteen measures have equal reliability across the four income groups. With the exception of black autonomy, the composite reliabilities are acceptable. And, the reliabilites for the constructs of negative stereotype and closeness to elites are fairly high.

Finally, the equivalence of the λs suggest that the various constructs are associated at the same level across the income groups. Also, as the most rigorous equivalence test of all, the errors in measure (ψ) are identical across the income groups.

Educational Differences

The same goodness-of-fit measures used previously were also applied here. They are presented in Table C.2, which shows that the χ^2 s in the first columns were all statistically significant at the 0.001 level. This suggests a less than adequate fit. But again, this is not surprising given the sample size considerations mentioned above. Nonetheless, the χ^2/df for all models except the null ranged from 2.55 to 3.13, giving a more positive indication of fit.

The third measure of fit comes from significance tests of the χ^2 differences under the various equivalence constraints. Relative to model 2, which assumed no equivalence constraints, the additional assumption of equivalence of factor loadings did increase the χ^2 relative to the increase in the degrees of freedom. Based on this measure, the assumption of equivalent factor loadings was not supported. Hence, statistically significant educational differences seem to exist in terms of factor loadings. However, the other measures of fit provide a slightly different and more positive picture. For while the Bentler—

Table C.2 Goodness-of-Fit of Models for Racial Belief System with Various Equivalence Constraints Across Education Levels

Likelihood χ^2	df	χ^2/df[a]	Incremental χ^2 χ^2	df	Bentler–Bonett Index	Corrected Normed Index	Hoelter's CN
Null Model (Model 1)							
8694.68	459	18.94					126.27
Model with No Equivalence Constraints (Model 2)							
957.98	375	2.55			0.89	0.93	1791.27
Model with Equivalence Constraints on Λ_y (Model 3)							
1023.12	401	2.55	65.02*	26	0.88	0.93	925.44
Model with Equivalence Constraints on Λ_Y, ψ (Model 4)							
1097.47	431	2.55	74.35*	30	0.87	0.92	923.76
Model with Equivalence Constraints on Λ_Y, ψ, 0ε (Model 5)							
1466.36	467	3.13	368.89*	36	0.83	0.90	746.62

[a]Likelihood ratios are significant at p < 0.001.
Source: National Study of Black Americans
adapted from *National Journal of Sociology* (1991) 6 (2), 157–186.

Bonett index is borderline (0.88), the correction of this index indicates an adequate fit (0.93). Also, the CN suggests an acceptable fit.

With somewhat ambiguous results for the above model, we decided not to interpret further any of the goodness-of-fit measures beyond this model. The other fit measures, however, are presented in Table C.2 for comparative purposes. The inadequacy of the subsequent models suggests that there is not an equivalence of error variance or error of measurement across the educational groups.

The findings from Table C.2 may be summarized thusly. If we judge them only on the likelihood ratios, none of the models demonstrates an adequate fit. Given the aforementioned conditions of its usefulness, this was not unexpected. While the CN and the corrected normed index all suggested that the models fit the data well, the χ^2 /df, the Bentler—Bonett indicated adequate model fits (models 2 and 3). The incremental χ^2 test suggests that there are differences in measurement errors across the educational groups (models 4 and 5). We therefore did not pursue further the analysis of models 4 and 5. The overall findings suggest that the constructs exist or have meaning for each group.

The composite reliability for each construct for each education group is as follows. For the three education groups, less than high school, high school, and more than high school, respectively, the reliability estimates are: black autonomy—0.526, 0.548, and 0.478, negative stereotypical belief—0.780, 0.809, and 0.839, positive stereotypical belief—0.635, 0.647, and 0.683, closeness to the masses—0.680, 0.603, and 0.612, and closeness to the elites—0.815, 0.787, and 0.774.

PART B

Structured Means

Income Differences

Since our hierarchical approach to factorial invariance indicated that adequate factorial invariance was reached, we moved to an examination of the structured or factor means. The analysis of structured means must be based on the moment rather than on the covariance matrix; thus, we added means values to the input data. In the upper panel of Table C.3, we show the omnibus test for mean differences across income groups. As shown in this table, the chi-square for the full model was compared to the model restriction $\gamma^{(1)} = \gamma^{(2)} = \gamma^{(3)} = \gamma^{(4)}$. The findings show that we must reject the null hypothesis of equal means across the groups with respect to our constructs of racial belief system ($\chi^2_{(15)} = 101.10$, p < 0.001). Thus, there are differences across income groups for at least one of the racial belief constructs.

Table C.3 Structural Equation Results for Model of an African American Racial Belief System: Omnibus Tests Across Four Income Groups

Omnibus Test	$\chi^2 = 1336.73$		
Full Model	$(414)\,\mathrm{p} < 0.001$		

$\gamma_1^{(1)} = 2.78$ (0.207)	$\gamma_1^{(2)} = 2.69$ (0.35)	$\gamma_1^{(3)} = 2.67$ (0.36)	$\gamma_1^{(4)} = 2.69$ (0.075)
$\gamma_2^{(1)} = 2.43$ (0.034)	$\gamma_2^{(2)} = 2.30$ (0.43)	$\gamma_2^{(3)} = 2.14$ (0.47)	$\gamma_2^{(4)} = 1.97$ (0.075)
$\gamma_3^{(1)} = 3.51$ (0.023)	$\gamma_3^{(2)} = 3.48$ (0.30)	$\gamma_3^{(3)} = 3.48$ (0.36)	$\gamma_3^{(4)} = 3.37$ (0.061)
$\gamma_4^{(1)} = 3.65$ (0.023)	$\gamma_4^{(2)} = 3.64$ (0.30)	$\gamma_4^{(3)} = 3.55$ (0.35)	$\gamma_4^{(4)} = 3.53$ (0.064)
$\gamma_5^{(1)} = 2.95$ (0.033)	$\gamma_5^{(2)} = 2.84$ (0.41)	$\gamma_5^{(3)} = 2.60$ (0.47)	$\gamma_5^{(4)} = 2.53$ (0.079)

Restricted model with $\gamma_i^{(1)} = \gamma_i^{(2)} = \gamma_i^{(3)} = \gamma_i^{(4)}$ for i = 1, 2, 3, 4, 5.
$$\chi^2 = 1437.83\,(567)\,\mathrm{p} < 0.05.$$
χ^2 Difference Text $\chi^2 = 101.10\,\mathrm{df} = 15\,\mathrm{p} < 0.001.$

The next step in the analysis was to determine which income group or groups were responsible for the mean differences for which of the five racial belief constructs. As is shown in the lower portion of Table C.4, no statistically significant differences exist across income categories for the black autonomy construct.

For the negative stereotype construct, statistically significant differences do exist. We find that for the two lowest income categories and for the two highest income categories there are no mean differences. However, mean differences are shown for the two highest income categories and the two lowest income categories. That is, those who make up to $5,000 a year are more likely to hold negative stereotypes concerning African Americans than those who earn from $10,000 to $19,999 a year. Also, those who make $5,000 or less hold more negative views of African Americans as compared to those who make $20,000 or more. While mean differences are demonstrated across income groups on the negative stereotype construct, no statistically significant differences exist across these income groups for the positive stereotype construct.

Educational Differences

Tables C.5 and C.6 show the structural equations results across the three education groups. The results show that we must reject the null hypothesis of equal means across the groups for our model. The χ^2 difference test domonstrates a statistically significant effect ($\chi^2 = 286.62$, 19df, p < 0.001). These results direct us to an examination of the factor means to determine where means are the same or different.

Table C.4 Structural Equation Results for Model of an African American Racial Belief System Across Four Income Groups

Test of Means Black Autonomy	Closeness to Elites
$\gamma_1^{(1)} = \gamma_1^{(2)}$	$\gamma_3^{(2)} = \gamma_3^{(1)}$
$\chi^2(553) = 1341.11$	$\chi^2(553) = 1337.22$
$\chi^2(552) = 1336.73$	$\chi^2(552) = 1336.73$
$\chi_d^2(1) = 0.438 \quad p < 0.05$	$\chi_d^2(1) = 0.48 \quad p < 0.05$
$\gamma_1^{(3)} = \gamma_1^{(1)}$	$\gamma_3^{(3)} = \gamma_3^{(1)}$
$\chi^2(553) = 1342.08$	$\chi^2(553) = 1337.22$
$\chi^2(552) = 1336.73$	$\chi^2(552) = 1336.73$
$\chi_d^2(1) = 5.36 \quad p < 0.05$	$\chi_d^2(1) = 0.49 \quad p < 0.01$
$\gamma_2^{(4)} = \gamma_2^{(2)}$	$\gamma_3^{(3)} = \gamma_3^{(2)}$
$\chi^2(553) = 1350.22$	$\chi^2(553) = 1336.73$
$\chi^2(552) = 1336.73$	$\chi^2(552) = 1336.73$
$\chi_d^2(1) = 13.49 \quad p < 0.05$	$\chi_d^2(1) = 0.00 \quad p < 0.05$
$\gamma_2^{(4)} = \gamma_2^{(3)}$	$\gamma_3^{(4)} = \gamma_3^{(2)}$
$\chi^2(553) = 1340.30$	$\chi^2(553) = 1339.31$
$\chi^2(552) = 1336.73$	$\chi^2(552) = 1336.73$
$\chi_d^2(1) = 3.57 \quad p < 0.05$	$\chi_d^2(1) = 2.58 \quad p < 0.05$
	$\gamma_3^{(4)} = \gamma_3^{(3)}$
	$\chi^2(553) = 1338.98$
	$\chi^2(552) = 1336.73$
	$\chi_d^2(1) = 2.25 \quad p < 0.05$
	$\gamma_5^{(2)} = \gamma_5^{(1)}$
$\gamma_4^{(2)} = \gamma_4^{(1)}$	$\chi^2(553) = 1341.60$
$\chi^2(553) = 1337.14$	$\chi^2(552) = 1336.73$
$\chi^2(552) = 1336.73$	$\chi_d^2(1) = 4.87 \quad p < 0.05$
$\chi_d^2(1) = 0.41 \quad p < 0.05$	$\gamma_5^{(3)} = \gamma_5^{(1)}$
$\gamma_4^{(3)} = \gamma_4^{(1)}$	$\chi^2(552) = 1336.73$
$\chi^2(553) = 1344.15$	$\chi_d^2(1) = 38.42 \quad p < 0.01$
$\chi^2(552) = 1336.73$	$\gamma_5^{(4)} = \gamma_5^{(1)}$
$\chi_d^2(1) = 7.42 \quad p < 0.05$	$\chi^2(553) = 1359.81$
$\gamma_4^{(4)} = \gamma_4^{(1)}$	$\chi^2(552) = 1336.73$
$\chi^2(553) = 1340.26$	$\chi_d^2(1) = 13.08 \quad p < 0.01$
$\chi^2(552) = 1336.73$	$\gamma_5^{(3)} = \gamma_5^{(2)}$
$\chi_d^2(1) = 3.53 \quad p < 0.05$	$\chi^2(553) = 1351.78$
$\gamma_4^{(3)} = \gamma_4^{(2)}$	$\chi^2(552) = 1336.73$
$\chi^2(553) = 1340.52$	$\chi_d^2(1) = 15.05 \quad p < 0.01$
$\chi_d^2(1) = 3.79 \quad p < 0.05$	$\gamma_5^{(4)} = \gamma_5^{(2)}$
$\gamma_4^{(4)} = \gamma_4^{(2)}$	$\chi^2(553) = 1348.42$
$\chi^2(553) = 1338.89$	$\chi^2(552) = 1336.73$
$\chi^2(552) = 1336.73$	$\chi_d^2(1) = 11.69 \quad p < 0.05$
$\chi_d^2(1) = 2.16 \quad p < 0.05$	

continued

Table C.4 *Continued*

Test of Means Black Autonomy	Closeness to Elites
$\gamma_4^{(3)} = \gamma_4^{(2)}$	$\gamma_5^{(3)} = \gamma_5^{(2)}$
$\chi^2(553) = 1336.77$	$\chi^2(553) = 1337.25$
$\chi^2(552) = 1336.73$	$\chi^2(552) = 1336.73$
$\chi_d^2(1) = 0.04 \quad p < 0.05$	$\chi_d^2(1) = 0.52 \quad p < 0.05$
$\gamma_4^{(1)} = \gamma_4^{(2)}$	$\gamma_5^{(1)} = \gamma_5^{(2)}$
$\chi^2(415) = 1286.83$	$\chi^2(415) = 1340.32$
$\chi^2(414) = 1266.57$	$\chi^2(414) = 1265.57$
$\chi_d^2(1) = 21.26 \quad p < 0.01$	$\chi_d^2(1) = 74.75 \quad p < 0.01$
$\gamma_4^{(1)} = \gamma_4^{(3)}$	$\gamma_5^{(1)} = \gamma_5^{(3)}$
$\chi^2(415) = 1329.33$	$\chi^2(415) = 1443.30$
$\chi^2(414) = 1265.57$	$\chi^2(414) = 1265.57$
$\chi_d^2(1) = 63.76 \quad p < 0.01$	$\chi_d^2(1) = 177.73 \quad p < 0.01$
$\gamma_4^{(2)} = \gamma_4^{(3)}$	$\gamma_5^{(2)} = \gamma_5^{(3)}$
$\chi^2(415) = 1282.83$	$\chi^2(415) = 1292.16$
$\chi^2(414) = 1265.57$	$\chi^2(414) = 1265.57$
$\chi_d^2(1) = 17.26 \quad p < 0.01$	$\chi_d^2(1) = 26.59 \quad p < 0.01$

When we examine the different pairs of means for each construct across the three education groups, the following relationships are revealed. For the black autonomy construct, as was shown in the case of income, there were no differences. The education groups exhibit the same level of black autonomy. Similar to the results for income, mean differences do not exist across education levels for the positive stereotype construct. Those with less than high school education, those with high school education, and those with college education or more all relate to the positive stereotype construct in the same way.

For the negative stereotype construct and the two closeness constructs (masses and elites), there are mean differences. While mean differences were also found for negative stereotypes and closeness to elites constructs across income, only for levels of education were mean differences obtained. The pattern of mean differences of the negative stereotype construct was such that for those with the least education and those with the most education (greater than high school), a statistically significant difference was found. The least educated group tends to hold stronger negative stereotypes than the most educated group. Further, a marked mean difference was found for those with a high school education tending to hold strong negative stereotypical views. The mean differences for those with less high school and those with high school education are very small and are not statistically significant.

Table C.5 Structural Equation Results for Model of an African American Racial Belief System Across Three Education Groups

Test of Means *Black Autonomy*	*Negative Stereotyping*	*Positive Stereotyping*
$\gamma_1^{(1)} = \gamma_1^{(2)}$	$\gamma_2^{(1)} = \gamma_2^{(2)}$	$\gamma_3^{(1)} = \gamma_3^{(2)}$
$\chi^2(415) = 1286.97$	$\chi^2(415) = 1269.45$	$\chi^2(415) = 1272.92$
$\chi^2(414) = 1285.57$	$\chi^2(414) = 1265.57$	$\chi^2(414) = 1265.57$
$\chi_d^2(1) = 3.40 \quad p < 0.05$	$\chi_d^2(1) = 3.85 \quad p < 0.05$	$\chi_d^2(1) = 7.35 \quad p < 0.01$
$\gamma_1^{(1)} = \gamma_1^{(3)}$	$\gamma_2^{(1)} = \gamma_2^{(3)}$	$\gamma_3^{(1)} = \gamma_3^{(3)}$
$\chi^2(415) = 1267.72$	$\chi^2(415) = 1344.53$	$\chi^2(415) = 1274.19$
$\chi^2(414) = 1265.57$	$\chi^2(414) = 1265.57$	$\chi^2(414) = 1265.57$
$\chi_d^2(1) = 1.15 \quad p < 0.05$	$\chi_d^2(1) = 78.96 \quad p < 0.01$	$\chi_d^2(1) = 8.62 \quad p < 0.01$
$\gamma_1^{(2)} = \gamma_1^{(3)}$	$\gamma_2^{(2)} = \gamma_2^{(3)}$	$\gamma_3^{(2)} = \gamma_3^{(3)}$
$\chi^2(415) = 1285.61$	$\chi^2(415) = 1314.94$	$\chi^2(415) = 1265.70$
$\chi^2(414) = 1265.57$	$\chi^2(414) = 1265.57$	$\chi^2(414) = 1265.57$
$\chi_d^2(1) = 0.04 \quad p < 0.05$	$\chi_d^2(1) = 59.37 \quad p < 0.01$	$\chi_d^2(1) = 0.13 \quad p < 0.01$

Table C.6 Structural Equation Results for Model of an African American Racial Belief System: Omnibus Test Across Three Education Groups

Omnibus Test *Full Model*		$\chi^2 = 1265.57$ $(414)\, p < 0.001$			
$\gamma_1^{(1)} = 2.76$	(0.029)	$\gamma_1^{(1)} = 2.68$	(0.029)	$\gamma_1^{(1)} = 2.69$	(0.034)
$\gamma_2^{(1)} = 2.46$	(0.036)	$\gamma_2^{(1)} = 2.36$	(0.036)	$\gamma_2^{(1)} = 1.99$	(0.038)
$\gamma_3^{(1)} = 3.55$	(0.023)	$\gamma_3^{(1)} = 3.45$	(0.026)	$\gamma_3^{(1)} = 3.44$	(0.028)
$\gamma_4^{(1)} = 3.76$	(0.021)	$\gamma_4^{(1)} = 3.61$	(0.025)	$\gamma_4^{(1)} = 3.43$	(0.034)
$\gamma_5^{(1)} = 3.15$	(0.033)	$\gamma_5^{(1)} = 2.72$	(0.036)	$\gamma_5^{(1)} = 2.45$	(0.038)

Restricted model with $\gamma_5^{(1)} = \gamma_5^{(2)} = \gamma_5^{(2)}$ for i = 1, 2, 3, 4, 5.

$$\chi^2 = 1552.19\,(424)\, p < 0.000.$$

χ^2 Difference Text $\chi^2 = 286.62\, df = 10\, p < 0.001.$

The pattern of mean differences for the closeness to the masses construct revealed that all the mean comparisons were statistically significant. The less than high school group exhibited greater closeness to the masses than the high school group and the greater than high school group. It is noteworthy that the greater than high school group showed not only less closeness to the masses but also less closeness to the elite groups in the African American community.

NOTES

Chapter 2. Conceptualization and Presentation of the Self-Concept

1. For a more detailed presentation of the advantages of structural equation modeling, see Bollen, 1989. While this technique has substantial value, for several questions posed in the first two chapters, other techniques or methodologies are more appropriate.

Chapter 3. Some Issues, Questions, and Problems Surrounding the Black Self-Concept: Self-Esteem

1. Given the nature of the sample (large and representative), it is possible to systematically examine the heterogeneity of the African American population. The focus of the survey pertained to fundamental social, economic, and psychological aspects of African American life. The questionnaire included items on family and friendship relationships, religious attitudes, job and employment history, and individual and group orientations, just to name a few. The techniques and procedures used in questionnaire development, sampling fieldwork, and coding culminated in a excellent and useful data set. For an expanded description and evaluation of this sample and others collected by those in the Program for Research on Black Americans, see Jackson, Tucker, and Bowman, 1982.
2. I assume that the existence of two factors for the Rosenberg self-esteem scale (one composed of the positively worded items and the other composed of the negatively worded items) is indicative of format effects. That is, self-esteem presented in negative terms is different from the effect found when it is stated in positive terms.
3. According to this model, these six items represent the two correlated dimensions of self-esteem, ξ_1 self-esteem (positively worded) and self-esteem, ξ_2 (negatively worded), each with three indicators. The model indicates that all the variables, observed and latent, are measured in deviations from their mean. Several assumptions were made. First, the errors in the factors are assumed to be uncorrelated with the exogenous latent variable, ξ. Second, the measurement errors, $\Theta\delta$, are assumed to be independent from ξ and ϕ, but they might be correlated among themselves. Finally, it is assumed that the observed indicators are multinormally distributed (Bollen & Long, 1992).

Chapter 4. Some Issues, Questions, and Problems Surrounding the Black Self-Concept: Group Identity

1. Much of the analysis and arguments in this chapter appear in "An African American racial belief system and social structural relationships: A test of invariance," *National Journal of Sociology*, 6, 157–186.

Chapter 5. What Identity Is Worth

1. As in my earlier analysis, I used structural equation models (also called co-variance structure analysis, causal modeling, and latent variable analysis) to test hypotheses concerning reliability and stability of a host of constructs, comparisons across groups, and reciprocal causation and the effects of a wide range of exogenous variables. Here I will focus on measurement and substantive issues and emphasize the use of structural equation modeling with respect to panel designs. In analyzing the data, four of the five basic steps were followed: (a) model specification, (b) identification, (c) estimation, (d) testing fit, and (e) respecification. This latter step must be carried out with a new set of data.

   In Figure 5.1, the relationship of self-esteem constructs to the closeness constructs at time 1 is making the causal argument that self-esteem leads to closeness and closeness leads to self-esteem, respectively. That same argument is being made with self-esteem and closeness at time 2 and self-esteem and closeness at time 3 and, of course, self-esteem and closeness at time 3 and self-esteem and closeness at time 4. The relationships are represented by βs. In this model, the following bs represent these relationships $\beta_{4,1}$, $\beta_{3,2}$, $\beta_{6,3}$, $\beta_{5,4}$, $\beta_{8,5}$, and $\beta_{7,6}$. The stability coefficients are also signified by the βs. It is the relationships of each of the self-constructs at time 1 to time 2, time 2 to time 3, and time 3 to time 4. For the self-esteem constructs, this is shown in the model by $\beta_{3,1}$, $\beta_{5,3}$, and $\beta_{7,5}$. The indirect relationships are shown by $\beta_{4,1}$, $\beta_{7,1}$, and $\beta_{7,3}$. For the closeness constructs, this is shown by $\beta_{4,2}$, $\beta_{6,4}$, and $\beta_{8,6}$. The indirect relationships are shown by $\beta_{6,2}$, $\beta_{8,2}$, and $\beta_{8,4}$. The ζs in the model indicate the error variance. The φs signify the correlations of these error variances. This may be interpreted as the amount of the error variance shared in common by these constructs due to omitted variables.

Chapter 6. Another Look From Another Angle

1. Using a subsample of the reported data, an earlier abbreviated version of this paper, entitled "Class, Communication, and the Black Self," appeared in *Research paradigms, television, and social behavior.* Joy Keiko Asamen and Gordon L. Berry (Eds.). Thousand Oaks, CA: Sage, 1998.

2. While the presumed individualist behavior of the European American often contrasts with observed individual behavior, there is a steadfast and widespread endorsement of individualism in its most extreme form.

3. From an empirical viewpoint, the black capitalist class is so small that it is difficult to include them in any survey analysis to assess their degree of cultural and political consciousness. That information is usually derived from participant observations. Boston (1988) estimated that today the black capitalist class consists of only a few thousand people, their paucity being a reflection of decades of a legalized system of racial segregation.

4. While these measures did not permit a distinction to be made between black-oriented media and black media as I have defined these terms, conceptually the distinction may be worthwhile. For example, when exploring some of the more race-conscious conceptions of identity, it is likely that the different kinds of media would have a different impact. Black media may be further clarified by distinguishing between, for example, the more leftist media and the nonleftist media, public affairs news media and nonpublic affairs.

5. Gray used these designations as a conceptual handle to categorize the television images of African Americans.

6. After a thorough item analysis, I removed the following items from my analysis.
   1. I don't necessarily feel like I am also being mistreated in a situation where I see another Black person being mistreated.
   2. Blacks in America should try harder to be American rather than practicing activities that link them up with their African cultural heritage.
   3. It is intelligent for Blacks in America to organize to educate and liberate themselves from white American domination.
   5. I feel little sense of commitment to Black people who are not close friends or relatives.

7. After a thorough item analysis, I removed the following items from my analysis.
   1. I like meeting and getting to know people from ethnic groups other than my own.
   2. I sometimes feel it would be better if different ethnic groups didn't try to mix together.
   3. I am not very clear about the role of my ethnicity in my life.
   4. I often spend time with people from ethnic groups other than my own.
   5. I really have not spent much time trying to learn more about the culture and history of my ethnic group.
   6. I don't try to become friends with people from other ethnic groups.
   7. I am involved in activities with people from other ethnic groups.
   8. I enjoy being around people from ethnic groups other than my own.

Appendix A. The Cross-Sectional Study

1. Although I received a good fit without correlating two sets of errors, we decided to correlate a set of errors in each dimension. For the self-esteem scale, with positive wording, I correlated items "I am a person of worth,"

and "I am a good person." For the self-esteem scale, with negative wording, I correlated items "I can't do anything right," and "I have nothing to be proud of." In the analysis of longitudinal data, the items were summed. The same practice will be followed in the subsequent analyses.

2. The examination of change in self-esteem (and subsequently group identity) over time was done with panel data, again, collected by the Program of Research on Black America (PRBA). The panel study consists of four waves. The first wave began in 1979 and the final wave ended in 1992. Most of the most crucial measures that we used in the earlier studies are contained in this panel study. Thus, I can more thoroughly and systematically examine the direction of the self-concepts and their stability over time.

REFERENCES

Adamss, B. D. (1978). Inferiorization and self-esteem. *Social Psychology, 41*, 47–53.

Adoni, H., & Mane, S. (1984). Media and the social construction of reality: Toward an integration of theory and research. *Communication Research, 11*, 323–340.

African Heritage Study Bible. (1993). Nashville: The James C. Winston Publishing Co.

Agassiz, L. (1850). The diversity of origin of the human races. *Christian Examiner, 49*, 110–145.

Akbar, N. (1984). *Chains and images of psychological slavery*. Jersey City, NJ: New Mind Productions.

Akbar, N. (1985). *The community of self*. Tallahassee, FL: Mind Productions & Associates.

Akbar, N. (1991a). The evolution of human psychology for African Americans. In R. Jones (Ed.), *Black psychology* (3rd ed., pp. 99–123). Berkeley, CA: Cobb & Henry Publishers.

Akbar, N. (1991b). Mental disorders among African Americans. In R. Jones (Ed.), *Black psychology* (3rd ed., pp. 339–352). Berkeley, CA: Cobb & Henry Publishers.

Akbar, N. (1995). *Natural psychology and human transformation*. Tallahassee, FL: Mind Productions & Associates.

Akbar, N. (1996). *Breaking the chains of psychological slavery*. Tallahassee, FL: Mind Productions & Associates.

Allen, R. L., Dawson, M. C., & Brown, R. E. (1989). A schema-based approach to modeling an African-American racial belief system. *American Political Science Review, 83*, 421–441.

Allen, R. L., & Hatchett, S. (1986). The media and social reality effects: Self and system orientations of Blacks. *Communication Research, 13*, 97–123.

Allen, R. L., Thornton, M., & Watkins, S. C. (1992). An African American racial belief system and social structural relationships: A test of invariance. *National Journal of Sociology, 6*, 157–186.

Allport, G. W. (1937). *Personality: A psychological interpretation*. New York: Holt.

Allport, G. W. (1954). *The nature of prejudice*. Cambridge, MA: Addison-Wesley.

Amin, S. (1989). *Eurocentrism*. New York: Monthly Review.

Aptheker, H. (1944). *American Negro slave revolts*. New York: International Publishers.

Azibo, D. A. (1989). Pitfalls and ameliorative strategies in African personality research. *Journal of Black Studies, 19*, 306–319.

203

Bagozzi, R. P. (1994). Measurement in marketing research: Basic principles of questionnaire design. In R. P. Bagozzi (Ed.), *Principles of marketing research* (pp. 1–49). Cambridge, MA: Blackwell.

Bagozzi, R. P., & Baumgartner, H. (1994). The evaluation of structural equation models and hypothesis testing. In R. P. Bagozzi (Ed.), *Principles of marketing research* (pp. 386–421). Cambridge, MA: Basil Blackwell.

Bagozzi, R. P., & Yi, Y. (1989). On the evaluation of structural equation models. *Journal of the Academy of Marketing Science, 16,* 74–94.

Baldwin, J. A. (1979). Theory and research concerning the notion of black self-hatred: A review and reinterpretation. *Journal of Black Psychology, 5,* 51–77.

Baldwin, J. A. (1981). Notes on an Africentric theory of black personality. *Western Journal of Black Studies, 5,* 172–179.

Baldwin, J. A., & Bell, Y. (1985). Psychology of Black Americans. *Western Journal of Black Studies, 9,* 61–68.

Baldwin, J. A., Brown, R., & Hopkins, R. (1991). The black self-hatred paradigm revisited: An Africentric analysis. In R. Jones (Ed.), *Black psychology* (3rd ed., pp. 141–166). Berkeley, CA: Cobb & Henry Publishers.

Banaji, M. R., & Prentice, D. A. (1994). The self in social contexts. *Annual Review of Psychology, 45,* 297–332.

Baraka, A. (1967). *Black music.* New York: Morrow.

Baraka, A. (1991). The changing same (r & b and new black music). In A. Baraka (Ed.), *The LeRoi Jones/Amiri Baraka reader* (pp. 186–209). New York: Thunder's Mouth.

Baraka, A., & Baraka, A. (1987). *The music.* New York: Morrow.

Barlow, W. (1993). Cashing in: 1900–1939. In J. L. Dates & W. Barlow (Eds.), *Split image: African Americans in the mass media* (pp. 25–55). Washington, DC: Howard University Press.

Bejar, I. (1980). Biased assessment of program impact due to psychometric artifacts. *Psychological Bulletin, 87,* 513–524.

Bell, D. (1987). *Faces at the bottom of the well.* New York: Basic Books.

Ben-Jochannan, Y. (1988). *Africa: Mother of western civilization.* Baltimore: Black Classic Press.

Ben-Jochannan, Y. (1991). *African origins of the major western religions.* Baltimore: Black Classic Press.

Bennett, L. (1962). *Before the Mayflower: A history of the Negro in America 1619–1964.* Baltimore: Pelican Books.

Bentler, P. M., & Bonett, D. G. (1980). Significance tests and goodness of fit in the analysis of covariance structures. *Psychological Bulletin, 88,* 588–606.

Bernal, M. (1991). *Black Athena: The denial of the Afro-Asiatic roots of Greece.* Ithaca, NY: Cornell University Press.

Black issues in higher education. (1987). Historian blamed for perpetuating bias—outgoing president challenges colleagues. *Black Issues in Higher Education, 4,* 2.

Blassingame, J. (1972). *The slave community.* New York: Oxford University Press.

Bogle, D. (1994). *Toms, coons, mulattoes, mammies, & bucks: An interpretive history of Black American films.* New York: Continuum.

Bollen, K. A. (1989). *Structural equations with latent variables.* New York: John Wiley & Sons.

Bollen, K. A., & Long, J. S. (1992). Tests for structural equation models: Introduction. *Sociological Methods & Research, 2,* 123–131.

Bollen, K. A., & Paxton, P. (1998). Detection and determinants of bias in subjective measures. *American Sociological Review, 63,* 465–478.

Boskin, J. (1986). *Sambo: The rise & demise of an American jester.* New York: Oxford University Press.

Boston, T. D. (1988). *Race, class & conservatism.* Boston: Unwin Hyman.

Boxill, B. R. (1992). The underclass and the race/class issue. In B. E. Lawson (Ed.), *The underclass question* (pp. 19–32). Philadelphia: Temple University Press.

Broman, C. L., Neighbors, H. W., & Jackson, J. S. (1988). Racial group identification among black adults. *Social Forces, 67,* 146–158.

Brown, S. A. (1968). Negro characters as seen by white authors. In J. A. Emanuel & T. L. Gross (Eds.), *Dark symphony* (pp. 139–171). New York: The Free Press.

Brown, W. O. (1931). The nature of race consciousness. *Social Forces, 10,* 90–97.

Byrnes, B. M., Shavelson, R. J., & Muthen, B. (1989). Testing for the equivalence of factor covariance and mean structures: The issues of partial measurement invariance. *Psychological Bulletin, 3,* 456–466.

Carmines, E. G., & McIver, J. P. (1981). Analyzing models with observed variables: Analysis of covariance structures. In G. W. Bohrnstedt & E. F. Borgatta (Eds.), *Social measurement* (pp. 65–115). Newbury Park, CA: Sage.

Cartwright, D. (1950). Emotional dimensions of group life. In M. L. Raymert (Ed.), *Feelings and emotions* (pp. 439–447). New York: McGraw-Hill.

Chapple, S., & Garofola, R. (1977). *Rock 'n roll is here to stay: The history and the politics of the music industry.* Chicago: Nelson-Hall.

Chinweizu. (1987). *Decolonising the African mind.* London: Sundoor.

Chomsky, H. (1989). *Necessary illusions.* Boston: South End Press.

Clark, K. B. (1965). *Dark ghetto: Dilemmas of social power.* New York: Harper and Row.

Clark, K. B., & Clark, M. P. (1947). Racial identification and preference in Negro children. In T. M. Newcomb & E. L. Hartley (Eds.), *Readings in social psychology* (pp. 169–178). New York: Holt.

Clark, K., & Clark, M. (1980). What do Blacks think of themselves. *Ebony,* November 1980, pp. 176–182.

Clarke, J. H. (1970). *Introduction to African civilization.* Secaucus, NJ: The Citadel Press.

Clarke, J. H. (1991). *Notes for an African world revolution: Africans at the crossroads.* Trenton, NJ: African World Press.

Clarke, J. H. (1994). *Who betrayed the African world revolution? and other speeches.* Chicago: Third World Press.

Cliff, N. (1980). Some cautions concerning the application of causal modeling methods. Paper presented at a National Institute for Justice Workshop on Research Methodology and Criminal Justice Program Evaluation, Baltimore, March 1980.

Cone, J. H. (1986). *Speaking the truth: Ecumenism, liberation and Black Theology.* Grand Rapids, MI: Eerdmans.

Cone, J. H. (1991). *The spirituals and the blues: An interpretation.* Maryknoll, NY: Orbis Books.

Cooley, C. (1902). *Human nature and the social order.* New York: Scribner.

Cripps, T. (1993). Film. In J. L. Dates & W. Barlow (Eds.). *Split image: African Americans in the mass media* (2nd ed., pp. 131–185). Washington, DC: Howard University Press.

Crocker, J., & Blanton, H. (1999). Social inequality and self-esteem: The moderating effects of social comparison, legitimacy, and contingencies of self-esteem. In T. R. Tyler, R. M. Kramer, & O. P. John (Eds.), *The psychology of the social self* (pp. 171–191). Mahwah, NJ: Lawrence Erlbaum.

Crocker, J., & Luhtanen, R. (1990). Collective self-esteem and ingroup bias. *Journal of Personality and Social Psychology, 58,* 60–67.

Crocker, J., & Major, B. (1989). Social stigma and self-esteem: The self-protective properties of stigma. *Psychological Review, 94,* 608–630.

Cross, W. E. (1985). Black identity: Rediscovering the distinction between personal identity and reference group orientation. In M. B. Spencer, G. K. Brookins, & W. R. Allen (Eds.), *Beginnings: The social and affective development of Black children* (pp. 155–171). New York: Lawrence Erlbaum.

Cross, W. E. (1988). The everyday functions of African identity. In J. K. Swim & C. Stranger (Eds.), *Prejudice: The target's perspective* (pp. 267–279). San Diego: Academic Press.

Cross, W. E. (1991). *Shades of black: Diversity in African-American identity.* Philadelphia: Temple University Press.

Cruse, H. (1972). *The crisis of the Negro intellectual.* New York: Quill.

Danziger, S., & Gottschalk, P. (1993). *Uneven tides: Rising inequality in America.* Cambridge, MA: Harvard University Press.

Danziger, S., & Gottschalk, P. (1995). *American unequal.* Cambridge, MA: Harvard University Press.

Dates, J. L. (1990a). Print news. In J. L. Dates & W. Barlow (Eds.), *Split image: African Americans in the mass media* (pp. 369–418). Washington, DC: Howard University Press.

Dates, J. L. (1990b). Public television news. In J. L. Dates & W. Barlow (Eds.), *Split image: African Americans in the mass media* (pp. 303–340). Washington, DC: Howard University Press.

Dates, J. L. (1990c). Commercial television. In J. L. Dates & W. Barlow (Eds.), *Split image: African Americans in the mass media* (pp. 253—302). Washington, DC: Howard University Press.

Dates, J. L., & Barlow, W. (1993). Introduction: A war of images. In J. L. Dates & W. Barlow (Eds.), *Split image: African Americans in the mass media* (2nd ed., pp. 1–21). Washington, DC: Howard University Press.

Davidson, B. (1991). The ancient world and Africa: Whose roots? In I. Van

Sertima (Ed.), *Egypt revisited* (pp. 39–54). New Brunswick, NJ: Transaction Publishers.

Dawson, M. C. (1994). *Behind the mule: Race and class in African-American politics.* Princeton, NJ: Princeton University Press.

Dawson, M. C., Brown, R. E., & Allen, R. L. (1990). Racial belief systems, religious guidance, and African American political participation. *National Review of Political Science, 2,* 22–44.

De Uriarte, M. L. (1994). Exploring (and exploding) the U.S. media prism. *Media Studies Journal, 8,* 163–175.

Demo, D. H., & Hughes, M. (1990). Socialization and racial identity among Black Americans. *Social Psychology Quarterly, 53,* 364–374.

Diop, C. A. (1974). *The African origin of civilization: Myth or reality.* New York: Lawrence Hill.

Diop, C. A. (1991). *Civilization or barbarism.* New York: Lawrence Hill.

Dixon, V. J. (1977). African-oriented and European-oriented worldviews: Research methodologies and economics. *Review of Black Political Economy, 7,* 119–156.

Douglass, F. (1857). West Indian Emancipation Speech, August 1857.

Drake, St. C. (1980). Anthropology and the black experience. *Black Scholar, 11,* 2–31.

Drake, St. C. (1987). *Black folk here and there* (Vol. 1). Los Angeles: University of California at Los Angeles.

Drake, St. C. (1990). *Black folk here and there* (Vol. 2). Los Angeles: University of California at Los Angeles.

Drake, St. C., & Cayton, H. (1945). *Black metropolis.* New York: Schocken.

Drasgow, F., & Kanfer, R. (1985). Equivalence of psychological measurement in heterogenous population. *Journal of Applied Psychology, 70,* 662–680.

DuBois, W. E. B. (1903). *The souls of black folk.* Chicago: A. C. McClurg.

DuBois, W. E. B. (1915). The African roots of war. *Atlantic Monthly, 115,* 707–714.

DuBois, W. E. B. (1935). *Black reconstruction in America 1860–1880.* New York: Atheneum.

DuBois, W. E. B. (1964). *The souls of black folk.* New York: Fawcett.

Dyson, M. (1989). Bill Cosby and the politics of race. *Z. Magazine,* September, 26–30.

Ellison, C. G. (1991). Identification and separatism: Religious involvement and racial orientations among Black Americans. *Sociological Quarterly, 32,* 477–494.

Entman, R. M. (1992). Blacks in the news: Television, modern racism, and cultural change. *Journalism Quarterly, 69,* 341–361.

Entman, R. M. (1994). African Americans according to TV news. *Media Studies Journal, 8,* 29–38.

Fanon, F. (1964). *The wretched of the earth.* New York: Grove Press.

Festinger, L. (1954). A theory of social comparison processes. *Human Relations, 7,* 71–82.

Finkenstaedt, R. L. (1994). *Face to face: Blacks in America: White perceptions and black realities.* New York: William Morrow.

Fischer, C. S., Hout, M., Jankowski, M. S., Lucas, S. R., Swidler, A., & Voss, K. (1996). *Inequality by design: Cracking the bell curve myth.* Princeton, NJ: Princeton University Press.

Franklin, R. S. (1991). *Shadows of race and class.* Minneapolis: University of Minnesota Press.

Frazier, E. F. (1974). *The Negro church in America.* New York: Schocken.

Fredrickson, G. M. (1971). *The black image in the white mind: The debate on Afro-American character and destiny, 1817–1914.* Hanover, NH: Wesleyan University Press.

Fredrickson, G. M. (1981). *White supremacy: A comparative study in American & South African history.* New York: Oxford University Press.

Gaines, S. O., & Reed, E. S. (1994). Two social psychologies of prejudice: Gordon W. Allport, W. E. B. DuBois and the legacy of Booker T. Washington. *Journal of Black Psychology, 20,* 8–28.

Gaines, S. O., & Reed, E. S. (1995). Prejudice: From Allport to DuBois. *American Psychologist, 50,* 96–103.

Gandy, O. H. (1994). From bad to worse—The media framing of race and risk. *Media Studies Journal, 8,* 39–48.

Garofalo, R. (1993). Crossing over: 1939–1992. Cashing in: 1900–1939. In J. L. Dates & W. Barlow (Eds.), *Split image: African Americans in the mass media* (pp. 57–127). Washington, DC: Howard University Press.

Gecas, V. (1982). The self-concept. *Annual Review of Sociology, 8,* 1–33.

Gecas, V., & Schwalbe, M. L. (1983). Beyond the looking-glass self: Social structure and efficacy based self-esteem. *Social Psychology Quarterly, 46,* 77–88.

Gerbner, G. (1990). Epilogue: Advancing on the path of righteousness (maybe). In N. Signorielli & M. Morgan (Eds.), *Cultivation analysis: New directions in media effects research* (pp. 249–262). Newbury Park, CA: Sage.

Gerbner, G., Gross, L., Morgan, M., & Signorielli, N. (1980). The "mainstreaming" of America: Violence profile no. 11. *Journal of Communication, 30,* 10–29.

Gerbner, G., Gross, L., Morgan, M., & Signorielli, N. (1982). Charting the mainstream: Television's contributions to political orientations. *Journal of Communication, 32,* 100–127.

Gomes, R. C., & Williams, L. F. (1990). Race and crime: The role of the media in perpetuating racism and classism in America. *Urban League Review, 14,* 57–69.

Gordon, V. (1977). *The self-concept of Black Americans.* Washington, DC: University Press of America.

Gossett, T. F. (1965). *Race: The history of an idea in America.* New York: Schocken Press.

Gould, S. J. (1977). *Ever since Darwin.* New York: W. W. Norton.

Gould, S. J. (1981). *The mismeasure of man.* New York: W. W. Norton.

Gould, S. J. (1993). American polygeny and craniometry before Darwin: Blacks and Indians as separate, inferior species. In S. Harding (Ed.), *The racial economy of science: Toward a democratic future* (pp. 84–115). Bloomington: Indiana University Press.

Gould, S. J. (1995). Mismeasure by any measure. In R. Jacoby & N. Glauberman (Eds.), *The bell curve debate: History, documents, opinions* (pp. 3–13). New York: Times Books.

Gray, H. (1995). *Watching race: Television and the struggle for "blackness."* Minneapolis: University of Minnesota Press.

Grier, W. H., & Cobbs, P. C. (1968). *Black rage.* New York: Basic Books.

Gurin, P., & Epps, E. (1975). *Black consciousness, identity, and achievement: A study of students in historically black colleges.* New York: John Wiley & Sons.

Gurin, P., Miller, A. H., & Gurin, G. (1980). Stratum identification and consciousness. *Social Psychology Quarterly, 43,* 30–47.

Harding, S. (1993). Introduction: Eurocentric scientific illiteracy—A challenge for the world community. In S. Harding (Ed.), *The racial economy of science: Toward a democratic future* (pp. 1–22). Bloomington: Indiana University Press.

Harris, J. E. (1987). *Africans and their history.* (rev. ed). New York: Mentro Book.

Hartman, S. V. (1997). *Scenes of subjection: Terror, slavery, and self-making in nineteenth-century America.* New York: Oxford University Press.

Hegel, G. W. F. (1901). *The philosophy of history* (2nd ed.). St. Louis: St. Louis Publishing Co.

Herkovits, M. J. (1958). *The myth of the Negro past.* Boston: Beacon Press.

Herman, E. S. (1997). Fog watch: Words, tricks and propaganda. *Z Magazine, 10,* 52–56.

Herman, E. S., & Chomsky, N. (1989). *Manufacturing consent: The political economy of the mass media.* New York: Pantheon.

Hilliard, A. G. (1995). *The maroon within us: Selected essays on African American community socialization.* Baltimore: Black Classic Press.

Hodge-Edelin, R. (1990). Curriculum and cultural identity. In A. G. Hilliard, L. Payton-Stewart, & L. O. Williams (Eds.), *Infusion of African and African American content in the school curriculum* (pp. 37–45). Morristown, NJ: Aaron Press.

Hoelter, J. W. (1983). The analysis of covariance structures: Goodness of fit indices. *Sociological Methods and Research, 11,* 325–344.

Holloway, J. E. (1990). The origins of African-American culture. In J. E. Holloway (Ed.), *Africanisms in American culture* (pp. 1–18). Bloomington: Indiana University Press.

Holt, T. C. (1990). The political use of alienation: W.E.B. DuBois on politics, race, and culture, 1903–1940. *American Quarterly, 42,* 301–323.

Holt, T. C. (1995). Marking: Race, race-making, and the writing of history. *American Historical Review, 100,* 1–20.

Hoyle, R. H. (1995). Structural equation modeling approach. In R. H. Hoyle (Ed.), *Structural equation modeling: Concepts, issues, and applications* (pp. 1–15). Thousand Oaks, CA: Sage.

Hughes, M., & Demo, D. H. (1989). Self-perceptions of Black Americans: Self-esteem and personal efficacy. *American Journal of Sociology, 95,* 132–159.

Hutchinson, E. O. (1994). *The assasination of the black male image.* Los Angeles: Middle Passage Press.

Ignatiev, N., & Garvey, J. (Eds.) (1996). *Race traitor.* New York: Routledge.

Jackson, J. G. (1970). *Introduction to African civilization.* Secaucus, NJ: The Citadel Press.

Jackson, J. G. (1972). *Man, God and Civilization.* Secaucas, NJ, Citadel.

Jackson, J. G. (1985). *Christianity before Christ.* Austin, TX: American Atheist Press.

Jackson, J. S., & Gurin, G. (1987). *National Survey of Black Americans, 1978–80.* Ann Arbor, MI: Inter-University Consortium for Political and Social Research, Institute for Social Research, University of Michigan.

Jackson, J. S., McCullough, W. R., Gurin, G., & Broman, C. L. (1981). Group identity development within black families. In H. P. McAdoo (Ed.), *Black families* (pp. 253–263). Newbury Park, CA: Sage.

Jackson, J. S., Tucker, M. B., & Bowman, P. J. (1982). Conceptual and methodological problems in survey research on Black Americans. In W. T. Liu (Ed.), *Methodological problems in minority research* (pp. 11–39). Occasional Paper No. 7, Pacific/Asian Mental Health Research Center.

Jamieson, K. (1990). Race, crime and political communication. Transcript of proceedings of Conference on Race, the Press, and Politics, Joan Shorenstein Barone Center on the Press, Politics and Public Policy, John F. Kennedy School of Government, Harvard University, Cambridge, MA, May 5, 1990.

Jenkins, A. H. (1982). *The psychology of the Afro-American: A humanistic approach.* New York: Pergamon Press.

Jhally, S., & Lewis, J. (1992). *Enlightened racism: The Bill Cosby Show, audiences, and the myth of the American Dream.* Boulder, CO: Westview.

Jones, M. (1992). The black underclass as systemic phenomenon. In J. Jennings (Ed.), *Race politics and economic development* (pp. 53–65). New York: Verso.

Joreskog, K. G., & Sorbom, D. (1984). *LISREL VI: Analysis of linear structural relationships by the method of maximum likelihood* (3rd ed.). Mooresville, IN: Scientific Software.

Joreskog, K. G., & Sorbom, D. (1988). *LISREL 7: A guide to the program and applications* (2nd ed.). Chicago: SPSS, Inc.

Joreskog, K. G., & Sorbom, D. (1989). *LISREL7: A guide to the program and applications.* Chicago: SPSS, Inc.

Kambon, K. K. K. (1992). *The African personality in America: An African-centered framework.* Tallahassee, FL: Nubian Nation Publication.

Kamin, L. J. (1974). *The science and politics of I.Q.* Potomac, MD: Erlbaum.

Kaplan, A. (1964). *The conduct of inquiry.* Scranton, PA: Chandler Publishing Company.

Kardiner, A., & Ovesey, L. (1951). *The mark of oppression.* New York: Norton.

Karenga, M. (1982). Society, culture and the problem of self-consciousness: A Kawaida analysis. In L. Harris (Ed.), *Philosophy born of struggle: Anthology of Afro-American philosophy from 1917* (pp. 212–228). Dubuque, IA: Kendall/Hunt.

Karenga, M. (1993). *Introduction to black studies.* Los Angeles: University of Sankore Press.

Kern-Foxworth, M. (1994). *Aunt Jemima, Uncle Ben, and Rastus: Blacks in advertising, yesterday, today, and tomorrow.* Westport, CT: Praeger.

Kerner Commission. (1968). *Report of the National Advisory Commission on Civil Disorders.* New York: Bantam Books.

Kitayama, S., & Markus, H. (In press). Construal of the self as a cultural frame: Implications for internationalizing psychology. In J. D'Arms, R. G. Hasties, S. E. Hoelscher, & H. K. Jacobson, (Eds.), *Becoming more international and global: Challenges for American higher education.*

Kitayama, S., Markus, H. R., & Matsumoto, H. (1997). Individual and collective processes in the construction of the self: Self-enhancement in the United States and self-criticism in Japan. *Journal of Personality and Social Psychology, 72,* 1245–1267.

Kohn, M. L., & Schooler, C. (1969). Class, occupation and orientation. *American Sociological Review, 34,* 659–678.

Kohn, M. L., & Schooler, C. (1983). *Work and personality: An inquiry into the impact of social stratification.* Norwood, NJ: Ablex.

Kovel, J. (1970). *White racism: A psychohistory.* New York: Pantheon.

Krings, M., Stone, A., Schmitz, R. W., Krainitzki, H., Stoneking, M., & Paabo, S. (1997). Neanderthal DNA sequences and the origin of modern humans. *Cell, 90,* 19–30.

Kuhnel, L. B. (1988). Testing MANOVA designs with LISREL. *Sociological Methods & Research, 16,* 504–523.

Landry, B. (1987). *The new black middle class.* Berkeley: University of California Press.

Latif, S. A., & Latif, N. (1994). *Slavery: The African American psychic trauma.* Chicago: Latif Communications Group.

Lawson, B. E. (1992). Uplifting the race: Middle class Blacks and the truly disadvantaged. Marooned in America: Black urban youth culture and social pathology. In B. E. Lawson (Ed.), *The underclass question* (pp. 90–113). Philadelphia: Temple University Press.

Lewin, K. (1948). *Resolving social conflicts.* New York: Harper.

Lewis, D. L. (1993). *W. E. B. DuBois: Biography of a race.* New York: Henry Holt.

Lewontin, R. C. (1992). *Biology as ideology.* New York: Harper Perennial.

Lewontin, R. C., Rose, S., &. Kamin, L. J. (1984). *Not in our genes.* New York: Pantheon Books.

Lewontin, R. C., Rose, S., & Kamin L. J. (1993). I.Q.: The rank ordering of the world. In S. Harding (Ed.). *The racial economy of science: Toward a democratic future* (pp. 142–160). Bloomington: Indiana University Press.

Liang, J., Tran, T. V., Krause, N., & Markides, K. S. (1989). Generational differences in the structure of the CES-D scale in Mexican Americans. *Journal of Gerontology, 44,* 110–120.

Lipsitz, G. (1998). *The possessive investment in whiteness: How white people profit from identity politics.* Philadelphia: Temple University Press.

Lott, T. L. (1992). Marooned in America: Black urban youth culture and social pathology. In B. E. Lawson (Ed.), *The underclass question* (pp. 70–89). Philadelphia: Temple University Press.

Lusane, C. (1991). *Pipe dream blues: Racism and the war on drugs.* Boston: South End Press.

MacDonald, J. F. (1992). *Blacks and white TV: African Americans in television since 1948* (2nd ed.). Chicago: Nelson-Hall.

Major, B. Sciacchitano, A. M., & Crocker, J. (1993). In-group versus out-group comparisons and self-esteem. *Personality and Social Psychology Bulletin, 19,* 711–721.

Marayuma, G., & McGarvey, B. (1980). Evaluating causal models: An application of maximum likelihood analysis of structural equations. *Psychological Bulletin, 87,* 502–512.

Markus, H. (1977). Self-schemas and processing information about the self. *Journal of Personality and Social Psychology, 35,* 63–78.

Markus, H. R., & Kitayama, S. (1991). Culture and the self: Implications for cognition, emotion and motivation. *Psychological Review, 98,* 224–253.

Markus, H. R., & Kitayama, S. (1994). A collective fear of the collective: Implications for selves and theories of selves. *Personality and Social Psychology Bulletin, 20,* 568–579.

Martin, J. N., Krizek, R. L., Nakayama, T. L., & Bradford, L. (1999). What do white people want to be called? In T. K. Nakayama & J. N. Martin (Eds.), *Whiteness: The communication of social identity* (pp. 27–50). Thousand Oaks, CA: Sage.

Massey, D. S., & Denton, N. A. (1993). *American apartheid: Segregation and the making of the underclass.* Cambridge, MA: Harvard University Press.

Mead, G. H. (1934). *Mind, self and society.* Chicago: University of Chicago Press.

Merton, R. K. (1948). The self-fulfilling prophecy. *Antioch Review, 8,* 193–210.

Meyers, L. J. (1998). The Afrocentric perspective: Ideology and method. In J. D. Hamlet (Ed.), *Afrocentric visions* (pp. 3–14). Thousand Oaks, CA: Sage.

Mincy, R. B. (1995). The underclass: Concept, controversy, and evidence. In S. Danziger, G. D. Sandefur, & D. H. Weinberg (Eds.), *Confronting poverty: Prescriptions for change.* New York: Russell Sage Foundation.

Morris, A. D. (1992). Political consciousness and collective action. A. Morris & C. M. Mueller (Eds.), *Frontiers in social movement theory* (pp. 351–373). New Haven, CT: Yale University Press.

Mruk, C. (1995). *Self-esteem: Research, theory, and practice.* New York: Springer.

Myers, L. J. (1993). *Understanding an Afrocentric worldview: Introduction to an optimal psychology*: Dubuque, IA: Kendall/Hunt.

Myers, L. J. (1998). The deep structure of culture: Relevance of traditional African culture in contemporary life. In J. D. Hamlet (Ed.), *Afrocentric vision* (pp. 3–14). Thousand Oaks, CA: Sage.

National Academy of Sciences (1993). Methods and values in science. In S. Harding (Ed.), *The racial economy of science: Toward a democratic future* (pp. 341–343). Bloomington: University of Indiana Press.

National Research Council (1989). *A common destiny: Blacks and American society.* Washington, DC: National Academy Press.

Neal, L. (1968). And shine swam on. In L. Jones & L. Neal (Eds.), *Black fire: An anthology of Afro-American writing* (pp. 637–656). New York: William Morrow.

Newby, I. A. (1969). *Challenge to the court. Social scientists and the defense of segregation, 1954–1966.* Baton Rouge: Louisiana State University Press.

Nkrumah, K. (1964). *Consciencism: Philosophy and ideology of decolonization.* New York: Monthly Review.

Nobles, W. W. (1973). Psychological research and the black self-concept: A critical review. *Journal of Social Issues, 29,* 11–31.

Nobles, W. W. (1986). *African psychology: Toward its reclamation, reascension and revitalization.* Oakland, CA: Black Family Institute Publication.

Nobles, W. W. (1989). Pyschological nigrescence: An Afrocentric review. *The Counseling Psychologist, 17,* 253–257.

Nobles, W. W. (1991a). Extended self: Rethinking the so-called Negro self-concept. In R. Jones (Ed.), *Black psychology* (3rd ed., pp. 295–302). Berkeley, CA: Cobb & Henry Publishers.

Nobles, W. W. (1991b). African philosophy: Foundations of black psychology. In R. Jones (Ed.), *Black psychology* (3rd ed., pp. 47–63). Berkeley, CA: Cobb & Henry Publishers.

Oliver, M. B. (1994). Portrayals of crime, race, and aggression in "reality-based" police shows: A content analysis. *Journal of Broadcasting & Electronic Media, 38,* 179–192.

Oliver, M. L., & Shapiro, T. M. (1995). *Black wealth/white wealth: New perspective on racial inequality.* New York: Routledge.

Oliver, M. L., & Shapiro, T. M. (1998). The racial asset gap. In L. Daniels (Ed.), *The state of Black America, 1998* (pp. 15–35). National Urban League.

Oyserman, D., Gant, L., & Ager, J. (1995). A socially contextualized model of African American identity: Possible selves and school persistence. *Journal of Personality and Social Psychology, 69,* 1216–1235.

Oyserman, D., & Markus, H. R. (1993). The sociocultural self. In J. Suls (Ed.), *Perspectives on the self,* volume 4: *The self in social perspective.* Hillsdale, NJ: Erlbaum.

Paris, P. (1995). *The spirituality of African peoples.* Minneapolis: Fortress Press.

Pettigrew, T. F. (1978). Placing Adam's argument in a broader perspective: Comment on the Adam paper. *Social psychology, 41,* 58–61.

Phinney, J. (1990). Ethnic identity in adolescents and adults; Review of research. *Psychological Bulletin, 108,* 499–514.

Phinney, J. S. (1991). Ethnic identity and self-esteem: A review and integration. *Hispanic Journal of Behavioral Science, 13,* 193–208.

Phinney, J. S., & Chivira, V. (1992). Ethnic identity and self-esteem: An exploratory longitudinal study. *Journal of Adolescence, 15,* 271–281.

Phinney, J. S., & Onwughalu, M. (1996). Racial identity and perception of American ideals among African American and African students in the United States. *International Journal of Intercultural Relations, 20,* 127–140.

Pierce, C. M. (1980). Social trace contaminants: Subtle indicators of racism in TV. In B. Withey & R. P. Abeles (Eds.), *Television and social behavior: Beyond violence and children* (pp. 249–257). Hillsdale, NJ: Erlbaum.

Pitts, J. P. (1974). The study of race consciousness: Comments on new directions. *American Journal of Sociology, 80,* 665–687.

Porter, J. R., & Washington, R. E. (1979). Black identity and self-esteem: A review of studies of the black self-concept, 1968–1978. *Annual Review of Sociology, 5,* 53–74.

Porter, J. R., & Washington, R. E. (1989). Developments in research on black identity and self-esteem: 1979–88. *Revue Internationale de Psychologie Sociale, 2,* 341–353.

Porter, J. R., & Washington, R. E. (1993). Minority identity and self-esteem. *Annual Review of Sociology, 19,* 139–161.

Proshansky, H., & Newton, P. (1968). The nature and meaning of Negro self-identity. In M. Deutsch, I. Katz, & A. R. Jensen (Eds.), *Social class, race, and psychological development* (pp. 178–218). New York: Holt, Rinehart and Winston.

Rainwater, L. (1966). Crucible of identity: The Negro lower-class family. *Daedalus, 95,* 172–216.

Ramseur, H. P. (1991). Psychologically healthy black adults. In R. Jones (Ed.), *Black psychology* (3rd ed., pp. 353—378). Berkeley, CA: Cobb & Henry Publishers.

Reed, A. L., Jr. (1998). *W. B. DuBois and American political thought.* New York: Oxford University Press.

Reeves, J., & Campbell, R. (1994). *Cracked coverage: Television news, the anticocaine crusade, and the Reagan legacy.* Durham, NC: Duke University Press.

Riggs, M. (1991a). *Ethnic notions (film).* San Francisco: California Newsreel.

Riggs, M. (1991b). *Color adjustment (film).* San Francisco: California Newsreel.

Robinson, C. J. (1983). *Black Marxism.* London: Zed Press.

Rodney, W. (1972). *How Europe underdeveloped Africa.* Washington, DC: Howard University Press.

Rosenberg, M. (1979). *Conceiving the self.* New York: Basic Books.

Rosenberg, M. (1981). The self-concept: Social product and social force. In M. Rosenberg & R. H. Turner (Eds.), *Social psychology: Sociological perspectives* (pp. 593–624). New York: Basic Books.

Rosenberg, M. (1985a). Self-concept and psychological well-being in adolescence. In R. L. Leahy (Ed.), *The development of the self* (pp. 205–246). Orlando: Academic Press.

Rosenberg, M. (1985b). The self-concept: Social product and social force. In M. Rosenberg & R. H. Turner (Eds.), *Social psychology: Sociological perspectives* (pp. 593–624). New York: Basic Books.

Rosenberg, M. (1986). *Conceiving the self.* Reprint Edition. Melbourne, FL: Krieger.

Rosenberg, M. (1989). Self-concept research: A historical overview. *Social Forces, 68,* 34–44.

Rosenberg, M., & Pearlin, L. (1978). Social class and self-esteem among children and adults. *American Journal of Sociology, 84,* 53–77.

Rosenberg, M., Schooler, C., & Schoenbach, C. (1989). Self-esteem and adolescent problems: Modeling reciprocal effects. *American Sociological Review, 54,* 1004–1018.

Rosenberg, M., Schooler, C., Schoenbach, C., & Rosenberg, F. (1995). Global self-esteem and specific self-esteem: Different concepts, different outcomes. *American Sociological Review, 60,* 141–156.

Rosenberg, M., & Simmons, R. G. (1971). Black and white self-esteem: The urban school child. Arnold and Caroline Rose monograph series in ecology. Washington, DC: American Sociological Association.

Semmes, C. E. (1992). *Cultural hegemony and African American development.* Westport, CT: Praeger.

Shweder, R. A., & Bourne, E. J. (1982). Does the concept of the person vary cross-culturally? In R. A. Shweder & R. A. LeVine (Eds.), *Culture theory: Essays on mind, self, and emotion* (pp. 158–199). Cambridge: Cambridge University Press.

Sinkler, G. (1972). *The racial attitudes of American presidents from Abraham Lincoln to Theodore Roosevelt.* New York: Doubleday Anchor Books.

Smith, R. C. (1995). *Racism in the post-civil rights era: Now you see it, now you don't.* Albany: State University of New York Press.

Steinberg, S. (1995). *Turning back: The retreat from racial justice in American thought and policy.* Boston: Beacon Press.

Sundquist, E. J. (1993). *To wake the nations: Race in the making of American literature.* London: Harvard University Press.

Tajfel, H. (1978). *Differentiation between social groups: Studies in the social psychology of intergroup relations.* New York: Academic Press.

Tajfel, H. (1981). *Human groups and social categories: Studies in social psychology.* Cambridge: Cambridge University Press.

Tajfel, H. (1982). Social psychology of intergroup relations. *Annual Review of Psychology, 33,* 1–39.

Tajfel, H. (1986). The social identity theory of intergroup behavior. In S. Worchel & W. Austion (Eds.), *Psychology of intergroup relations* (2nd ed., pp. 7–24). Chicago: Nelson-Hall.

Tajfel, H., & Turner, J. (1979). An integrative theory of intergroup conflict. In W. G. Austin & S. Worchel (Eds.), *The social psychology of intergroup relations* (pp. 33–47). Monterey, CA: Brooks/Cole.

Tajfel, H., & Turner, J. (1986). The social identity theory of intergroup behavior. In S. Worchel & W. G. Austin (Eds.), *Psychology of intergroup relations* (2nd ed., pp. 7–24). Chicago: Nelson-Hall.

Taylor, D. M., & Moghaddam, F. M. (1994). *Theories of intergroup relations: International social psychological perspectives* (2nd ed.). Westport, CT: Praeger.

Taylor, M. C., & Walsh, E. J. (1979). Explanations of black self-esteem: Some empirical tests. *Social Psychology Quarterly, 42,* 242–253.

Taylor, R. J., & Chatters, L. M. (1991). Religious life. In J. S. Jackson (Ed.), *Life in Black America* (pp. 105–123). Newbury Park, CA: Sage.

Tesser, A., & Campbell, J. (1983). Self-definition and self-evaluation mainte-nance. In J. Suls & A. Greenwald (Eds.), *Psychological perspectives on the self* (pp. 1–31). Hillsdale, NJ: Erlbaum.

Thiong'o, N. W. (1986). *Decolonising the mind: The politics of language in African literature.* London: James Currey.

Thompson, R. F. (1984). *Flash of the spirit: African & Afro-American art & philosophy.* New York: Vintage Press.

Tishkoff, S. A., Dietzsch, E., Speed, W., Pakstis, A. J., Kidd, J. R., Cheung, K., Bonne-Tamir, B., Santachiara-Benerecetti, S. S., Moral. P., Krings, M., Paabo, S., Watson, E., Risch, N., Jenkins, T., & Kidd, T. T. (1996). Global patterns of linkage disequilibrium at the CD4 locus and modern human origins. *Science, 271*, 1380–1387.

Tonry, M. (1995). *Malign neglect: Race, crime, and punishment in America.* New York: Oxford University Press.

Torres, M. (1992). New addition to the data collection of PRBA: NSBA wave iv. *Program for Research on Black Americans, 1*, 3.

Triandis, H. C. (1989). Self and social behavior in differing cultural contexts. *Psychological Review, 96*, 269–289.

Triandis, H. C. (1994). *Culture and social behavior.* New York: McGraw-Hill.

Triandis, H. C., Bontempo, R., Villareal, M.J. Asai, M., & Lucca, N. (1988). Individualism and collectivism: Cross-cultural perspectives on self-ingroup relationships. *Journal of Personality and Social Psychology, 54*, 323–338.

Triandis, H. C., McCusker, C., & Hui, C. H. (1990). *Journal of Personality and Social Psychology, 59*, 1006–1020.

Ture, K., & Hamilton, C. V. (1992). *Black power: The politics of liberation in America* (2nd ed.). New York: Vintage Books.

Tyler, T. R., Kramer, R. M., & John, O. P. (1999). What does studying the psychology of the social self have to offer to psychologists? In T. R. Tyler, R. M. Kramer, & O. P. John, *The psychology of the social self.* Mahwah, NJ: Lawrence Erlbaum.

Unger, S., & Gergen, D. (1991). *Africa and the American media.* Occasional Paper No. 9. New York: The Freedom Forum Media Studies Center.

Van Sertima, I. (1989). Nile Valley Civilizations. Proceedings of the Nile Valley Conference, Atlanta, GA, September 26–30, 1984.

Watkins, V. (1997). Womanism and black feminism: Issues in the manipulation of African historiography. In J. H. Carruthers & L. C. Harris (Eds.), *The African world history project: The preliminary challenge* (pp. 245–284). Los Angeles: Association for the Study of Classical African Civilizations.

West, C. (1982). *Prophecy deliverance: An Afro-American revolutionary Christian-ity.* Philadelphia: Westminster.

White, J. L., & Parham, T. A. (1990). *The psychology of Blacks: An African-American perspective* (2nd ed.). Englewood Cliffs, NJ: Prentice-Hall.

Wilson, A. N. (1990). *Black-on-black violence: The psychodynamics of black self-annihilation in service of white domination.* Brooklyn: African World Information Systems.

Wilson, C. C., & Gutierrez, F. (1995). *Race, multiculturalism and the media: From mass to class communication* (2nd ed.). Thousand Oaks, CA: Sage.

Wilson, J. (1983). *Social theory.* Englewood Cliffs, NJ: Prentice-Hall.

Wilson, J. W. (1978). *The declining significance of race: Blacks and changing American institutions.* Chicago: University of Chicago Press.

Wilson, J. W. (1987). *The truly disadvantaged: The inner city, the underclass, and public policy.* Chicago: University of Chicago Press.

Wilson, W. J. (1980). *The declining significance of race* (2nd ed.). Chicago: University of Chicago Press.

Winant, H. (1998). Racial dualism at century's end. In W. Lubiano (Ed.). *The house that race build* (pp.87–115). New York: Vintage.

Winston, M. R. (1982). Racial consciousness and the evaluation of mass communications in the United States, *Daedalus, 3,* 171–182.

Wolford, M., & Torres, M. (1994). Nonresponse adjustment in a longitudinal survey of African Americans. Unpublished paper. University of Michigan.

Woodson, C. G. (1933). *The miseducation of the Negro.* Trenton, NJ: African World Press.

Wright, B. H. (1985). The effects of racial self-esteem on the personal self-esteem of black youth. *International Journal of Intercultural Relations, 9,* 19–30.

Wright, E. O. (1985). *Classes.* London: Verso.

Wright, E. O., Hachen, D., Costello, C., & Sprague, J. (1982). *American Sociological Review, 47,* 709–726.

Wright, E. O., & Perrone, L. (1977). Marxist class categories and income inequality. *American Sociological Review, 42,* 32–55.

Wylie, R. (1977). *The self-concept: A review of methodological considerations and measuring instruments.* Lincoln: University of Nebraska Press.

X, Malcolm (1990). *Malcolm X on Afro-American history* (3rd ed.). New York: Pathfinder.

Zinn, H. (1995). *A people's history of the United States 1492—present.* New York: Harper.

INDEX

racial group identification, 95
racial identification, 87
racial self-esteem, 95
Rainwater, L., 57
Ramseur, H. P. 72
reciprocal causation, 109
reconstruction period, 164
Reed, E. S., 29, 55
"reference group measures," 63
reference group orientation, 52–53, 68–69, 86
reflective appraisal, 48, 73
Robeson, Paul, 162
Robinson, C. J., 25
Rodney, W., 28
Rosenberg, M., 48, 58, 61, 74, 76, 109
Rosenberg global self-esteem scale, 76–77,
    148, 199n. 2; dimensionality of, 78;
    reliability of, 81–82

Schoenbach, C., 48, 108
Schooler, C., 48, 77, 78, 108
self-attribution, 48, 73
self-concept, approaches to, 45–48; behavioral,
    47; existential, 47; global assumptions
    concerning, 126; phenomenological,
    47; symbolic interactional, 47; Western
    theories, 125
self-conceptions, 52
self-construals, 55
self-enhancement motive. See self-esteem
    theory
self-esteem, 48–49, 50, 68, 82–83, 159;
    efficacy-based, 73–74; and group identity,
    51–53, 108; racial, 52; personal, 52; social
    structure and, 78–82; studies of, 50–51
self-esteem studies, limitations of, 61–62
self-esteem theory, 48, 73–74
self-evaluation, 52
self-fulfilling prophecy, 73
self-hatred, 74, 75–76
"self-knowledge," 55
self-maintenance motive. See self-esteem
    theory
self-schemas, 46, 56
Semmes, C. E., 33–34, 54
Shapiro, 137–38
Shaw, George Bernard, 22
Shweder, R. A., 127
Simmons, R. G., 58, 76
slave trade, 18
slavery, 18, 26–28, 172–73
Smith, R. C., 75–76
social comparison, 48

social equity hypothesis, 74
social evaluation theory, 70
social exchange theory, 74
social identity theory, 49, 74, 87–88, 107–8
social interaction, 48
Sorbom, D., 93
Spain, 25
Steinberg, S., 164
stereotyping, 96
"stigmatized" groups, 48–49, 50
structural equation modeling (SEM), 63, 171,
    199n. 1, 200n. 1
Stuart, Charles, 34
Sundquist, E. J., 30
supportive African American community
    theory, 72, 131
system-blame, 71, 72

Tajfel, H., 49, 88, 96
tangle of pathology theory, 71–72
Taylor, D. M., 87–88
Taylor, M. C., 75
Thompson, R. F., 128
Thornton, M., 93
Toynbee, Arnold, 21
Triandis, H. C., 55
Ture, K., 28
Turner, J., 49

umuntu umuntu ngabantu, 47
"underclass," 134, 136
United States: economic conditions, 133–34;
    and human rights, 164; racial conditions,
    25, 28

Villareal, M. J., 55
Voice from the South, A (Cooper), 31

Walsh, E. J., 75
Washington, R. E., 52, 60, 70, 71–72, 87, 89,
    90–91, 131
Watkins, S. C., 33, 93
Wells, Ida B., 32
"we-ness," 160
White, J. L., 75
white supremacy, 107, 164
"whiteness," 51
Wilson, A. N., 45
Wilson, W. J., 135
Winston, M. R., 36
Woodson, C. G., 26, 35–36
Wright, B. H., 60, 108

Books in the African American Life Series

Coleman Young and Detroit Politics: From Social Activist to Power Broker, by Wilbur Rich, 1988.

Great Black Russian: A Novel on the Life and Times of Alexander Pushkin, by John Oliver Killens. 1989.

Indignant Heart: A Black Worker's Journal, by Charles Denby, 1989 (reprint)

The Spook Who Sat by the Door, by Sam Greenlee, 1989 (reprint)

Roots of African American Drama: An Anthology of Early Plays, 1858–1938, edited by Leo Hamalian and James V. Hatch, 1990

Walls: Essays, 1985–1990, by Kenneth McClane, 1991

Voices of the Self: A Study of Language Competence, by Keith Gilyard, 1991

Say Amen, Brother! Old-Time Negro Preaching: A Study in American Frustration, by William H. Pipes, 1991 (reprint)

The Politics of Black Empowerment: The Transformation of Black Activism in Urban America, by James Jennings, 1992

Pan Africanism in the African Diaspora: An Analysis of Modern Afrocentric Political Movements, by Ronald Walters, 1993

Three Plays: The Broken Calabash, Parables for a Season, and The Reign of Wazobia, by Tesss Akaeke Onwueme, 1993

Untold Tales, Unsung Heroes: An Oral History of Detroit's African American Community, 1918–1967, by Elaine Latzman Moon, Detroit Urban League, Inc., 1994.

Discarded Legacy: Politics and Poetics in the Life of Frances E. W. Harper, 1825–1911, by Melba Joyce Boyd, 1994

African American Women Speak Out on Anita Hill–Clarence Thomas, edited by Geneva Smitherman, 1995

Lost Plays of the Harlem Renaissance, 1920–1940, edited by James V. Hatch and Leo Hamalian, 1996

Let's Flip the Script: An African American Discourse on Language, Literature, and Learning, by Keith Gilyard, 1996

A History of the African American People: The History, Traditions, and Culture of African Americans, edited by James Oliver Horton and Lois E. Horton, 1997 (reprint)

Tell It to Women: An Epic Drama for Women, by Osonye Tess Onwueme, 1997

Ed Bullins: A Literary Biography, by Samuel Hay, 1997

Walkin' over Medicine, by Loudelle F. Snow, 1998 (reprint)

Negroes with Guns, by Robert F. Williams, 1998 (reprint)

A Study of Walter Rodney's Intellectual and Political Thought, by Rupert Lewis, 1998

Ideology and Change: The Transformation of the Caribbean Left, by Perry Mars, 1998

"Winds Can Wake up the Dead": An Eric D. Walrond Reader, edited by Louis Parascandola, 1998

Race & Ideology: Language, Symbolism, and Popular Culture, edited by Arthur Spears, 1999

Without Hatreds or Fears: Jorge Artel and the Struggle for Black Literary Expression in Columbia, by Laurence E. Prescott, 2000

African Americans, Labor, and Society: Organizing for a New Agenda, edited by Patrick L. Mason, 2001

The Concept of Self: A Study of Black Identity and Self-Esteem, by Richard L. Allen, 2001